KT-486-633

ERROL MORRIS

INTERVIEWS

CONVERSATIONS WITH FILMMAKERS SERIES
PETER BRUNETTE, GENERAL EDITOR

'10 JUN 2024

York St John

3 8025 00580126 4

ERROL MORRIS
INTERVIEWS

EDITED BY LIVIA BLOOM

YORK ST. JOHN
LIBRARY & INFORMATION
SERVICES

UNIVERSITY PRESS OF MISSISSIPPI / JACKSON

www.upress.state.ms.us

The University Press of Mississippi is a member of the Association of American University Presses.

Copyright © 2010 by University Press of Mississippi
All rights reserved
Manufactured in the United States of America

First printing 2010

∞

Library of Congress Cataloging-in-Publication Data

Errol Morris : interviews / edited by Livia Bloom.
     p. cm. — (Conversations with filmmakers series)
   Includes index.
   ISBN 978-1-60473-372-3 (cloth : alk. paper) — ISBN 978-1-60473-373-0 (pbk. : alk. paper) 1. Morris, Errol—Interviews. 2. Motion picture producers and directors—United States—Interviews. I. Bloom, Livia.
   PN1998.3.M684E77 2010
   791.4302'33092—dc22

                                                           2009022460

British Library Cataloging-in-Publication Data available

CONTENTS

INTRODUCTION

C A N N E S , 2 0 0 3 . A door bursts open in the midst of pleasantries. "We need someone to interview Errol Morris. Tomorrow. Tomorrow morning." My editor turns, grins. "Lucky you," she says, and the assignment is mine. I smile and nod my way out into the evening . . . wondering how on earth to conduct this interview, and who on earth Errol Morris might be.

I see Errol's new film, *The Fog of War*, at an unannounced screening and take copious, barely legible notes. The film, which is playing Out of Competition, is based on Errol's extensive, exclusive interviews with Robert S. McNamara, Secretary of Defense under Kennedy and Johnson and an architect of the Vietnam War. Not having lived through Vietnam turns out to be a significant disadvantage, as my background on the topic is largely courtesy of *The Deer Hunter* (1978), *Apocalypse Now* (1979), *Platoon* (1986), *Full Metal Jacket* (1987), and *Good Morning Vietnam* (1987). I contact everyone I know for information, time difference be damned.

And from film friends across the globe, juicy morsels of information on the Morris oeuvre accumulate in my inbox like ingredients for a stone soup. I am delighted to discover that I've actually seen quite a number of his films over the years. For instance, Mr. Martinelli bravely blurred the line between film and filmstrip by showing *A Brief History of Time* to my eleventh-grade physics class; *Fast, Cheap and Out of Control* once played at a slumber party. I trundle to the makeshift Cannes computer lab and memorize everything there is about Errol Morris, researching late into that night.

A self-described "weird kid," Errol Morris was born into a Jewish family in New York State. When Errol was two, his father Abner, a doctor, died.

He was raised by his Yiddish-speaking, pianist mother, Cinnabelle; his scientist elder brother, Noel; his sizable British nanny, Hardy; and Roz, his schizophrenic, movie-loving aunt. Errol attended public school in a wealthy area of Long Island. "It was one of the richest communities in America," he said, "But we did not have money. I never lived in Richville, and I never had the kind of money that other people had." Growing up, he played the cello, both in duets with his mother and later at The Julliard School, where his mother had also studied. "She could sight-read anything—the two Mendelssohn sonatas, the Rachmaninoff sonata, and on and on . . . ," he told me. "I didn't realize that every mom couldn't play *Carnival* perfectly; I just didn't have any basis for comparison."

A prodigious learner and an autodidact, Errol nevertheless had a relationship to academic institutions that proved to be complicated. "Errol is, well, Errol," said Ann Petrone, his co-producer and main researcher for the past eleven years. "Brilliant, mercurial, obsessive, and one of the best-read people I've ever meet—and I was in rare books, so I don't say this lightly." Though his family was Jewish and he had his Bar Mitzvah at the local Congregation Sons of Israel, Errol attended a diverse public school growing up. "There were all kinds of kids. There was even the apartment building around the corner where someone called me a Christ Killer when I was eleven or ten, and I had to go and ask what that was. Now when someone calls me a Christ Killer I think I should say, 'I'm sorry, and I promise never to do it again.'"

Errol later attended The Putney School, a boarding school in Vermont, graduated from the University of Wisconsin, and studied fitfully in graduate school, including the University of California-Berkeley and Princeton University. "I couldn't earn a living until I was forty, or close to it. I probably started earning a living when I got my job as a private detective well into my thirties," Errol explained. "Ben, my stepfather, liked me and gave me money for *Gates of Heaven*. It never would have happened without his encouragement." Both film and detective enterprises engaged Errol's passion for detail, for history, and perhaps for poetic justice. "One of the funny things about my private detective work, when I was an out-of-work-filmmaker," he told me, "is that I wasn't doing anything different from what I was doing all along: just talking to people, getting them to talk to me, and trying to remember stuff."

At Berkeley, Errol frequented the Pacific Film Archive, becoming more than just a regular. "He quickly became one of the *regular, regular, regulars*," said film programmer Tom Luddy, former head of programming for the PFA and the co-founder of the Telluride Film Festival.

He was coming almost every day to whatever I showed. He was interested in much darker things then, and he would walk around with
transcripts of interviews he had done with mass murderers. Sometimes he would show me a little bit of them. At the Archive, we had
many variously obsessed people, but Errol was also a little strange
because even in hot weather he would wear a dark jacket and dress
in kind of geeky clothes. He looked like somebody who had never . . .
taken advantage of the outdoor life in California.

We had an incident once when my theater manager asked me to
ban him from the theater because he kept sneaking in without pay-
ing. He insulted her, and insulted the staff. He just said, "I have to
see movies." She said she would quit unless I banned him. But then
I sat down and talked with him. He explained that he didn't have
much money and that he had to see these films. I said, "Well, if
you'll apologize to Bonnie and help me do some research or write a
few program notes, I'll give you a free pass." So we made that kind
of a deal. Bonnie didn't quit, and I started trying to bring him into
the fold. He wasn't an employee, he was a volunteer; I just needed
something for him to do to justify to my staff why he was getting
in free.

James Schamus, president of Focus Features, was an undergraduate Philosophy major at Berkeley when Errol was in graduate school there. James
remembers Errol's notoriety: "As a film nut, I was at the PFA all the time,
and Errol was known as the guy who just refused to pay. People would
say, 'Oh, there's the guy who doesn't pay . . .' whereas I was too shy; I always had to pay."

Tom Luddy also shared the inside story of the making of Errol's first
film, *Gates of Heaven*, the chronicle of two dueling California pet cemeteries:

When he came to me and said he wanted to start shooting the burial
of pets, he seemed like one of many people who said they would
do something you would never in a million years believe that they
would do. But he wanted me to get him a cameraman who would
shoot for free, so I found a guy who owed me a favor. The next day,
he said, "This asshole fired me! I'm doing it for free with my own
camera; he takes the film that I shot, and says I don't want to work
with you anymore!" This was an experienced cameraman, and Errol
had never done anything. I called Ed Lachman, who's a famous
cameraman now; he just did Todd Haynes's *I'm Not There* (2007),

and at the time, he had already worked with Herzog and Bertolucci. I talked Ed into flying up from L.A. to shoot for Errol, and the same thing happened again: after one day, Errol fired him—from an unpaid job!

I said to Errol, "Three strikes and you're out. I'll try one more time." I'd been working with Godard quite a bit by then, and the camera operator on *Tout va bien* (1972) was an American who happened to be visiting his girlfriend in Berkeley. He had with him an Éclair camera, so I called up Ned Burgess and said, "I have a friend with a bizarre project . . . It's about burying pets." Errol liked him, and Ned Burgess stayed till the end.

When I saw the film, I was really blown away. We showed it in Berkeley in our big eight-hundred-seat venue. And in those days, I was one of the five people selecting films for the New York Film Festival, so I told Richard Roud and everybody, "I've got this film to show you, by this guy out of nowhere." Once they saw it, I didn't have to convince them. I got it into the New York festival, and I got Dan Talbot [founder of New Yorker Films], who was a good friend of mine, to see it and distribute it. That launched Errol.

Critic Roger Ebert named *Gates of Heaven* one of his ten best films of all time and became one of the most important champions of Errol's work. "[*Gates of Heaven*] is surrounded by layer upon layer of comedy, pathos, irony, and human nature. I have seen this film perhaps thirty times, and am still not anywhere near the bottom of it," he wrote. "This eighty-five-minute film about pet cemeteries has given me more to think about over the past twenty years than most of the other films I've seen." When the two spoke at Ebertfest, Roger's annual film festival in Champaign, Illinois, Errol explained, "It was unclear if [*Gates of Heaven*] would have any distribution at all. It was accepted at the New York Film Festival, but it was the year of the newspaper strikes, so there were no reviews and no publicity. Roger put it on his 'Ten Best' List. I remember scanning the list and thinking, 'The other nine directors are wondering whether or not to take a plunge into the pool . . . and I am wondering whether or not to take a plunge out the window.' Roger really has kept me going over the years. With each new film that I make, I ask myself, 'How much less is he going to like this than *Gates of Heaven*?'"

Following New York Film Festival screenings, filmmakers traditionally take audience questions. Reid Rosefelt, of whom Errol said, "If publicity was a religion, and I believe it is, Reid Rosefelt would be the High Priest," recounted an anecdote in which one audience member encountered not only Errol's groundbreaking film, but his rapier wit. "A woman raised her hand and said to Errol, 'Your film would be a lot better if it was cut in two.' Errol just said, 'So would you.' "

Not all film festivals went quite as smoothly as the NYFF, however. "Errol used to hate Sundance," Rosefelt explained. "Once he flew to Salt Lake City and rented a car and drove all the way to Park City. When he got out of his car in Park City, the first thing he saw was one of the cinematographers he had fired from *Gates of Heaven*. And he thought, 'It's cold; my ex-cinematographer is here . . .' So he got back in the car, drove back to Salt Lake and flew home. True story. That was before I worked with him at Sundance for the first time with *Fast, Cheap and Out of Control*. One of my responsibilities was to keep him from leaving. Errol also used to say that he prepared for Sundance by standing in a walk-in freezer next to someone who was shouting on a cell phone."

Errol went on to make *Vernon, Florida* (1981), another New York Film Festival selection and a film widely recognized as an important antecedent to comedies like Christopher Guest's *Waiting for Guffman* (1996) and *Best in Show* (2000); documentaries like *Wonderland* (1997), John O'Hagan's portrait of Levittown, New York; and satires like Larry Charles's *Borat* (2006) and *Religulous* (2008), among others. The film was also considered by many to have blurred the fine line between laughing with and laughing at subjects, though Janet Maslin defended this aspect of it in her *New York Times* review: "At his New York Film Festival news conference, Mr. Morris came under fire for making fun of his subjects, but that seems not to have been his idea at all. The fancifulness of his subjects is something he appears to appreciate and enjoy."

Errol further address the question himself in discussion with Roger Ebert:

There was this question that kept being repeated again and again and again: "Are you making fun of people?" Actually it was in the form of accusation: "You are making fun of people; why are you doing that?" Over the years, I have reacted to this question in many different ways. I went through a period of simply denying I was making fun of them, which didn't seem entirely ingenuous. Then I pointed out that the fact that I was making fun of them did not mean I didn't have other feelings for them—complex feelings for them. Maybe the fact that these people were funny didn't mean that that's all they were for me. When I was a little boy, I remember my mother telling me, "The lowest kind of humor is making fun of other people." And I said to her, "Wait a second, what other kind of humor is there? I must be missing something."

Errol married art historian Julia Sheehan in 1984, and went on to make *The Thin Blue Line* (1988), arguably his most influential film. The investigation of a murder case, it exonerated an innocent man from death row, documented the confession of the real killer, and did it all with the intrigue of an Agatha Christie novel. The first film to solve a real-life crime, *The Thin Blue Line* set a new bar for what a documentary could be and do. Technically, it is also recognized for its seminal use of dramatic reenactments, and it marked the beginning of a fruitful, much imitated collaboration between Errol and composer Philip Glass, who created its modernist atmospheric soundscapes.

The subjects of *A Brief History of Time* (1990), physicist Stephen Hawking and his scientific theories and method, are so well suited to Morris's deep interest in metaphysical questions that it's surprising the film was done for hire, with Steven Spielberg as executive producer. It is a highly mobile film made of an immobile subject: though Hawking, who suffers from ALS, is paralyzed, his synthesized voice narrates dynamic visuals. On this film there was never a suggestion of condescension. As Ebert writes, "With Stephen Hawking, [Errol Morris] met his match. He approaches his subject with great seriousness [and] has no doubts about [Hawking's] importance or greatness."

The little-seen film *The Dark Wind* (1991) is Errol's only narrative effort to date, although he has considered making many others over the years. Based on a book by Tony Hillerman, it tells the story of yet another sort of detective: Lou Diamond Philips, who plays a young man investigating crime on a Native American reservation. The project united Errol with the titan of independent film, producer Robert Redford, with whom he had a contentious relationship. Errol reports never having seen the finished film, which was not commercially successful. To me, he said, "I would have loved to have made a movie that was not bad from one of [Tony Hillerman's] novels. I like those novels; I've always liked those novels. When I was hired, I read them all. Every single one of them."

In *Fast, Cheap and Out of Control* (1997), the stories of four disparate characters are collected, juxtaposed, and interposed, despite (or because of) their vastly different professions and interests: a wild animal trainer; a topiary gardener; a mole-rat specialist; and a robotics scientist. Although the objects of these men's intellectual and professional affections seem unrelated, each private world nevertheless carries visual echoes of all the others. With masterful work by lead editors Karen Schmeer and Shondra Merrill, as the film progresses the iconography associated with a given subject—circus imagery to illustrate and signify the lion tamer, for instance—slips over into the realm of the other subjects, as do each of the men's voices in interview. "People are afraid of new, different, strange; but to me it isn't something to be feared. It's something to be looked at, wondered at, and explored . . . perhaps communicated with," says the mole-rat specialist of his subjects. His words apply to all the men— including even Errol himself.

Perhaps unsurprisingly, implications of mortality also highlight commonalities among the film's protagonists. "I tried understudies; I've had several understudies. But they lose interest in it. Very few of them want to do the same thing too long. It's been more than half my life . . . and I'd hate to see anything happen to it," a man says, while a grainy on-screen magician makes a colored scarf disappear. The imagery belongs to the lion tamer, but the gardener speaks the words, and the sentiment could belong to any of them. Errol considers the film an elegy, and dedicated it to his mother and stepfather, both of whom had recently passed away.

His subsequent film, *Mr. Death* (1999), placed another subject who loves his job in Errol's hot seat: Fred Leutcher, a self-proclaimed expert designer of electric chairs and execution equipment. The film is about the Holocaust, corruption in the criminal justice system, capital punishment, and the extremity of one man's self-delusion. Yet despite the gravitas of the subject, it did not receive an Oscar nomination. Errol says he was unsurprised. "I was not nominated for *The Thin Blue Line*, which seemed kind of like a movie that you would nominate somebody for; I wasn't nominated for *Brief History*; I wasn't nominated for *Fast, Cheap*; and I wasn't nominated for *Mr. Death*. I used to joke when I was making *Mr. Death* that it was going to be the first Holocaust-related film that was not nominated for anything."

First Person (2000) was a bid for a commercial television audience. The series, which is available, like all of Errol's films, on DVD, exploited the sheer variety and vast number of its director's interests. Each new episode focused on another unlikely hero plucked from society's fringes, from a lawyer for the mob to the man who opened his life to the online world for his experiment, "We Live in Public" (now the subject of a feature film by Ondi Timoner).

Based on the strength of Errol's previous work, the distribution deal with Sony Pictures Classics for *The Fog of War* (2003) was signed before co-presidents Michael Barker and Tom Bernard had even seen the film. As Barker explained to me:

> My partner and I are consistently staggered by Errol's intelligence and this kind of balance between cynicism and humor that I don't think even Billy Wilder could have pulled off. I come from Texas, and I remember seeing *The Thin Blue Line* very early on. I still think it's the single greatest, clearest, truest portrayal of Texans ever made. We signed the deal for *Fast, Cheap and Out of Control* at the Sundance Film Festival in the bathroom of the Egyptian theater five minutes before the film screened, and before anyone in the world had ever seen a single frame of the film. It's true. Some time later, he showed us fourteen minutes of an interview he did with Robert McNamara. Tom and I said to him, "Let's do this one together, from the beginning." And we did. Our goal in life was to get Errol Morris the Oscar, and we felt that he would have a shot with this film. That was always our intention, for it to be a contender for him.

Their work paid off: *The Fog of War* won the 2004 Academy Award for Best Documentary. Errol then went on to make *Standard Operating Procedure* (2008) about the infamous torture photographs from Abu Ghraib; the film won the Silver Bear at the Berlin Film Festival; co-authored a book, also called *Standard Operating Procedure*, with Philip Gourevitch; and directed spots supporting Barack Obama's presidential campaign, *People in the Middle for Obama* (2008), and cancer-awareness, *Stand Up to Cancer* (2008). Throughout this career, Errol also directed commercials for diverse corporate clients, some of which have featured his friends, neighbors, and even his son, Hamilton.

This development came as a particular surprise to Tom Luddy. "The last thing I would ever have believed was that Errol would be helping to keep our corporations afloat. The Errol that I first met, if you had said to me, 'This man is going to be selling United Airlines, Heineken beer, and Apple computers?' I never would have imagined he'd be interested in that. He was deep into the counter culture in Berkeley. You wouldn't have thought that the big powers of the establishment would find their main salesman in him." As Errol explained, however, it's his very outsider status that makes him valuable to the advertising world. "I often get hired to do nontraditional advertising jobs. The straighter the job, the less likely that it will be offered to me. Which is good. It means that I get to *do something* as opposed to following a set of [story]boards." Errol won an Emmy for directing the commercial "Photobooth" for PBS; he was nominated by the Director's Guild of America (DGA) for Best Commercial Director; and *Adweek* named him one of the brightest talents in advertising.

Also significantly, Errol started a blog for the *New York Times* called *Zoom*, despite the fact that writing has proved difficult over the years. "My stepfather wanted me to write a book on *The Thin Blue Line*—and I wanted to write a *Thin Blue Line* book—but I couldn't do it. I had endless notes and hundreds of pages of this, that, and the other thing, and I just couldn't do it," he said. "He even wrote part of this book, my stepfather did, to try to encourage me to write it, or to rewrite it. I just simply couldn't do it . . . just like all of the other books that I couldn't write."

When told that today he seems a fountain of creativity, he replied, "I'm actually working harder. . . . Or maybe I'm just *functioning* better. I don't know what it is. I had writer's block for probably thirty years." "What changed?" I asked. "Someone asked me to write, and offered to pay me to write. I think it's as simple as that. The *Times* asked me to do this. I didn't think I could. And then I started to write. It seems magical to me. I hope it doesn't change."

No introduction of Errol Morris would be complete without mentioning his filming apparatus, the Interrotron. Using this system of double video Teleprompters, subjects speak to a live digital feed of the director's image rather than to the director himself, thus gazing directly into the camera. This gives the recorded interrogations uncanny directness and strong visual consistency, qualities that are particularly important in films that often include a wide variety of source formats.

His fascination with different ways of seeing has physiological and familial implications as well as cinematic ones, as Errol explained to me. Our recent interview was the first time that he ever publically discussed, in mesmerizing detail, the fact he is legally blind in his left eye and lacks stereopsis, or depth perception. It's a revelation to know this about him; perhaps it puts him in visual accord with the elite directors like Fritz Lang, John Ford, and Raoul Walsh, each of whom wore an eye patch and may have experienced a similar lack of stereopsis. Errol's explanation of this subject is also a wonderful illustration of the clarity of his understanding and the depths of his insight into scientific, philosophical, and psychological causes and effects.

There are two terms: amblyopia and strabismus. Amblyopia refers to the suppression of vision; strabismus is when the eyes are physically out of alignment. So cross-eyed, wall-eyed: strabismus. [As a child,] I was wall-eyed. I had the Jean-Paul Sartre problem.

You do *have the Jean-Paul Sartre problem.* (Laughter)

They don't completely understand this, but the idea is that if the eyes can't be physically brought into alignment, the brain is going to see two different images it can't integrate. So it suppresses one of those images; usually the eye that is out of kilter. Not physically out of kilter; it's a normal eye, it's just misaligned. In the 1950s—and I think still today, though I'm still [researching this]—they operated on the muscles of the eye to bring it back into position. Then they would put a patch on the good eye, forcing you to use the lazy eye. It encouraged the brain to get up to speed.

My stepfather, Ben Esterman, was an ophthalmologist. He married my mom when I was twenty-three years old. In many ways, he was my dad, though I never called him dad. He was the family eye doctor; I think he was always interested in my mom, that's what I think. He operated on my eyes when I was two. I would call it the Reverse Oedipus myth because he blinded me and married my mom. (Laughs)

I would never wear my patch; I always tore my patch off. My eyes are aligned, but I don't have stereoptic vision; the two eyes never integrated, and this [left] eye has always been very weak. I can barely read with it; I can see out of this eye, but I can barely read an "E" on an eye chart.

There's a whole corpus of literature on whether vision can be restored to the eye. Most recent studies say yes, to a certain extent, but they used to say that if it hadn't developed by the age of eight or nine it would never develop, kind of like language acquisition. So when I was three, shortly after my father died, I was operated on and my eyes were bandaged. While my eyes were bandaged, my mother came to visit me. My stepfather told her that she shouldn't say anything to me because I would be disturbed to know that she was there if I couldn't see her. So she came to visit me and *said nothing*. I've always wondered about the fact that my father had dropped dead not so many months before, and my mother had vanished as well. What did that do? (Laughs) I think my stepfather should have let her talk to me.

[In a letter written about stereopsis to neurologist and *New Yorker* writer Oliver Sacks,] I said at the end, "Better to be Hume-ian than to be human." If stereopsis made you feel like you were one with the world, that you were floating in the world, the lack of stereopsis perhaps created a sense of being apart from the world, and skeptical of it. I believe that stereopsis is wonderful; I can never know first hand. I suppose it's like trying to describe the color red to someone who's blind. I don't have stereopsis and I most likely will never have it, so I can only imagine what it's like.

But most of the ways that people test for stereopsis are optical illusions—gimmicks—created by the fact that we have these two singular flat images on our retinas that are integrated to create the illusion of three-dimensionality. Say I go into a 3-D movie: I can't appreciate it because in order to see it properly, you have to have the red and the green glasses, and you have to have stereopsis. If I go in, I just see a double image on the screen. But is the person who sees it *with* stereopsis seeing something that's veridical—as opposed to me? (Laughs) An optical illusion of three-dimensionality is created for people who have this ability, whereas I *cannot* be tricked in that way.

Back in Cannes, 2003, it is finally morning. I am at the Carlton, an elaborate frosted white wedding cake of a grand hotel on the Riviera. It's where my grandparents stayed on trips to the festival during another era; it is miles from my tiny room. The Mediterranean sun beats down from the heavens, and I am roasting when I arrive in my black suit, teetering in professional high heels. I am armed with pages of questions, each copied and refined an infinite number of times.

"You'll each have just about ten minutes," a publicist says to the long line of journalists. My heart sinks, and thousands of potential queries erase themselves from my notes as if they had been written in disappearing ink. When miraculously, it is our turn, my videographer rolls, and I clear my throat. "Mr. Morris, I'm delighted to talk to you about *The Fog of War.* Can you describe how you got involved with . . . ?" All at once, I am abruptly cut off.

"Why did you like it?" he says. "Let me ask you."

"Why did I like it?" I stammer, stalling for time; thrown violently off guard. "Well, hmm. . . . Can I tell you at the end of the interview?" (This part is still hard for me to watch on tape.)

"No!" He is teasing, indignant, and emphatic. His eyes twinkle mysteriously, judgmentally.

"I have to tell you now?"

"Yeah," he laughs. "I'm curious."

And with that, I am hooked. I stammer through an explanation, and mercifully, he seems satisfied; our conversation continues to the ten-minute mark and beyond. I receive a compliment, of all things, for having "done my homework." Frantic publicists come and go; he waves them off like flies for forty minutes—no, more—while he thinks and rethinks his answers, turning each one upside down and inside out. Errol has a searching, searing intellect, and he listens to each question with the passion of an eight-year-old on a new bike, riding up and down the block long after he has been called in for dinner; long after the other kids have gone home. He is not only master interviewer; he is also master interviewee.

Thank you to my smart, curious contributors, and to their original publications and editors. Thanks also to Jay Allison and Viki Merrick, Transcom.org; Alice Arshalooys Kelikian, Brandeis University; Amy Austin, *Washington City Paper*; Drew Avery and Leigh Montville, the *New Yorker*; Gary Crowdus, *Cineaste* magazine; Jeff Hill and Jessica Uzzan, International House of Publicity; Michael Hopkins, *New York Times*; Virginia Hutton, Sony Pictures Classics; Lucy Laird and Jason Sanders, Pacific Film Archive; Shana Liebman and Michele Meek, *The Independent*; the estate of Joel E. Siegel; Carole Rosenberg, FilmFestivals.com; Karl Rozemeyer, Hachette Filipacchi Media U.S.; Gavin Smith, *Film Comment* magazine; and Erica Varela, *Newsday*. The Grump was named and first published by Ren Weschler in his magazine, *Omnivore*.

Thank you to Michael Barker, Roger Ebert, Werner Herzog, Tom Luddy, Ann Petrone, Reid Rosefelt, and James Schamus for their candid and humorous original interviews.

This volume was made possible by Paul Cronin, a filmmaker, an historian, and a lover of art and rebellion. He worked on an interview with Errol Morris, in personal and written collaboration, between 2003 and 2006. Their extensive interview, which Errol considers the best that has been done with him, is published for the first time in this volume.

The cover photograph was taken by Nubar Alexanian. His book, *Nonfiction: Images from the Film Sets of Errol Morris*, is available from Walker Creek Press.

Thank you to my publishers, Walter Biggins, Seetha Srinivasan, and the wonderful Leila Salisbury of the University Press of Mississippi.

I am aided, abetted, and inspired by my brother Avery Bloom; by my parents, Loren and Mayra Bloom; by my grandparents, Martin and Clara Bloom, and Sheldon and Luz Gunsberg; by Erika Brutsaert, Mary Fessenden, Natalia Fidelholtz, Joanne Koch, Andrew Lampert, Greg Laufer, Donna Lerner, Dennis Lim, Laura Maccabee, Ilona Parkansky, Richard Peña, Mark Peranson, Santiago Portillo, Joshua Rothkopf, David Schwartz, A. O. Scott, Amy Villarejo, and of course, Errol Morris.

Thank you for fire and music in endless supply.

LB

CHRONOLOGY

Errol's parents were Cinnabelle Burzinsky and Abner Morris. Abner, a doctor, grew up in Far Rockaway, New York, and was educated at Queens College and the University of Edinburgh Medical School. Cinnabelle, a piano and French teacher, grew up on the Lower East Side and was educated at Hunter College, the Juilliard School, and Columbia University.

1942	Noel, Errol's only sibling, born 4 November, Hewlett, New York, and educated at MIT. He died in 1984. Noel was a computer scientist who was one of the inventors of email. He was considered by his brother (and a lot of other people) to be the genius of the family.
1948	Born 5 February, Hewlett, New York.
1950	Death of Abner Morris.
1954	Studies at the Hewlett Elementary School, Hewlett, Long Island. Woodmere Junior High School, Woodmere, Long Island.
1959	Studies cello at the Juilliard School, receives 87 on IQ test. Mr. Flick, the guidance counselor, tells Errol that he seems to be a lot smarter than he really is. You might consider this the story of his life.
1964	Studies musical harmony and cello at the Conservatoire Americain in Fontainebleau with Nadia Boulanger, who decides he is either a slacker or devoid of musical talent.
1965	Graduates from the Putney School, Putney, Vermont, after being threatened with expulsion for three years. Everyone, including Errol, is surprised—not by the threats of expulsion but by the graduation.
1969	Graduates from University of Wisconsin, Madison, as a history major. Studies with George Mosse, Harvey Goldberg, and

William Appleman Williams. Spends most of his time rock-climbing in Yosemite Valley, the Tetons, and the Canadian Rockies. Writes the climber's guide to Devil's Lake, Wisconsin. Made-up an ancient proverb for the frontispiece: "He who does not climb, does not fall."

1971   Graduate student in the Program in the History and Philosophy of Science at Princeton University. Attends Saul Kripke's seminar on "Naming and Necessity." Studies with Thomas Kuhn. Finds Kuhn's brand of post-modernism tiresome. Kuhn has him expelled from the program.

1973   Student in the Department of Philosophy at the University of California, Berkeley. Finds this department most depressing of all and starts programming films for Tom Luddy, the director of the Pacific Film Archive.

1974   Starts interviewing mass murderers Ed Gein and Ed Kemper under the auspices of Bernard Diamond, head of the School of Criminology at Berkeley. Arrested trying to break into a mental hospital in Winnebago, Wisconsin.

1975   First attempts at filmmaking. Shoots several scenes of an unfinished movie, *A Chance to Live and a Chance to Die*, involving a number of characters that fascinated him at the time, including the soprano who sings only one note.

1976   Works with Werner Herzog on the production of Herzog's *Stroszek*. Herzog and Morris plan the exhumation of Gein's mother's grave in Plainfield Cemetery. Morris makes the first of several trips to Vernon, Florida, also known as "Nub City," to interview insurance investigators because of the extraordinary incidence of local insurance fraud involving self-mutilation.

1978   *Gates of Heaven*, described by critic Roger Ebert as one of the ten best films of all time.

1981   *Vernon, Florida*.

1982   Begins to work as a private investigator in New York. No one wants to give him money for movies.

1984   Death of brother Noel.

1985   Marries art historian Julia Sheehan.

1987   Son Hamilton born.

1988   *The Thin Blue Line*, voted best film of the year in a *Washington Post* survey of over a hundred critics; winner of the New York Film Critics Circle Best Documentary Award; Edgar Award from the Mystery Writers of America.

1990   Receives a MacArthur "Genius" Fellowship and a Guggenheim Fellowship.

1991   *A Brief History of Time*, inspired by the Stephen Hawking book of the same name, wins the Sundance Grand Jury Prize for documentaries. Morris's only narrative film, *The Dark Wind*, is released. Morris still hasn't watched it.

1997   *Fast, Cheap and Out of Control*. Wins Best Documentary from the National Board of Review and Best Non-Fiction Film from the New York Film Critics Circle. Morris becomes the first documentary filmmaker in the history of the IFP Gotham Awards to receive their Filmmaker Award.

1999   *Mr. Death: The Rise and Fall of Fred A. Leuchter, Jr.* Retrospectives at the Museum of Modern Art and LACMA.

2000   First season of *First Person* appears on Bravo. *A Brief History of Errol Morris* by Kevin Macdonald airs on IFC.

2001   Special tribute at the Sundance Film Festival; wins Emmy for PBS "Photobooth" commercial; second season of *First Person* airs on IFC.

2002   Short film screened for the opening of the Academy Awards.

2003   *The Fog of War: Eleven Lessons from the Life of Robert S. McNamara*. The film wins the Academy Award for Best Documentary. Listed as one of the best ten directors in the world by *The Guardian*.

2004   Commercials for MoveOn.

2006   Listed as one of the most important people in advertising by *Creativity*.

2007   Another short film for the opening of the Academy Awards. Starts writing *Zoom*, a column on film and photography for the *New York Times*.

2008   *S.O.P.: Standard Operating Procedure* premieres at the Berlinale (Berlin Film Festival), wins Jury Grand Prize, Silver Bear. Commercials for Obama, *People in the Middle*, released.

FILMOGRAPHY

1978
GATES OF HEAVEN
Producer: **Errol Morris**
Director: **Errol Morris**
Cinematography: Ned Burgess
Editor: **Errol Morris**
Music: Dan Harbarts
Featuring: Lucille Billingsley, Zella Graham, Cal Harbarts, Dan Harbarts, Phil
Harbarts, Scottie Harbarts, Florence Rasmussen
85 minutes

1981
VERNON, FLORIDA
Producer: David Loxton, **Errol Morris** (Errol Morris Films, WNET, ZDF)
Director: **Errol Morris**
Cinematography: Ned Burgess
Editor: Brad Fuller
Music: Claude Register
Featuring: Albert Bitterling, Claude Register, Snake Reynolds, Henry Shipes
56 minutes

1988
THE THIN BLUE LINE
Producer: Lindsay Law, Mark Lipson (American Playhouse, Channel 4, Third
Floor Productions)
Director: **Errol Morris**
Cinematography: Robert Chappell, Stefan Czapsky
Editor: Paul Barnes

Music: Philip Glass
Production Design: Ted Bafaloukos
Featuring: Randall Adams, David Harris, Gus Rose, Jackie Johnson, Emily Miller
103 minutes

1991
A BRIEF HISTORY OF TIME
Producers: Colin Ewing, Gordon Freedman, David Hickman, Kathleen Kennedy,
Steven Spielberg (Anglia Television, Channel 4, NBC, TBS)
Director: **Errol Morris**
Cinematography: John Bailey, Stefan Czapsky
Editor: Brad Fuller
Music: Philip Glass
Production Design: Ted Bafaloukos
Featuring: Stephen Hawking, Isobel Hawking, Roger Penrose, John Wheeler
80 minutes

1991
THE DARK WIND
Producers: Bonni Lee, Patrick Markey, Robert Redford (Seven Arts, Silver
Pictures)
Director: **Errol Morris**
Writers: Neal Jimenez, Eric Bergren (based on the novel by Tony Hillerman)
Cinematography: Stefan Czapsky
Editor: Freeman Davies
Music: Michel Colombier
Production Design: Ted Bafaloukos
Cast: Lou Diamond Phillips (Jim Chee), Gary Farmer (Albert Dashee), Fred
Ward (Joe Leaphorn), Guy Boyd (Agent Johnson), John Karlen (Jake West), Jane
Loranger (Gail Pauling), Gary Basaraba (Larry), Blake Clark (Ben)
111 minutes

1995
ERROL MORRIS: INTERROTRON STORIES *(television)*
Producer: Donald Kushner, Peter Locke, **Errol Morris** (The Kushner-Locke
Company, Fourth Floor Pictures)
Director: **Errol Morris**
Cinematography: Christophe Lanzenberg
Editor: Shondra Merrill
Music: John Kusiak, Caleb Sampson
Production Design: Ted Bafaloukos
With: Diane Alexander, Jack Shows

1997
FAST, CHEAP AND OUT OF CONTROL
Producers: Lindsay Law, Mark Lipson, **Errol Morris**, Julia Sheehan, Kathy Trustman (American Playhouse, Fourth Floor Pictures)
Director: **Errol Morris**
Cinematography: Robert Richardson
Editor: Sondra Merrill, Karen Schmeer
Music: Caleb Sampson
Production Design: Ted Bafaloukos
Featuring: Dave Hoover, George Mendonça, Raymond A. Mendez, Rodney Brooks
80 minutes

1999
MR. DEATH: THE RISE AND FALL OF FRED A. LEUCHTER, JR.
Producers: Dorothy Aufiero, David Collins, Caroline Kaplan, **Errol Morris**, Jonathan Sehring, John Sloss, Kathy Trustman, Michael Williams (Channel Four, Fourth Floor Pictures, IFC, Scout)
Director: **Errol Morris**
Cinematography: Peter Donahue
Editor: Karen Schmeer
Music: Caleb Sampson
Production Design: Ted Bafaloukos
Featuring: Fred A. Leuchter, Jr., Robert Jan Van Pelt, David Irving, Caroline Leuchter, James Roth, Shelly Shapiro, Suzanne Tabasky, Ernst Zündel
91 minutes

2000–2001
FIRST PERSON *(television)*
Producers: Dorothy Aufiero, David Collins, Caroline Kaplan, **Errol Morris**, Alison Palmer Bourke, Jonathan Sehring, John Sloss, Michael Williams
Director: **Errol Morris**
Cinematography: Martin Albert, Robert Chappell, Ian Kincaid, Christoph Lazenberg, Walt Lloyd, Tom Krueger
Editors: Doug Abel, Shondra Burke, Schuyler Cayton, Tom Hill, Chyld King, Juliana Peroni, Karen Schmeer, Sylvia Waliga
Music: Caleb Sampson, John Kusiak
Featuring: Temple Grandin ("Stairway to Heaven"), Saul Kent ("I Dismember Mama"), Sondra London ("The Killer Inside Me"), Bill Kinsley ("The Stalker"), Bony Saludes, Evelyn Bruce, Annette Bridges-Klausing, Victoria Witzowsky, Jim Lenhart ("The Parrot"), Clyde Roper ("Eyeball to Eyeball"), Gretchen Worden ("Smiling in a Jar"), Gary Greenberg ("In the Kingdom of the Unabomber"),

Joan Dougherty ("You're Soaking in It"), Antonio Mendez ("The Little Gray Man"), Josh Harris ("Harvesting Me," 30 minutes), Chris Langan ("The Smartest Man in the World," 29 minutes), Murray Richman ("The Only Truth," 29 minutes), Rick Rosner ("One in a Million Trillion," 56 minutes), Michael Stone ("Mr. Personality," 28 minutes), Denny Fitch ("Leaving the Earth," 55 minutes)
24 minutes per episode, unless otherwise indicated

2003
THE FOG OF WAR: ELEVEN LESSONS FROM THE LIFE OF ROBERT S. MCNAMARA
Producers: Julie Bilson Ahlberg, Jon Kamen, Jack Lechner, Robert May, **Errol Morris**, Frank Scherma, John Sloss, Michael Williams (Sony Pictures Classics, @radical.media, SenArt Films, The Globe Department Store)
Director: **Errol Morris**
Cinematography: Robert Chappell, Peter Donahue
Editors: Doug Abel, Chyld King, Karen Schmeer
Music: Philip Glass
Production Design: Ted Bafaloukos
Featuring: Robert McNamara
106 minutes

2008
S.O.P.: STANDARD OPERATING PROCEDURE
Producers: Julie Bilson Ahlberg, Robert Fernandez, **Errol Morris**, Diane Weyerman (Participant Productions, Sony Pictures Classics)
Director: **Errol Morris**
Cinematography: Robert Chapell, Robert Richardson
Editors: Andy Grieve, Steven Hathaway, Dan Mooney
Music: Danny Elfman
Production Design: Steve Hardie
Featuring: Megan Ambuhl Graner, Ken Davis, Javal Davis, Tony Diaz, Tim Dugan, Lynndie England, Jeffrey Frost, Sabrina Harman, Janis Karpinski, Roman Krol, Jeremy Sivitz, Brent Pack
116 minutes

ERROL MORRIS

INTERVIEWS

Director: Errol Morris

ELLEN HOPKINS/1987

ERROL MORRIS makes documentaries about ordinary people. At least his subjects seem ordinary; then they open their mouths. In *Vernon, Florida*, Morris's profile of a small southern town, a phlegmatic husband and wife describe a trip they once took through the desert, and the wife ambles off to get her souvenir jar of sand. So far, a scene of the most banal normalcy. Then she begins to talk about the sand: "I had just a little bit of this, and now, you see, my jar is nearly full. It grows, it grows, it crawls up the side of the jar. In two more years, it'll fill up this jar." Her husband never blinks.

"My rule of thumb is leave people alone, let them talk, and in two or three minutes, they'll show you how crazy they really are," says Morris, a shaggy thirty-nine-year-old. Over the years, Morris's films have acquired a small but loyal following: critic Roger Ebert numbers *Gates of Heaven* among his top ten movies of all time. (That film, Morris's first, chronicles the fortunes of two California pet cemeteries.) Yet this year marks the first time *Gates of Heaven* and *Vernon, Florida* have been available on videocassette. Perhaps because he's so difficult to categorize, Morris has had more than the ordinary problems getting financing. His latest film, *The Thin Blue Line*, due for release in a few months, documents what Morris believes to be a miscarriage of justice in a Texas murder case. The film cost about $1 million (Morris's first two were in the $200,000 range) and is his first in almost six years. "I think I was given money for this film by mistake," he says, "because it has a number of themes that are easily recognized as 'important': the death penalty, the miscarriage of justice. But I think the movie is interesting independent of all that."

There's an existential malaise to Morris's landscapes—but that's hardly

From *Premiere*, December 1987.

surprising for a filmmaker who was once a graduate student in philosophy. He had planned on writing his thesis on criminal responsibility and the insanity plea, and started interviewing murderers with a cassette tape recorder. The thesis was abandoned and he developed his idiosyncratic documentary technique instead. "I began to realize the tapes I was proudest of were the ones that would run on for hours without my voice on them," he says. "It became a style—trying to convince people to talk as long as possible."

And how does he do it? By not listening. "If your main interest is Keeping People Talking"—he recites the formula with reverence—"the important thing is to look like you're listening, not necessarily to listen. Because if you really start to listen, you feel you have to respond in some way."

Morris's documentaries don't look like conventional documentaries, either. His subjects sit squarely in the space they've chosen, however warily, to occupy, and looking directly into the camera, they talk. There's no interviewer, no narration, no recreated action. "There's a whole style to *cinéma-vérité*—you take very light equipment, use available light, follow the action, remain as unobtrusive as possible. I do the exact opposite," says Morris. "These people are performing for the camera. They're perfectly aware of what's going on."

Morris avoids the punch line, the underlying smirk, refusing to suggest "appropriate" reactions to his subjects. Three cinematographers were fired from *Gates of Heaven* before Morris was able to find one (Ned Burgess) who could resist the temptation to editorialize with the zoom. It's this refusal to smooth away the ambiguities that has led some critics to accuse Morris of ridiculing his subjects. "Just because the films are funny doesn't mean I'm poking fun at people," Morris protests. "Although . . . I think it would be something of a lie to say I'm not *aware* these people are funny. But I don't see myself as any less ridiculous or any less desperate than the people I put on film."

The Thin Blue Line was first conceived as a documentary about a Dallas psychiatrist who often serves as an expert witness in trials of capital crimes. But Morris became sidetracked by the story of one of the prisoners who's been sentenced to die at least in part because of the doctor's testimony. "I started investigating his case—at the time it was the longest unsolved police killing in Dallas history—and eventually I became part of the story itself," Morris says. He believes the wrong man was convicted; because of new evidence that Morris uncovered, that man is no longer under sentence of death and may eventually be released.

"*The Thin Blue Line* is the ultimate paranoid dream," says Morris. "It's like my other movies in its style, but the stakes are much higher here—a man's life. It's the only film I know of where the investigation was actually done with a camera." It wasn't Morris's first experience with skulduggery. During the lean years between *Vernon, Florida* and *The Thin Blue Line*, he spent time as a private detective. "I'd go to expensive restaurants with the guy I'd be investigating, and we'd eat a lot of expensive food and he'd say nothing. I was always frightened because I never seemed to find anything out." Morris says his most important piece of detecting equipment was his K2R stain remover: "It was the only way I kept my suits looking nice enough for those dinners. Then I got the money to make *The Thin Blue Line*. Not only was it an opportunity to do a film again, it was an opportunity to do a real investigation. And I got to put my stain remover away."

Errol Morris's *Cinéma-Realité*

JOEL E. SIEGEL/1988

AT FIRST GLANCE, Errol Morris seems so excessively normal—owlish, black rimmed glasses, nondescript dark jacket, plaid shirt, and khakis—one can't help thinking that he's concealing something. He looks like a CPA who secretly plays the horses with his clients' funds, or maybe a math professor with a foot fetish. Getting to know him, over an Indian dinner—he likes it *extremely hot*—and a Sunday evening walk through Georgetown, these suspicions proved to be correct. Morris's studiously conventional exterior hides—but not very effectively—a first-rate mind, an original creative talent, and incorruptible artistic ideals, the very qualities that *must* be concealed nowadays by any serious filmmaker who hopes to find backing for his projects.

Again, the facts: The forty-year-old filmmaker, who lives with his wife and son in New York City, studied at the University of Wisconsin, Princeton, and the University of California and holds a B.A. in history and an M.A. in philosophy.

His first film was the highly praised *Gates of Heaven* (1978), a dryly funny, oddly moving portrait of two California pet cemeteries—one successful and one failed. (PBS broadcast *Gates of Heaven* last Tuesday as part of its *P.O.V.* series.) Instead of parading the expected Evelyn Waughish gallery of grotesques, Morris's movie probes private dreams, sorrows, and intimations of eternity. His second film, *Vernon, Florida* (1981), is a series of obsessive monologues by the residents of a rural Southern town, another exploration of the mysteries of existence. (The filmmaker consider it the best of his films, "a very pure kind of movie about ideas.") Since making these pictures, Morris has supported himself as a door-to-

From *Washington City Paper*, 2 September 1988. Reprinted by permission.

door cable television salesman and a private detective, while trying to secure backing for his work. Having completed *The Thin Blue Line*, he is currently editing *Dr. Death*, an omnibus film about people like Dr. Grigson who "confront the Beast," and is preparing his first fiction feature, *The Trial of King Boots*, based on a true story of an Old English sheepdog put on trial for murder.

Morris feels rather uncomfortable being characterized as a documentarian and makes a point of calling his new movie "a nonfiction feature." He's unenthusiastic about the documentary film tradition, and considers the work of American documentary godfather Robert Flaherty "unwatchable," an opinion my own unhappy experience confirms.

"I have very little interest in documentary per se, if by that you mean the prevailing style of *cinéma-vérité* filmmaking you see occasionally in theatrical release and very often on television," he says. "*Gates of Heaven* was intentionally designed to reverse most of the tenets of *cinéma-vérité*. Instead of using the lightest and most unobtrusive equipment, I used the heaviest and *most* obtrusive equipment available. After all, part of making films is controlling what you are doing. The idea of being at the mercy of reality is a very unappealing notion, in life as well as in filmmaking. The idea that you are supposed to sit around waiting for things to happen is, to me, all wrong. The belief that style—or the absence of it—somehow guarantees truth is an especially pernicious assumption of *cinéma-vérité*. Style is style, and truth is truth and, as such, isn't guaranteed by anything."

The few documentaries that appeal to Morris are as personal and subjective as his own work—the films of Chris Marker and Frederick Wiseman. He also admires Werner Herzog's documentaries—valuing them above Herzog's better known feature films—and has some enthusiastic things to say about two little seen documentaries by Godard's former associate, Jean-Pierre Gorin. He suggests that the roots of the nonfiction feature "go back to the neo-realist idea of Bresson, Dreyer, and Rossellini. I'm a great fan of Bresson—he's one of my heroes. These directors have found very personal ways of combining realistic material with storytelling." He expresses no fondness at all for two films by directors who have credited *his* work as influences on their own—Diane Keaton, whose dreadful *Heaven* was "inspired" by *Gates of Heaven*, and David Byrne, whose *True Stories* draws heavily on *Vernon, Florida*. ("It isn't true and it isn't a story," Morris snorts.)

Morris is articulate in extracting the ideas that connect his work.

"All the characters in my three films are people who are not really sure what's out there in the world. You're very much aware of the gulf between peoples' fantasies and the realities of their lives. The young guitar-playing guy in *Gates of Heaven* performing a rock concert for the universe of dead pets, the man in *Vernon, Florida* who is hunting for turkeys that might be there or might not be there, that really aren't there but he wishes were there, the old man at the beginning of *Vernon, Florida* with his various Cartesian concerns—the jewel that could be a jewel but might not be a jewel. All of these disjunctures between the world as real and as imagined. *The Thin Blue Line* is somewhat different in the sense that, though it is also about a world of confusion, error, and self-deception, I was forced to face the question of what really *did* happen on that cold November night in Dallas.

"I interviewed over two hundred people in the course of investigating *The Thin Blue Line*. Then I filmed twenty-four interviews, twenty of which were used in the final film. The transcription of those interviews alone runs to close to two thousand single-spaced pages which I typed myself, an enormous undertaking. The eventual transcript of the finished movie is forty-one pages.

"All of this detail is very important. One of the purposes of the re-enactments in the movie is to call attention to the fact that our knowledge is composed of tiny atomic details, some related, some unrelated. The spilled milkshake, the flashlight, the tire marks on the pavement, the two movies Adams and Harris saw that night—*Student Body* and *Swinging Cheerleaders*—all seem to point to clues. Although we don't know the meaning of all those clues, certain things we can be fairly sure of—for example, that the police car was *behind* the blue compact. Then there are things like the milkshake that we don't know the meaning of. The milkshake might be a clue as to whether Teresa Turko had remained in the car while her partner was shot, or whether she was where she claimed to be—standing outside in back of the blue car. Every detail potentially points to a deeper understanding."

Since 1981, Morris has been struggling, with little success, to continue making movies. "I had Hollywood development deals writing screenplays for Dino De Laurentiis and Ed Pressman, but none ever got made. I went to HBO to pitch an idea for a film called *Whatever Happened to Einstein's Brain?*, based on the true story of a brain that took on a life of its own after it ceased to think. They listened very closely, then said, 'It's a wonderful idea, but we can't use it because we're already doing a movie

about transplants.' I pointed out that Einstein's brain hasn't been transplanted yet, but they were unswayed.

"Part of the reason why I haven't been making films for years is that
what I'm trying to do isn't easy to categorize. The person most responsible for seeing that *The Thin Blue Line* got made was Sue Weil, who is se-
nior vice-president for Public Broadcasting here in Washington," he says,
crediting her with keeping the cash flowing. "After *The Thin Blue Line* fin-
ishes its theatrical run and is released on home video, it will be shown on
PBS's *American Playhouse*, but that won't be until the end of next season,
at the earliest."

Although Morris extracts his films from reality, he is very conscious
of cinematic form, especially in how he shoots his interviews. "In one
sense you can say they are unstaged. People aren't told what to say and
are encouraged to talk without interruption. But they *are* staged in the
sense that I take great care in framing them. Very often I have my 'characters' change clothing to suit my color scheme. The shots are very carefully composed and designed.

"Part of the problem of being a 'director-detective'—investigating a
case about which I was also making a film—is that I didn't feel I could
ask people direct questions about the case until I was actually shooting
them. That could annoy them and consequently make arrangements for
a filmed interview impossible. Also, when someone has previously told
you something, it's almost unavoidable they'll lose their spontaneity,
that they will say, 'As I told you . . .' while the camera is running. So, you
see, I never really know what the interviews are going to contain until
the camera rolls."

What compelled Morris to devote two-and-a-half years of his life to
the Randall Adams case, he says, was the wealth of undiscovered material in the case. "The feeling that Adams might be telling me the truth
and, later, *was* telling the truth. The feeling that David Harris could have
been the killer and, later, *was* the killer. The feeling that there was a terrible story behind Doug Mulder's prosecution of Adams. For a long time,
nobody in Dallas seemed to understand or care about what I was doing.
Then, at a certain point, I ran afoul of the Dallas Police Department, who
came to feel I was asking too many questions."

Left untold in *The Thin Blue Line* are the stories of how Morris investigated the case, how he tracked down the mystery witnesses, his relationships with Adams's family and Harris's family, and the tale of how he first
met David Harris while Harris was wandering around free.

"Harris broke our first appointment for a filmed interview because he was out killing somebody. After he was arrested, he broke our second appointment because he was using me in a spectacular escape attempt from Jefferson County Jail in Beaumont, Texas. He kept calling me in New York to see if I could intercede with the prison authorities to let him wear street clothing for the interview. With my usual perceptivity, I assumed he wanted to avoid the stigma of looking like a prisoner. Instead, he slipped on the street clothes and hid in the heating duct system of the jail for seventeen hours. He couldn't find a way out, so finally he got hungry and crawled back down into his cell."

"I waited over a year and half, from out initial meeting in April 1985, to put David Harris on film. I realized I was going to have great trouble filming him while he was awaiting trial for murder. Then, after he was convicted and sentenced to death, I learned that the Texas Department of Corrections put severe restrictions on filming death row inmates. You were only permitted to film them Wednesday mornings as part of a press pool, behind thick glass impregnated with chicken wire. Doing this would have broken with the entire style of my movie, and I refused to do it. I tortured myself for six months, trying to talk myself into accepting those rules. But I really wanted to shoot him sitting in my chair just like everyone else, with proper lights and at the same distance from the lens.

"Finally, David Harris was brought back to Dallas for a writ hearing in federal court concerning the Adams case. I was allowed to film him in jail on the day after the hearing. It was a Friday, I arrived with forty reels of film, prepared to shoot all day and all night if necessary. After several hours, the camera's motor seized. I tried but couldn't get a new camera, it would have to be sent from New York or Los Angeles. I went out to dinner, then came back and told David I would try to return the next day with another camera. He started telling me all these things I didn't want to hear. He indicated that he was about to confess to the killing of Robert Wood. I kept thinking, "Don't tell me that! Wait!" The next day, I came back with two tape recorders. The interview lasted two hours during which he admitted he was alone in the car on the night Wood was killed, which, to me, is tantamount to a confession.

"As a result of *The Thin Blue Line*, a large number of reporters have made this trip down to Huntsville to talk with David Harris. He's been interviewed by the *New York Times*, two Dallas papers, several television programs, even the *Geraldo* show." (Morris grimaces.) "Each time, he comes a little bit closer to saying he killed Robert Wood. He's told people that he pulled the gun from under the seat of the car, that he had his hand on the trigger, and so forth. It's like a crazy game: When will David Harris say the Magic Words?"

"Ironically, whatever David Harris says has no consequence on whether Randall Adams gets released from prison. Harris has no credibility, a death row inmate has nothing to lose. He can confess to this crime one thousand times over without affecting Randall Adams's future in the slightest way. What I have done is to uncover new details about this case to show that Adams did not receive a fair trial in 1977. These details *can* get Adams out of jail if enough people are made aware of them and can force the Texas judiciary to acknowledge them and do something about them.

"I believe that there has been a terrible miscarriage of justice and am hopeful that sooner or later someone will rectify it. There were five witnesses against Adams—David Harris, Teresa Turko, and those three wacko eye-witnesses," he says. "Turko is not a credible witness. . . . Since she claimed she saw only one person in the blue compact, she's actually a better witness for the defense than the prosecution. And David Harris is a convicted murderer. The minute a judge rules that the 1977 trial was unfair, Adams will walk and never be retried for a very simple reason. It would be absurd since there is no evidence against him and never *was* any evidence against him.

"My film is over, but I have an ongoing responsibility to Randall Adams. It would be irresponsible, knowing what I know, to walk away from this case. In a strange way, I have become incarcerated by my own film. Randall Adams believes in me and I, in turn, believe in him. I won't rest until I see him out of jail and exonerated of this crime."

Predilections

MARK SINGER/1989

AMONG THE NONFICTION movies that Errol Morris has at one time or another been eager to make but has temporarily abandoned for lack of investor enthusiasm are *Ablaze!* (or *Fire from Heaven*), an examination of the phenomenon of spontaneous human combustion; *Whatever Happened to Einstein's Brain?* (portions of the cerebellum and the cerebral cortex are thought to be in the possession of a doctor in North Carolina, other parts are floating around here and there); *Road*, the story of one man's attempt to build across northern Minnesota an interstate highway that no one else wanted; *Insanity Inside Out*, based on the book of the same title, by Kenneth Donaldson, a man who, in his forties, was wrongly committed by his parents to a mental hospital and got stuck there for fifteen years; *Weirdo*, about the breeding of a giant chicken; *The Wizard of Wendover*, about Robert K. Golka and his laser-induced fireball experiments in Utah; and a perusal of Yap, a South Pacific island where stone money is the traditional currency.

Some months ago, Morris attended a meeting with executives of Home Box Office, his primary motive being, as they say in the movie business, to pitch an idea—in that case, the one involving Einstein's brain. The meeting did not go particularly well. An HBO person at one point said admonishingly, "You know, your movies are ironic. Our viewers just don't like irony."

Groping for a more tactful evasion, another HBO person said, "We're already doing a transplant movie."

"But wait a second," Morris replied. "This brain hasn't *been* transplanted—*yet*."

From *The New Yorker*, 6 February 1989. Reprinted by permission of Mark Singer.

Unapologetically, Morris draws his films fresh from the substance of the real world, where irony has a way of running riot. Describing his work, he goes to some lengths to avoid using the term "documentary" ("the 'D' word," he will say, in a pinch), but he has not yet coined an alternative label that a Hollywood publicist might use to characterize a generic Errol Morris movie. During the past twelve years, he has directed and released three films: *Gates of Heaven*, about two pet cemeteries in Northern California; *Vernon, Florida*, a series of interviews with several residents of a swamp town in Florida; and *The Thin Blue Line*, which arrived in theatres around the country last summer and fall, and which Morris has described, not immodestly, as "the first murder mystery that actually solves a murder." An Errol Morris movie features real people talking uninterrupted, mainly about literal objects or events, only occasionally about feelings or ideas; trafficking in entertaining truths as well as in equally entertaining transparent prevarications; free-associating, it often seems, as if the camera were a psychotherapist whose expensive time it would be a pity to squander on silence.

Near the midpoint of *Gates of Heaven*, which was completed in 1978, a woman with a pinched mouth whose age might be anywhere from seventy to eighty-five sits in a chair before an open doorway. She is never identified, but, it happens, her name is Florence Rasmussen. In a manner that alternates between passive and bold, accented by facial expressions that range from beatific to sinister, Florence Rasmussen soliloquizes elegiacally:

"I'm raised on a farm, we had chickens and pigs and cows and sheep and everything. But down here I've been lost. Now they've taken them all away from here up to that—What's the name of that place? Up above here a little ways? That town? Commences with a 'B.' Blue. It's—Blue Hill Cemetery, I think the name of it is. Not too far, I guess, about maybe twenty miles from here. A little town there, a little place. You know where it's at. But I was really surprised when I heard they were getting rid of the cemetery over here. Gonna put in buildings or something over there. Ah well, I know people been very good to me, you know. Well, they see my condition, I guess, must of felt sorry for me. But it's real, my condition is. It's not put on. That's for sure! Boy, if I could only walk. If I could only get out. Drive my car. I'd get *another* car. Ya . . . and my son, if he was only better to me. After I bought him that car. He's got a nice car. I bought it myself just a short time ago. I don't know. These kids—the more you do for them. . . . He's my grandson, but I raised him from two years old. . . . I don't see him very often. And he just got the car. I didn't pay for all of it. I gave him four hundred dollars. Pretty good! His boss knows it. Well, he's not working for that outfit now. He's changed. He's gone back on his old job—hauling sand. *No*, not hauling sand; he's working in the office. That's right. He took over the office job. His boss told me that on the phone. But, you know, he should help me more. He's all I got. He's the one who brought me up here. And then put me here by myself among strangers. It's terrible, you stop and think of it. I've been without so much, when I first come up here. Ya. It's what half of my trouble is from—him not being home with me. Didn't cost him nothing to stay here. Every time he need money, he'd always come, 'Mom, can I have this? Can I have that?' But he never pays back. Too good, too easy—that's what everybody tells me. I quit now. I quit. Now he's got the office job, I'm going after him. I'm going after him good, too—if I have to go in . . . in a different way. He's going to pay that money. He's got the office job now. And he makes good money anyway. And he has no kids. He has not married. Never get married, he says. He was married once—they're divorced. Well, she tried to take him for the kid, but she didn't. They went to court. It was somebody else's kid. She was nothing but a tramp in the first place. I told him that. He wouldn't listen to me. I says, 'I know what she is.' I said, 'Richard, please, listen to me.' He wouldn't listen. He knew it all, he knew everything. Big shot! But he soon found out. Now that's all over with. I've been through so much I don't know how I'm staying alive. Really, for my age . . . if you're young, it's different. But I've always said I'm never going to grow old. I've always had that, and the people that I tell how old I am, they don't believe me, because people my age as a rule don't get around like I do."

With an arresting instinct for symmetry, Florence Rasmussen manages to contradict most of what she has to say. It seems that she knows certain things, but then, in the next moment, she trots out contrary information: I have roots with the earth; I'm lost in this world. People have been very good to me; I'm all alone, surrounded by strangers, my own flesh and blood treats me badly. I have a health problem that's real; I protest too much. I'd like to drive my car; but I might not even have a car any longer, might have to buy a new one. I bought my son—O.K., he's not my son, he's my grandson—a new car; well, I didn't pay for the whole thing, I gave him four hundred dollars, but anyway I want my money back. His boss—Hold on, he has a different boss. He hauls sand for a living; nope, he's got that office job now. He's not the marrying kind; he was married once. He has no children; he's been involved in a paternity suit. I'll never grow old; I'm so old people can't believe it. Even though I can't walk, people my age as a rule don't get around like I do.

Gates of Heaven gives an account of a pet cemetery that fails and one that succeeds; Mrs. Rasmussen refers to each in only a glancing manner. The first day that Morris set out as a bona-fide film director with an actual film crew was the day the residents of the failed pet cemetery were being exhumed, so that they could be transferred to the other cemetery. The cinematographer Morris had engaged to shoot *Gates of Heaven* he fired that same day—a consequence of serious philosophical differences that culminated in a physical struggle for the camera. ("It's *mine!*" "No, it's *mine!*") Day Two, Morris met Florence Rasmussen, and she became the first person with whom he ever filmed an interview. The footage from that interview didn't make it into the final cut, however, because the replacement camera operator, a woman, felt compelled to engage the interviewee in a dialogue. When Mrs. Rasmussen mused, "Well, here today, gone tomorrow. Right?" the camerawoman said, "No. Wrong." Morris couldn't decide which made him angrier—that the camerawoman had interfered with the interview or that her notions about death and the hereafter were so misguided. In any event, he fired her on the spot and hired a replacement, who lasted three or four days.

One of Morris's techniques is to situate his interview subject in a chair (when possible, a specific chair: a lightweight canvas-and-metal-frame low-back Regista) that is a precise distance (forty-nine inches) from the camera, which is equipped with a 25mm Zeiss high-speed prime lens—a lens of fixed focal length, which is one that cannot zoom—and is secured to a tripod, so that the camera cannot pan. When Morris went back to reshoot Mrs. Rasmussen—accompanied by Ned Burgess, his fourth, and final, cinematographer—she rewarded him with what has become the emblem of the Morris style: a seamless monologue from someone who has been allowed to talk until the truth naturally sorts itself out. Quotidian lies, the little fabrications that make the commerce of daily life possible, if not always palatable, are laid on the surface by the speaker. A muted strain of implicit skepticism—the silent voice of the filmmaker— bubbles along just beneath that. Peripheral stuff turns out to matter. "I like the idea of making films about ostensibly absolutely nothing," Morris says. "I like the irrelevant, the tangential, the sidebar excursion to nowhere that suddenly becomes revelatory. That's what all my movies are about. That and the idea that we're in possession of certainty, truth, infallible knowledge, when actually we're just a bunch of apes running around. My films are about people who think they're connected to something, although they're really not."

Gates of Heaven is the only one of Morris's films that can be said to have emerged with its original subject matter intact. *The Thin Blue Line*, which at its inception was to have been a study of Dr. James Grigson, a Texas psychiatrist who regularly testifies for the prosecution in death-penalty cases, instead became a horrifyingly satiric examination of the wrongful murder conviction and near-execution of an innocent man. *Vernon, Florida*, which is essentially plotless—a pastiche of interviews with a turkey hunter, a policeman, a retired couple who are convinced that a glass jar in their possession contains radioactive sand that grows, a wild-animal collector, a Holy Roller preacher, a worm farmer, and others—evolved haphazardly, almost desperately, from an unwieldy idea Morris had of making a fiction film based upon a bizarre insurance scam. A loquacious man named Albert Bitterling, who appears intermittently throughout *Vernon, Florida*, has held a pair of opera glasses against the lens of a camera and photographed the night sky. In one scene, displaying the opaque result, he says, "Of course, as you can see is that picture ain't too good, it's a cheap camera, you get a cheap picture." Then, speaking literally and in metaphor, he encapsulates the filmmaker's dilemma: "Well, of course, you see, when you have a camera. . . . You have a camera and you point it at a certain—just like if you had a gun. You don't shoot, do you? Well, if you had a gun and you pointed it at something, you're liable to hit what you're pointing at, and then again you might not."

Vernon, Florida has been, as a practical matter, the least accessible of Morris's films; it was completed in 1981, but a commercial videocassette version of it has just been released. Videocassettes of *Gates of Heaven* became available only a few months ago. *The Thin Blue Line* is the first of Morris's films to be widely distributed in theatres. A word that regularly comes up when Morris discusses the until quite recent low-orbit trajectory of his career is "disturbing." The frustration of making movies that only modest numbers of people have seen, or even heard of, has encouraged Morris to cultivate a melodramatic haplessness. In a less ironically disposed person, this tendency might be taken for neurotic self-indulgence. When Morris consents to be the interviewee—when it becomes his turn to sort the truth out—he ends up quoting Shakespeare ("But since the affairs of men rest still uncertain, let's reason with the worst that may befall") or himself ("The fact that the world is, like, utterly insane makes it tolerable"). Once, when I made the mistake of asking, in an offhand manner, how he'd been feeling lately, he said, "I've been horribly depressed, which, as you know, can be terribly time-consuming. I mean, if you're going to do it right, that is." Another time, en route to a preview screening of *The Thin Blue Line*, he said, "I hope this won't be terribly embarrassing." A pause, then: "No, actually, I remember, when I was a teen-ager, thinking there was no point in going on, but then I realized that life is just an endless series of embarrassments and I'd hate to miss out on all that."

The first time I met Morris was in an airport, on a day in early 1987, when he was still working on *The Thin Blue Line* and was flying to Dallas to attend a federal-court hearing. He wore a navy pin-striped suit, carried a briefcase, and could easily have masqueraded as a typical traveling litigator except that he was not flying first class. Days when he doesn't wear a suit, he dresses like a permanent graduate student—khakis, Black Watch blazer or tweed jacket, button-down shirt, dark-framed dark Kentish eyeglasses. He has short dark-brown hair, which often looks as if it had been slept on the wrong way, and a rueful, asymmetrical smile. Although he is six-one, imperfect posture renders his presence less than imposing. Photographs make him appear either darkly handsome or dolefully goofy. Morris is now forty-one years old. He grew up in Hewlett, on the South Shore of Long Island. His father, a doctor, died when he was two, and his mother, a Juilliard graduate, who did not remarry for more than twenty years, supported him and an older brother by teaching music in a public school. Errol studied cello, read with a passion the forty-odd *Oz* books, watched a lot of television, and on a regular basis went with a doting but not quite right maiden aunt ("I guess you'd have to say that Aunt Roz was somewhat demented") to Saturday matinees, where he saw stuff like *This Island Earth* (1955) and *Creature from the Black Lagoon* (1954)—horror movies that, viewed again thirty years later, still seem scary to him. "I don't really understand how Errol got drawn to these gothic themes that interest him—maybe that he lost his father," his mother, Cinnabelle Esterman, told me not long ago. "I remember the first time we went on a trip out West. We had to take a flight to Chicago, and a friend drove us to the airport. And I noticed that along the way, in the car, Errol was reading the *World Almanac*, studying about air crashes." In the tenth grade, he was enrolled in the Putney School, in Vermont. Part of what had drawn him to Putney was its highly regarded music program. Morris's most vivid memories, however, include having a forbidden radio confiscated because one evening he made the mistake of loudly singing along while listening to Birgit Nilsson perform the immolation scene from *Götterdammerung*. On another occasion, for an offense that he cannot recall, a dormitory proctor deprived him of his cello.

Next came the University of Wisconsin, where he excelled academically ("the first time I did really well at anything, except elementary school") and, in 1969, received a degree in history. For a couple of years, he drifted about, earning money as a cable-television salesman in Wisconsin and as a term-paper writer in Massachusetts and "trying to get accepted at different graduate schools just by showing up on their doorstep." This strategy, which did not succeed at Oxford and Harvard, finally worked at Princeton, but graduate school soon proved to have been not such a hot idea. Morris's mistake was in pursuing academic disciplines—at Princeton, the history of science—in which he had "absolutely no background."

"I did enter Princeton actually thinking I was going to get a doctorate," he says. "I was wrong. I had big fights with my adviser. I was supposed to be concentrating on the history of physics. And, naturally, my adviser expected me to take all these courses in physics. But the classes were always full of fourteen-year-old Chinese prodigies, with their hands in the air—'Call on me! Call on me!' I couldn't do it. I reneged on some of my commitments. At the end, my adviser actually assaulted me. He was on sabbatical and had an office at the Institute for Advanced Study. I remember thinking, This is the Institute for Advanced Study, and he's *assaulting* me. I'd written a thirty-page double-spaced paper, and he produced thirty single-spaced pages of his own criticizing it. The bile just flowed out of him. I accused him of not even finishing reading what I'd written. It turns out I *was* a problem, but at least I wasn't a drudge, and that school was filled with drudges. I remember saying to my adviser, 'You won't even look through my telescope.' And his response was 'Errol, it's not a telescope, it's a kaleidoscope.'"

In 1972, Morris moved to Berkeley, where he had been accepted as a Ph.D. candidate in philosophy at the University of California. His recollections of that experience also lack a warm glow, but something fundamentally positive did take place, which was that he discovered the Pacific Film Archive, a cinemathèque/library/revival house/symposium center, and the only place in the Bay Area with the ability to devote several days to a retrospective of, say, the cinema of Senegal. Tom Luddy, a film producer, who was then the director of the Archive, recently said, "There were a bunch of regulars and a bunch of eccentric regulars, and Errol was one of the eccentrics. I often had to defend him to my staff. What made him eccentric? Well, for one thing, he dressed strangely. Remember, this is Berkeley in the early seventies. And Errol was wearing dark suits with pants that were too short, white dress shirts, and heavy shoes. He looked like a New York person gone to seed. Then, I let him use our library for research, and he was always getting into little frictions with the staff. He felt he could both use the Archive and put it down. He would leave messes. He never bothered to re-shelve books. I found myself defending him, which was often difficult, because he would attack me for the programming. He was a *film noir* nut. He claimed we weren't showing the *real* film noir. So I challenged him to write the program notes. Then, there was his habit of sneaking into the films and denying that he was sneaking in. I told him if he was sneaking in he should at least admit he was doing it."

The Archive opened each afternoon at five-thirty. Among the other eccentrics were a superannuated Berkeley professor who had a habit of showing up at 5:30 A.M.; the narcoleptic who used to come for the first show, immediately fall asleep, and remain that way through the final feature; a disconcertingly loud laugher, known as the Cackler; and a misanthropic woman who, with her dog, lived in a van outside the Archive.

Meanwhile, Morris's academic career failed to thrive. "Berkeley was just a world of pedants," he says. "It was truly shocking. I spent two or three years in the philosophy program. I have very bad feelings about it." His own flaw, he believes, was that he was "an odd combination of the academic and the prurient." While he was supposed to be concentrating on the philosophy of science, his attention became diverted by an extracurricular interest in the insanity plea. A quotation from *The Black Cat*—a story in which Edgar Allan Poe writes of "the spirit of perverseness . . . this unfathomable longing of the soul *to vex itself* . . . to do wrong for the wrong's sake only"—had become resonant for him, and he began to ponder the metaphysics of mass murder. In 1975, he returned to Wisconsin long enough to have several interviews with Ed Gein, the real-life prototype for the Norman Bates character in *Psycho* and a Midwestern legend. "You couldn't spend long in Wisconsin, especially with my predilection, without hearing a lot about Ed Gein," Morris says. Gein was then confined to Central State Hospital, in Waupun, a maximum-security institution for the criminally insane. Evidently, Morris was the first person in quite a while to make a special effort to talk with him. What perhaps discouraged other potential visitors was that Gein not only murdered people but also was a cannibal, a grave robber, and an amateur taxidermist. Morris found his way to Dr. George Arndt, a Geinologist and the author of a study—a catalogue of Ed Gein jokes, basically—titled *Community Reaction to a Horrifying Event.*

"I go and meet Dr. Arndt," Morris says. "Almost from the beginning, I entertain serious doubts about the wholesomeness of Dr. Arndt's interest in the Gein case. Dr. Arndt seems real excited that there's this kindred spirit interested in the Ed Gein story. I tell him I've been spending a lot of time in Plainfield, Wisconsin, where Ed Gein lived and committed his crimes. I tell him I've been to the Plainfield cemetery to look at graves. I had the names of the graves whose occupants Ed had exhumed. I noticed that those graves made a circle around his mother's grave. Dr. Arndt looks at me and says, 'You know what that means, don't you?' I say, 'No, sir.' He says, 'It's a kind of sublimation. Transference. He couldn't go down directly after his mother. He had to go down through the other graves.' He says, 'There may be underground tunnels leading to his mother's grave.' So we go in his Cadillac to the Plainfield cemetery. When we're almost there, he pulls over and starts looking around in the brush for something, and he comes up with a big thick stick. We get to the cemetery, we find the graves where the exhumations took place, and he has me put my ear to the ground near Mrs. Gein's grave. While I do that, Dr. Arndt walks around beating the ground, searching for hollow sounds. I hear nothing. Finally, I ask, 'Dr. Arndt, why didn't he just dig straight into Mrs. Gein's grave?' And Dr. Arndt gives me this look and says, *'Too devious.'* "

During his research, Morris stumbled across the provocative fact that Plainfield, with a population of seven hundred, had within a ten-year period been home to several multiple killers, and that Gein's depredations had antedated the others', almost as if he had driven the town mad.

"One of the things that have always fascinated me about abnormal behavior is that we can't really explain it to our satisfaction," Morris says. "Almost everything I do now in my work is about epistemic concerns: how do we come by certain kinds of knowledge? Take the insanity plea—we talk about insane acts and insane people. When we talk about insane acts, we're saying we don't understand something about the act itself. When we say someone is insane, we're either saying, one, 'That person could be mentally ill,' or, two, 'I don't *know* why that person does what he does.' Rather than expressing a knowledge, we're expressing a *lack* of knowledge. I wrote an essay on the insanity plea and movie monsters and certain mechanistic fantasies we have about criminal behavior. I very much wanted to write a doctoral thesis on this stuff, and it hurt my feelings when Berkeley just sort of kicked my ass out of there."

The demise of Morris's academic career was a protracted matter, and he stayed at the university long enough to get a master's degree in phi-losophy. All the while, he was a devotee of the Pacific Film Archive. Tom Luddy introduced him to Werner Herzog, the German director, whose fascination with fanatics, losers, Nazi supermen, and dwarfs dovetailed with Morris's outside-the-mainstream preoccupations. Once, making the film *Even Dwarfs Started Small* (1970), Herzog inadvertently set a dwarf afire; the dwarf survived, and Herzog did penance by throwing himself onto a cactus. At the time he and Morris met, Morris's reading diet included, in addition to his academic texts, the *National Enquirer* and *Weekly World News*. For listeners whom he deemed worthy, he had as-sembled an endlessly aggressive repertoire that included eyewitness tales of Geinology and other vignettes of American dementia.

"Werner was very taken with Errol," Luddy recalls, adding that, de-spite Morris's never having shot a single foot of film, "Werner treated him as an equal."

Morris and Herzog discussed the question that Morris and Dr. Arndt had left unanswered—whether or not Gein had disinterred his mother—and they set a date for a rendezvous in Plainfield in the summer of 1975. The idea was that, with shovels, in the moonlight, they would satisfy their curiosity. When Herzog arrived in Plainfield, however—he had been working on a film in Alaska and was now driving toward New York—no familiar face was there to greet him. He made a phone call to California and learned that Morris had had second thoughts. A few months later, Morris did return to Plainfield, alone, and rented a room from Ed Gein's next-door neighbors. This time, he stayed almost a year, during which he conducted hundreds of hours of interviews with some of the other homicidally inclined local talent. He had no focused idea of what to do with the material. Maybe he would make a film about Ed Gein called *Digging Up the Past*, or maybe he would write a book. Although he still had a fellowship at the University of California, he didn't have enough money to transcribe all his interview tapes. Some supplemen-tary financial support came from his family, but it was not unqualified support. "My mother was worried about what I was doing," he says. "She has this wonderfully euphemistic way of talking to me. At one point, she said, 'Errol, can't you spend more time with people your own age?' And I said, 'But, Mom, some of these mass murderers are my own age.'"

It didn't do Morris any good when, in order to talk to one of the Plain-field murderers, he made his way illegally into a state mental hospital, got caught, and was reported to his academic supervisors at Berkeley. In the fall of 1976, while Morris was still in Plainfield, Herzog unexpectedly returned. During Herzog's visit the previous year, his car had broken down, and he had discovered an automobile-repair shop—a grim place set against a grim, flat natural backdrop—that struck him as an excellent movie location. So now he had come to finish a film, *Stroszek* (1977), most of which had been shot in Berlin. He asked Morris to work with him, but Morris felt that he had been abused. "Stealing a *landscape*," he complained. "The worst kind of plagiarism." On the other hand, he had never made a film himself, and here was a chance to observe a master. So he stuck around, and when the shooting was completed, Herzog, afflicted with some measure of guilt, handed him an envelope stuffed with cash. They were in a motel room. Morris went to a window and tossed the envelope into a parking lot. After retrieving the money, Herzog offered it once more, saying, "Please don't do that again."

The envelope contained about two thousand dollars—more than enough to finance a two-week trip Morris had been planning. Recently, he had read a newspaper article about an insurance investigator which mentioned, in passing, how several people in an unidentified Southern town had tried to collect benefits after "accidentally" losing limbs. Morris had tracked down the insurance investigator and learned that the town was Vernon (population 883), in the Florida panhandle. Vernon's unofficial nickname was now Nub City. In the hierarchy of nubbiedom, the supremely rewarding self-sacrifice was the loss of a right leg and a left arm, because, so the theory went, "afterward, you could still write your name and still have a foot to press the gas pedal of your Cadillac." Morris stayed in Vernon long enough to read some files at the courthouse, talk to an insurance broker and several nubbies, and receive at least one unambiguous death threat. At the Cat's Eye Tavern one night, a citizen twice Morris's size smiled as he extinguished a cigarette on the lapel of Morris's blazer. Morris remembers thinking that perhaps he had packed the wrong clothes. Also, "I remember it hurt my feelings, because it seemed that, you know, maybe the people in Vernon didn't like me." Rarely did murders take place in Vernon, because, someone explained, "down here, people don't get murdered—they just disappear."

Back in Berkeley, Morris tried to write a script for a fiction feature to be called *Nub City*. Mainly, he had a pitch line—*Nub City* would be "about people who, in order to achieve the American dream, literally become a fraction of themselves"—but the plot elements were still gestating. Months went by and he made only slight progress. One afternoon while waiting for inspiration to descend, he was eating lunch in the Swallow, a restaurant in the same building as the Pacific Film Archive, and he saw a headline in the San Francisco *Chronicle* that said, "450 DEAD PETS GOING TO NAPA VALLEY." Suddenly, he had an altogether different idea for a film; *Nub City* would have to wait.

It was enough that in deciding to make *Gates of Heaven* Morris selected a subject that, on its surface, seemed highly likely to repel. He also insisted on making a documentary film "the opposite of how you were supposed to." That meant being static and obtrusive—using artificial light and heavy, earthbound equipment rather than the standard hand-held, mobile tools of *cinéma vérité*. After Morris hooked up with Ned Burgess, a compliant cinematographer, the making of *Gates of Heaven* progressed in a straightforward fashion. The film was shot in the spring and summer of 1977 and cost $120,000 to make; the money came from a wealthy graduate-school classmate and from Morris's family.

Getting to know mass murderers and their relatives in Wisconsin, Morris had developed an interview technique that, reduced to basics, amounted to: Shut up and let people talk. "Listening to what people were saying wasn't even important," he says. "But it was important to *look* as if you were listening to what people were saying. Actually, listening to what people are saying, to me, interferes with looking as if you were listening to what people are saying."

The first half of *Gates of Heaven* explores the broken dream of a man named Floyd McClure, who lives in Los Altos, a peninsula town thirty miles south of San Francisco. In the opening frames, McClure describes, in a sincere but unmaudlin manner, how the accidental death of a beloved collie in his childhood inspired his vision of a pet cemetery. Choosing a site, he settled on what he calls "the most beautiful piece of land, as far as I was concerned, in the whole valley." (Never mind that the land was situated right next to a freeway; it also happened to be across the street from his house.) "A pet-cemetery business is not a fast-buck scheme, it's not a suede-shoe game," McClure says. "It's a good, solid business enterprise. And in order to have this concept it has to be in your heart, not in your billfold. And these are the type of people I wanted in business with me, in the pet-cemetery concept." His co-investors in the by-now-failed enterprise allow themselves to be interviewed, the owner of a rendering plant talks, families of departed pets have their say, Florence Rasmussen appears. Monologues tend not to parse. At one point, McClure says, "And this is the part of the inspiration of getting our little pets . . . into a cemetery. Something that we could be proud of, of saying, 'My little pet did his chore here—that God has sent him to us to do a chore—love and be loved and serve his master.' And, boy, these little pets that did that. . . . Like I said before—death is for the living and not for the dead."

The second half of *Gates of Heaven* focuses on the Harberts family— Cal and his wife, Scottie, and their sons, Dan and Phil—who are the proprietors of Bubbling Well Pet Memorial Park, the *final* final resting place of the displaced tenants of Floyd McClure's doomed pet-cemetery *concept*. Dan, the younger son, has been employed in the family business for a few years. Phil has recently given up selling insurance in Utah (his idol is W. Clement Stone, the Chicago insurance tycoon and an avatar of the Positive Mental Attitude) and has repatriated to the Napa Valley.

Cal Harberts says, "We created the Garden of Honor. And in this garden we will bury a Seeing Eye dog or a police dog killed in the line of duty at *no* cost—*if* it's killed in the line of duty. And for anybody else who wants to share this garden then we created a price which amounts to more than any other garden that we have."

Phil, who manifests what might or might not be symptoms of an incipient existential crisis—possibly a consequence of having listened to and delivered too many motivational lectures—says, "I have to say to myself: What does it mean to me? What does *this* mean to me? What is it going to mean to me? I recognize this and— A couple of things when I was instructing motivation back in Salt Lake City is that if we don't stop and ask ourselves a question once in a while to probe our subconscious or to probe our conscious . . . I used to teach it. It's a plain, simple formula. We reduced everything to a formula, memorized it, and therefore we were able to repeat it constantly. I used to call it the R2-A2 formula: Recognize, Relate, Assimilate, and put into Action! Like, I could be driving down the freeway and see a 450 SL. I could say, 'Hey, I like that. What does that mean to me? What would I have to do to get it? How can I do it?' And then go to work for it. And strive for it. It kind of makes life easy. I think that's why a lot of people don't— They get frustrated. They have emotional problems, it's that they don't know how to cope with their— *mind*. There are three things that I've got to do and that if anybody wants to do to be successful, to have the desire, the want-to. Why do you go to work in the morning? *Gee, why am I here?* Because you want to. But that's obvious. And then the next very important ingredient is something that a lot of people and a lot of businesses fail to delve into. It's the activity knowledge. It would be the equation to a mathematical problem. It would be equal to the chemist's ability to emulsify chemicals—you know, properly, the valences. But the knowledge of it, the whole scope. Everything in detail. And then the third element would be, of course, the know-how or the experience. I have the inspiration to action. I don't have the activity knowledge, but I'm getting the know-how before I'm getting the activity knowledge. As a matter of fact, I'm getting more know-how than I'm getting activity knowledge. But they can be correlated together. They can be overlapped."

Dan Harberts says, "As far as preparation—a hole has to be dug, prepared. We have to make sure that the hole is going to fit the size of the casket. Because you don't want to make it too large, because you're going to waste space. And you don't want to make it too small, because you can't get the thing in there."

Gates of Heaven was first shown during the 1978 New York Film Festival, which happened to coincide with a newspaper strike. In other words, *Gates of Heaven* sprang into a void. When the film opened in Berkeley, that same year, a glowing review by Michael Covino appeared in the *East Bay Express*. (Covino later retooled the essay, and it was published in *Film Quarterly*.) More than two years elapsed before *Gates of Heaven* was seen again, in New York or anywhere else—before anyone paid significant attention. In the spring of 1981, New Yorker Films arranged a limited national distribution. The notices were favorable—in several instances, extravagantly so. Perhaps the most ardent champion of *Gates of Heaven* across the years has been Roger Ebert, who includes it in his list of the ten best films of all time and calls it "compulsively watchable, a film that has engaged me as no other movie has in my twenty-one years as a movie critic." When Ebert is invited to give a speech and is told that he can screen a film of his choosing, he selects *Gates of Heaven*, which he regards as "a film about hope—hope held by the loneliest people who have ever been on film." Ebert estimates that he has seen it at least fifty times—often enough to have memorized long passages. "Every time I show this, it plays differently," he says. "Some people think it's about animals. Some people think it's about life and death. I've shown it to a group of bankers, who believe it raises all kinds of questions about success, about starting a small business. People think it's funny or sad or deadpan or satirical. They think that Errol Morris loved the people in the film, or that he was being very cruel to them. I've never yet had a person tell me that it's a bad film or a film that doesn't interest them."

Werner Herzog commemorated the Berkeley premiere of *Gates of Heaven* by eating one of his shoes—a poached desert boot—in a public ceremony. Though less spectacular than flinging oneself upon a cactus, this event was sufficiently momentous for the documentary filmmaker Les Blank to record it in a twenty-minute short titled *Werner Herzog Eats*

His Shoe (1980). A haze of myth enshrouds the genesis of the shoe-eating. Tom Luddy's version has Herzog, while one day arguing with Morris in a hallway of the Pacific Film Archive, saying, "You'll never make a film, but if you do I'll come and eat my shoe at the premiere." Herzog maintains that it happened in a more encouraging manner, as in "You are going to make a film. And the day I am going to see the film in a theatre I will eat the shoes I am wearing." Morris, who claims not to recall any of the above, says the entire stunt was concocted by Luddy.

"I didn't make *Gates of Heaven* so that Werner Herzog would have to eat his shoe," he says. "It's not as if I decided to realize my potential as a human being in order to get somebody to ingest something distasteful. I specifically asked Werner *not* to eat his shoe." Morris was supposed to fly from New York to Berkeley to attend the screening and to appear in Les Blank's film. At Kennedy Airport, he boarded a plane, but when a mechanical problem forced all the passengers to get off he decided not to go. "As a result, I don't appear in *Werner Herzog Eats His Shoe*," he says. "I suppose I regret that reticence. Why be so prissy? Why try so hard to control things? I'm not even sure what that's all about. Probably, as a result of my petulant behavior, fewer people have seen *Gates of Heaven* than otherwise would have. In fact, I'm still surprised when anyone tells me he's seen it."

In the winter of 1979, Morris went back to Vernon, Florida, and for very little money he was able to rent one of the biggest houses in the county. Vernon was no less xenophobic than any other small Southern town. When the locals asked Morris why he had come there and he gave vague, misleading answers, the typical response was "No, you're here because of the Nub City stuff." He spent much of his time attending revival meetings and driving around to places that had interesting names— Blackhead, Lizard Lake, the Ebro Dog Track. Although he was still enamored of the Nub City idea, he had not yet written a workable screenplay. If he were to try to make a nonfiction film about the Nub City episode, "it would turn into one of those bad investigative documentaries where people are slamming doors in your face." Finally, after several months of insisting "I'm not here about Nub City, I'm not making a film about Nub City," guilt overwhelmed him, he indeed became incapable of making a film about Nub City, and he left town.

A year later, he returned, rented the same big house, and spun his wheels some more. Now, however, vacillation carried a steeper price tag, because he had financial help from German television and from WNET, the public-television affiliate in New York. A crew of recent graduates from the New York University film school drove to Vernon in a rented van, bringing with them equipment so heavy that the van blew out two sets of tires on the drive south. When they arrived, Morris had still not decided what the film would be about. A controversy had arisen involving the firing and rehiring of one of the local police officers. Morris felt that the officer's travails were connected with "the Napoleonic ambitions of the king of the nubbies." The king of the nubbies had advised Morris to leave town within twenty-four hours or leave in a casket. When Morris failed to oblige, the king made what seemed a sincere effort to run down Ned Burgess, the cinematographer, with a truck. More or less in desperation—to get the king of the nubbies off his back, to give the public-television people something, *anything*, for their money—Morris began to film interviews with various interesting citizens of Vernon, among them Roscoe Collins, the cop; Joe Payne, the collector of wild animals (opossum, gopher, tortoise, rattlesnake); Albert Bitterling, the cosmologist with the opera glasses ("Reality—you mean, *this* is the real world? Ha, ha, ha. I never thought of that"); George Harris and Claude Register, two geezers who discuss how an acquaintance put a shotgun to his forehead and pulled the trigger with his big toe ("And he said, that day, he says, 'That'll be the last thing I ever do is to shoot myself.' Which it was"), *Vernon, Florida* contains not a single reference to Nub City. Rather, as with *Gates of Heaven*, the film's subjects are the American vernacular and the malleability of truth. Morris presents Vernon, Florida, as is—no special effects, what you see is what you get—as if he had stumbled across, and without editorial intrusion had agreed to share, an unexplored settlement full of Florence Rasmussens.

Howard Pettis, the worm farmer, says, "I've never studied no book on these wigglers. What I know about 'em is just self-experience. They got books on 'em, but them books is wrong. They don't teach you right. They don't teach you right on 'em. Teach you what kind of feed to feed 'em. How to do 'em and all, there. And it's all wrong, in my book."

Henry Shipes, the turkey hunter ("I can't tell you how it feel. It's just a hell of a sport, that's all"), sits in a chair in his living room and, with enormous relish, recounts the gut-stirring thrills of each of a series of trophy kills. While the viewer is not prohibited from imputing deep meanings to the images or the monologues of Henry Shipes, one ultimately gets the feeling that if turkey hunting stands as a metaphor for anything it is probably turkey hunting. In the film's final scene, Henry Shipes, on a hunt, surveys a crowd of buzzards roosting on a cypress tree and counts them aloud—thirty-five. "Listen to that sound," he says. "That *fwoop fwoop*. Hear that sound? Getting in and out of the trees? That flop-flop sound? Mmm-hmm. That sound'll sure mistake you for turkeys. Listen! Hear that flop- flop? Limbs breaking. Hear that good flop then? Listening to that gives me the *turkey fever*. Mmm-hmm. I wish there's as many turkeys as there are buzzards."

Like *Gates of Heaven*, *Vernon* had its premiere at the New York Film Festival—the 1981 edition. Werner Herzog called it "an invention of cinema, a discovery of one side of cinema that all of us have not known yet." A review in *Newsweek* said it was "a film as odd and mysterious as its subjects, and quite unforgettable—unforgettable, that is, for those who laid eyes on it. Because it had a running time of only sixty minutes, no national distributor materialized, and not until the summer of 1982, when it was shown on public television, did significant numbers of viewers or critics take notice. Meanwhile, Morris was, as usual, low on funds. He was living in Manhattan, occupying rooms in a series of not quite elegant hotels— the Carter, the Bryant, the Edison, the Wellington—before finally settling in a building in the West Fifties, where he still keeps an apartment. The more dire his fiscal circumstances grew, the better he got to know a Mr. Montori, an employee of a collection agency. Mr. Montori seemed to derive pleasure from gracing Morris's telephone-answering machine with one-a-day rhetorical questions like "Mr. Morris, have you no sense of shame?" and "Mr. Morris, were you really brought up to act this way?" Then the calls abruptly ceased. After several months had passed, Morris phoned the collection agency, asked, "Is Mr. Montori okay?" and learned that his tormentor had moved on to a more rewarding position elsewhere.

In earnest, Morris sought backing for what turned out to be some of his most resistible film projects: *Road*, the story of the northern Minnesota interstate-highway folly; Robert K. Golka, the laser-induced-fireball wizard in Utah; Centralia, Pennsylvania, the coal town where an inextinguishable subterranean fire began burning in 1962. Morris concluded that "people who tend to be interested in documentary filmmaking weren't interested in my films, because they didn't look like documentary films." The theme of *Road*, in particular—a man wants to create a complicated and expensive thing for which absolutely no need exists— was, he says, "disturbingly self-reflective."

As his debts accumulated, his stepfather advised him that the time had come to "turn yourself in to the phone company." Instead, Morris permitted himself a brief Hollywood interlude. In 1983, Edward Pressman, a producer whose credits include films by Brian De Palma, Terrence Malick, and Oliver Stone, agreed to finance the development of a screenplay about the exploits of John and Jim Pardue, brothers from Missouri who, fifteen years earlier, had killed their father, their grandmother, and two accomplices and robbed five banks, in two instances using dynamite. Pitching the film, Morris would say, "The great bank-robbery sprees always take place at a time when something is going wrong in the country. Bonnie and Clyde were apolitical, but it's impossible to imagine them without the Depression as a back-drop. The Pardue brothers were apolitical, but it's impossible to imagine them without Vietnam." Pressman underwrote a sojourn at the Chateau Marmont, a Hollywood hotel that is famous in part because John Belushi died there (not because Errol Morris wrote anything memorable while in residence). Morris enlisted Tom Waits and Mickey Rourke to portray the Pardue brothers, and got as far as writing a treatment before the project derailed.

Next, Morris was set to direct a Pressman film called *The King Lives*, about an Elvis Presley impersonator; this venture proceeded not very far before Morris was fired. For Dino De Laurentiis, Morris agreed to work on an adaptation of a Stephen King short story. Then De Laurentiis changed his mind and asked him to adapt a different King short story. Then he changed his mind again and gave Morris two and a half weeks to write a screenplay based on King's *Cycle of the Werewolf*. Around the time that De Laurentiis rejected the script—because it "wasn't frightening enough"— Morris's brother and only sibling, Noel, died suddenly of a heart attack, at age forty. "I was very depressed," Morris says. His apartment in Manhattan was a couple of blocks from the Ed Sullivan Theatre, from whose studios fund-raising telethons were often broadcast. He found himself dropping in. "My favorite was the Stop Arthritis Telethon," he says. "When I would go to these things, I would always see the same people in the audience, and I'd look upon them with some pity, and then I realized that I was one of them."

In 1984, Morris married Julia Sheehan, an art historian, whom he had met in Wisconsin in the mid-seventies, during his Ed Gein phase. Julia had tried to get a friend to introduce them, but the friend "made such a mess of it I actually approached Errol to apologize," she says. "I wanted to meet him because I'd heard he had been interviewing murderers. I didn't know anyone else who knew any murderers. It was quiet in Wisconsin— the sixties were over, not much was going on—so somebody who had met murderers sounded good." Morris recalls saying to her, early in their relationship, "I was talking to a mass murderer but I was thinking of you," and immediately fearing that this might not have sounded affectionate. Julia, however, was flattered: "I thought, really, that was one of the nicest things anyone ever said to me. It was hard to go out with other guys after that." They share a vivid and fond memory of their wedding, which took place in the Criminal Court Building in Brooklyn.

"They frisked us on the way in, which was very romantic," Julia says.

"We got married between two prostitution cases," Morris says. "And we celebrated with a whale-shaped cake from Carvel."

They have since become the parents of Nathaniel Hamilton Morris, and Julia has come to understand her husband well. Some time ago, she stopped in at the Strand Bookstore to pick up an order for him. The clerk who was helping her couldn't find the books and asked whether she knew the subject matter. "I don't know any of the titles," she said. "But they're probably about either insanity or murder or Nazis." Indeed, there was one of each.

"The Nazis, of course, are interesting to me," Morris once told me. "I just finished reading Joseph Goebbels' diary. You know a movie director Goebbels really liked? Frank Capra. I have this heart-warming image of Goebbels sneaking away from the office in mid-afternoon to go watch *Meet John Doe* (1941) or *Mr. Deeds Goes to Town* (1936)."

What Morris likes to call his "predilections" led him, in early 1985, to Dr. James Grigson, a Dallas psychiatrist. Under Texas law, a jury cannot impose the death penalty unless it is confident that a convicted person will commit future violent crimes. To encourage juries to arrive at that conclusion, Dr. Grigson for more than fifteen years regularly appeared as a prosecution witness in capital cases. In almost every instance, Dr. Grigson would, after examining a defendant, testify that he had found the individual in question to be an incurable sociopath, who it was "one hundred percent certain" would kill again. When Morris first went to see Dr. Grigson, it was with the idea of making a film titled *Dr. Death.* Grigson proved to be as obliging to Morris as he had been to the prosecutors he served, and encouraged him to interview several men who, helped along by Dr. Grigson's testimony, had received the death penalty. Don't be surprised if these fellows profess their innocence, Dr. Grigson warned; that, after all, is how sociopaths behave.

A number of the twenty-five or so inmates with whom Morris spoke made such a claim. One was a thirty-six-year-old man named Randall Dale Adams, who was an inmate of the Eastham Unit, a maximum-security prison in southeast Texas. In the spring of 1977, Adams had been convicted of and sentenced to die for the murder, the previous fall, of Robert Wood, a Dallas police officer. Wood had been shot five times by the driver of a car that he and his partner, Teresa Turko, had stopped in west Dallas for a minor traffic violation. Nearly a month elapsed between the murder of Wood and Adams's arrest. Adams told Morris that he had been framed, and that the actual killer was David Harris—"the kid," he kept calling him during that first conversation—who had been the principal prosecution witness at Adams's trial. Morris had not gone to Texas with the purpose of finding and becoming an advocate for innocent incarcerated men; he had gone there because of his fascination with Dr. Grigson. He didn't really believe the story Adams told him, because he had no particular reason to believe it. Nevertheless, he went to Austin three weeks later and read the transcripts of several trials. A number of passages in the Adams transcript aroused the possibility that Adams was telling the truth. After Morris met David Harris, two weeks later, in a bar outside Beaumont, his doubts about Adams's guilt and his curiosity about the case deepened.

This came at a time when Morris's film career was in another lull. Suzanne Weil, then the head of programming for the Public Broadcasting System and a generous believer in Morris and his work, had arranged a grant sufficient for him to begin his research on *Dr. Death*. (She once told me, "Errol is the one person in the world who, if he now came to me and said, 'I want to make a documentary titled *My Grandmother Remembers* or *So-and-So: Potter of the South-west*, I would tell, 'Go ahead.'") Morris's main source of income at that point was free-lance employment with a private detective agency that specialized in Wall Street securities and commodities cases. Most of the agency's referrals came from law firms.

"When I worked as a detective, I felt like this well-paid conceptual cleaning lady for lawyers," he has said. "It's like— There seems to be hair clogging the drain. My job was to clean it out and find out if it was really hair. I had one particular problem: people would start talking to me and when I'd leave I often couldn't remember what they had said. I wanted to use a tape recorder, but my employer was totally opposed. So I worried about whether I was getting valuable information. I also worried about getting stains on my clothes—I had to wear suits all the time. Because I couldn't use a tape recorder, my most important piece of equipment was my can of K2R spot remover."

The owner of the detective agency, who prefers anonymity, told me that what he valued most about Morris was his talent as a listener—the talent that has served him so effectively as a filmmaker. What happened next was that Morris began to employ in his film work certain skills he was honing as a detective. As a "director-detective"—a phrase Morris used to describe himself when he was promoting *The Thin Blue Line*—not the least of his accomplishments was cultivating Henry Wade, for thirty-six years the District Attorney of Dallas County. Instead of handling the Adams prosecution himself, Wade assigned it to Douglas Mulder, one of his most experienced assistants. After gaining access to the files in Wade's office, Morris became convinced that Mulder had seriously tampered with the truth and that Adams had received anything but a fair trial.

Randall Adams and David Harris met by chance the morning before Officer Wood was killed. Adams had run out of gas and was walking along a road in west Dallas when Harris, a sixteen-year-old with an extensive criminal record, driving a car that he had stolen in his home town of Vidor, Texas, pulled over and offered to help him refill the tank. They spent the rest of the day, a Saturday, together—bumming around a shopping mall, drinking beer, visiting pawnshops, shooting pool, smoking marijuana. That evening, they ended up at a drive-in theatre that featured two soft-core-porn movies. Officer Wood was shot at twelve-thirty Sunday morning—almost three hours after Harris, according to Adams's testimony, had dropped him off at the motel where he was living. That became Adams's alibi: he was home asleep when the crime was committed.

Teresa Turko proved to be a poor eyewitness to the slaying of her patrol partner, and gave an inaccurate description of the car that the killer had been driving. The first break in the case came because David Harris, back in Vidor, told several friends that he had killed a policeman in Dallas. After being arrested and leading the Vidor police to the murder weapon, a .22-calibre handgun that belonged to his father, Harris was turned over to the Dallas police. At this point, he changed his story and said that he had only been bragging—that the real killer was a hitchhiker he had picked up and spent the day with. Which is how Adams, who had no prior criminal record, came to be charged with murder.

Initially, Adams was represented by Edith James, a lawyer whose criminal-trial experience included no homicide-defense work. She brought in as co-counsel a general practitioner named Dennis White. In one of White's previous head-to-heads with Doug Mulder, things had ended badly for his clients—two brothers named Ransonette who had made the mistake of kidnapping the daughter-in-law of a Dallas newspaper publisher. At the sentencing hearing in that case, White argued that the victim had not been harmed by her captors, and suggested a lenient prison term of five years. The prosecution mentioned a term of five thousand years. The jury, aspiring to Solomonic wisdom, said, in effect, "Okay. Let's compromise," and sentenced each defendant to five thousand and five years. Dennis White was simply no match for Doug Mulder, who is said to have once boasted, "Anybody can convict a guilty man. It takes talent to convict an innocent man."

Testifying during Adams's trial, David Harris offered a chronology of the events surrounding the murder that varied from Adams's version by approximately two and a half hours. Adams and Harris agreed that they had left the drive-in theatre during a movie called *Swinging Cheerleaders* (1974). Mulder elicited from Harris testimony that their departure had occurred shortly after midnight; Adams said they left around nine-thirty. In the D.A.'s files, Morris discovered a memorandum from Mulder's own chief investigator stating that there had been no late showing of *Swinging Cheerleaders* that night and that the final feature had ended shortly after ten o'clock.

This was the sort of serious defect in Harris's version of the facts that Mulder apparently had no intention of allowing to interfere with his prosecution of Adams—who, at twenty-eight, was eligible for capital punishment, whereas Harris, at sixteen, was not. It was also, unfortunately, the sort of discrepancy that Adams's attorneys failed to make clear to the jury. Nor were Edith James and Dennis White prepared when Mulder produced three mysterious witnesses, all of whom testified that they had driven past the scene of the crime moments before Officer Wood was murdered and that Randall Adams was in the driver's seat—the position from which the shots were fired. The three witnesses, Emily Miller, Robert Miller, and Michael Randell, all of whom were aware of a five-figure reward for information leading to the conviction of the killer, appeared in court on a Friday and impressed the jury. White, outmaneuvered by Mulder's strategy of presenting his "eyewitnesses" during the rebuttal phase rather than as part of his case-in-chief, conducted an ineffectual cross-examination. That weekend, White received a call from a woman named Elba Carr, who knew Emily and Robert Miller and expressed the opinion that "Emily Miller had never told the truth, in her life." When, back in court the following Monday, White asked to question the Millers and Michael Randell further, Mulder told the judge that all three had left town or were otherwise unreachable. Actually, all three witnesses were still in Dallas. The Millers, in fact, were ensconced in the Alamo Plaza Motel as guests of Dallas County. Not until nine years later, when Morris came along and found in the District Attorney's files bills for phone calls that the Millers had made from the Alamo Plaza, did Mulder's role in this apparent deception become evident.

Toward the end of *The Thin Blue Line*, Errol Morris asks David Harris, "Would you say that Adams is a pretty unlucky fellow?" and Harris responds, "Definitely—if it wasn't for bad luck, he wouldn't have had none." Ironically, of course, Harris's reply is accurate only up to the moment when Morris met Adams. Not only did Morris discover important evidence in the prosecution's files; he discovered the absence of some important documents—specifically, the official record of a police lineup at which, according to Emily Miller's trial testimony, she had positively identified Randall Adams. Most significantly, Morris tracked down the three rebuttal witnesses themselves and persuaded them to appear on film. Emily Miller, a bleached blonde, whose childhood ambition was to be a detective or the wife of a detective, told Morris that she had failed to identify Adams in the lineup but that a policeman had told her the correct suspect, "so that I wouldn't make that mistake again." Robert Miller told him, "I really didn't see anything." Michael Randell, who had testified in 1977 that he was on his way home from playing basketball when he drove past the murder scene, told Morris that in fact he had spent that evening in an adulterous endeavor and that he was drunk "out of my mind." Each of the state's rebuttal witnesses, it therefore appeared, had committed damaging perjury. Putting David Harris on film posed a significant challenge. The first interview appointment, Morris says, Harris missed "because he was off killing somebody"—Mark Walter Mays, a Beaumont citizen, whose apartment Harris had broken into, and whose girlfriend he had abducted. Another interview had to be postponed when Harris tried to use Morris in an escape attempt from the jail where he was awaiting trial for these crimes. The climactic interview finally took place in the Lou Sterret Jail, in Dallas, by which time Harris had been convicted and sentenced to death for the Mays murder, and it included this exchange:

MORRIS: Is he [Adams] innocent?
HARRIS: Did you ask him?
MORRIS: Well, he's always said he's been innocent.
HARRIS: There you go. Didn't believe him, huh? Criminals always lie.
MORRIS: Well, what do you think about whether or not he's innocent?
HARRIS: I'm sure he is.
MORRIS: How can you be sure?
HARRIS: Because I'm the one that knows.

On a straightforward, realistic level, *The Thin Blue Line* is the story of how Adams got railroaded, the story of an innocent man wrongly accused. Its aura, however, is that of a dreadful fantasy, a mixture of the ghastly and the absurd. By any standard, it breaches the conventional definition of "documentary." Tom Luddy has said that *The Thin Blue Line* illustrates Morris's belief that *cinéma-vérité* is "too mundane—that there is a way to heighten the structure of the facts." To accomplish this, Morris combines straight interviews—his unblinking talking-heads technique, from *Gates of Heaven* and *Vernon, Florida*—with artful restagings of certain incidents. The restaged episodes correspond to conflicting versions of "the facts" proposed by the people who appear in the interviews. Also, inserted throughout the film are closeups—of a gun, a mouth and a straw, a milkshake spilling, popcorn popping—that have a fetishistic quality, an exaggerated objectivity (evidence of Morris's passion for film noir). The *Rashômon* (1950)-like result is something considerably creepier than the cold-blooded murder that *The Thin Blue Line* explores.

The day before the interview with Harris, which took place December 5, 1986, Morris appeared in the courtroom of John Tolle, a federal magistrate in Dallas, who was presiding over a habeas-corpus hearing—an effort by Adams to win a new trial. In addition to Morris's oral testimony, unedited footage from his interviews with the prosecution witnesses became part of the court record. Watching these interviews—either unedited or as they appear in the final cut of *The Thin Blue Line*—one marvels at Morris's ability to win the confidence of so many people so prone to self-incrimination. On film, the witnesses against Adams seem to suffer collectively from the actor's nightmare—an instinctive fear of silence, terror at the thought of forgetting one's lines. Talking to Morris, they manage to discredit themselves thoroughly.

Under oath in Magistrate Tolle's courtroom, however, Emily Miller and Michael Randell tried to recant their statements to the filmmaker. Among the questions raised by Adams's habeas-corpus motion were: Had Adams been denied due process because he had not been effectively represented by his attorneys during his original trial, because of certain evidence that was illegally withheld from the jury during that trial, and because in 1980, when the United States Supreme Court overturned his death sentence (on a technical point involving jury selection), he received from the governor of Texas a commutation of the death sentence to life imprisonment rather than a new trial?

Morris returned to Magistrate Tolle's courtroom a month later, for the second, and last, day of the habeas-corpus hearing. Doug Mulder, by now a highly successful defense attorney, testified, responding to un-welcome questions from Adams's appellate lawyer, Randy Schaffer, with mumbled replies and lapses of memory. As the hearing ended, reason dictated that the magistrate would rule on Adams's petition within a few weeks. Tolle, however, turned out to be an even more, gifted procrasti-nator than Morris. The New York Film Festival committee had expressed interest in showing *The Thin Blue Line* in September of 1987, but Mor-ris failed to meet the deadline. Finally, on March 18, 1988, *The Thin Blue Line* had its premiere, at the San Francisco Film Festival. Morris appeared to be in buoyant spirits that day, and I asked him what he expected to do after the screening. "Oh, I imagine the usual lithium treatments," he said. "Followed by a period of hospitalization." A month later, *The Thin Blue Line* led off the USA Film Festival, in Dallas. Magistrate Tolle had yet to be heard from. Two more weeks passed—sixteen months had elapsed since the conclusion of the habeas-corpus hearing—and Tolle at last ren-dered his judgment: "All relief requested . . . denied." As far as Morris's role in the case was concerned, Tolle wrote, "much could be said about those videotape interviews, but nothing that would have any bearing on the matter before this court."

A week later, Randy Schaffer filed a motion asking that Tolle's opinion be set aside, because an astonishing fact had come to light: In the spring of 1977, on the heels of Adams's conviction for the murder of Officer Wood, Dennis White had filed a five-million-dollar lawsuit against Doug Mulder and Henry Wade, alleging that the District Attorney's conduct during the trial had violated the defendant's civil rights. John Tolle then worked in the civil division of the Dallas County District Attorney's of-fice. White's suit had been briskly dismissed by a federal judge. After the screening at the USA Film Festival, Dennis White mentioned to Mor-ris that he recalled Tolle's having been involved in the 1977 civil suit. The records of that litigation were dredged from a file, and, sure enough, John Tolle's name was all over them: John Tolle had triumphantly repre-sented Mulder and Wade. Somehow, not quite ten years later, Magistrate Tolle had decided that this coincidence did not disqualify him from ren-dering an opinion on Adams's habeas-corpus petition. Rather, he had chosen to hear the case, and had then sat on it for seventeen months be-fore eventually ruling, in effect, in favor of his former client. The embar-rassing revelation of Tolle's conflict of interest forced him to withdraw his recommendation; thus, an additional year and a half of Adams's life had been consumed by a proceeding that ultimately yielded irrelevance. Rather than start all over again in federal court, before a different magistrate, Schaffer decided to formally withdraw the writ and re-file it in state court, citing new evidence that Adams had never received a fair trial.

Officer Robert Wood was murdered Thanksgiving weekend in 1976. Twelve years later almost to the day, Adams and his attorneys returned to the room where he had been convicted of the murder and handed a death sentence—Criminal District Court No. 2, on the fourth floor of the Dallas County Courthouse. By Texas statute, the judge who presides at a trial—in this instance, District Judge Don Metcalfe, whose evidentiary rulings against Adams formed part of the basis for the writ—also presides at any subsequent appellate-writ hearing. Adams's bad luck, while consistent, was not absolute, however, and Metcalfe had since left the bench. In 1984, he was succeeded by Larry W. Baraka, a respected former prosecutor and defense attorney, whose special distinction is that he is the only member of the Texas judiciary who is black, a Muslim, and a Republican.

On the eve of the hearing, I had a phone conversation with Morris. In New York the previous day, he told me, his secretary had taken a call from a stranger who said, "An important message for Errol Morris: Stay away from the hearing in Dallas on Wednesday. You might disappear"—a forewarning that brought to mind his experience in Vernon, Florida, a decade earlier, where, he had been informed, unfortunate people had a tendency to "just disappear."

"My stepfather told my wife I should wear two bulletproof vests, so that one covers the seams of the other," he continued. "I don't mind a death threat, as such, but I do mind the idea of disappearing. That's like the 'delete' button on your personal computer—'We deleted that character.' Disappearing suggests a whole set of unsavory possibilities."

As it turned out, I couldn't be in Dallas the opening day of the writ hearing, and thereby missed a memorable striptease by David Harris. Testifying for three hours, Harris said that he had been alone in a stolen car and in possession of a stolen gun when Wood pulled him over. In a videotaped interview that was introduced as evidence, he said that he had had his finger on the trigger as Wood approached him. Judge Baraka, no quibbler, announced, "As far as the court is concerned, he's in fact telling me he did it." Randy Schaffer read aloud a letter from Harris to his mother, written in September, 1988—just two months earlier—that said, "It seems like my whole life is surrounded by 'wrongs' of some kind and it seems like I've never done the right thing when I could and should have. Absolving Randall Dale Adams of any guilt is a difficult thing for me to do, but I must try to do so because he is innocent. That is the truth."

Next, Schaffer called Teresa Turko, Robert Wood's patrol partner, as a witness. He wanted to make plain to the judge that Turko's initial description of the killer, recorded immediately after the shooting, differed measurably from the one she had offered at Adams's trial. Dennis White had not cross-examined Turko about the first statement, because, in violation of a cardinal principle of criminal-trial procedure, Mulder had not given him a copy. Nor would the document have come to light, of course, if Morris had not insinuated himself into the Dallas District Attorney's good graces and scrutinized Mulder's old files.

When I caught up with Morris, at the end of the first day of the hearing, his mood was upbeat but not entirely sanguine. The drama of Harris's confession notwithstanding, it did not, in a technical sense, really help Adams. In Texas, evidence of innocence is insufficient to win a new trial. What Schaffer had to prove was that Adams's original trial had been "unfair" on constitutional grounds. Even if Baraka were to grant Adams's writ, his ruling would have the effect only of a recommendation to the Texas Court of Criminal Appeals, a nine-judge panel, which in 1977 had unanimously upheld Adams's conviction. Harris's testimony was useful, however, in bolstering some of the other claims in the writ— most significantly, that Harris and Mulder had an understanding in 1977 whereby in exchange for testimony against Adams unresolved criminal charges against Harris in another county would be dropped. (Under cross-examination at the original trial, Harris had insisted that no quid pro quo existed—an avowal that Mulder has always maintained. Further harm to Adams was done when Judge Metcalfe refused even to allow into evidence the fact that Harris had such charges pending.)

Randall Adams wore the same outfit to court all three days of the hearing—a bright-orange jumpsuit with "DALLAS COUNTY JAIL" in black block letters stenciled on the back; leg irons; and handcuffs, which were attached to a chain around his waist. When Adams was escorted into the courtroom on Day Two, Morris had already arrived and taken a seat in the front row of the spectator section, between Adams's mother, Mildred, and his two sisters, Nancy Bapst and Mary Baugess. Two of Mildred Adams's sisters and their husbands had also come to Dallas for the hearing. George Preston, a lawyer who was assisting Randy Schaffer, leaned across a low partition that separated the spectators from the business end of the courtroom and showed Morris a printed sheet of paper, portions of which had been highlighted in yellow.

"This is from the Bar Association code," he said. "It regards tampering with witnesses and suppression of evidence."

"I'd like a copy of that," Morris said.

"Our Xerox machine broke, so I had to tear this page out of the book," Preston said.

"That page must have been missing from Doug Mulder's copy, too," Morris said.

The first witness on Day Two was Emily Miller. Randy Schaffer expected to score several points while she was on the stand: her failure to identify Adams in a lineup; the intervention of the Dallas policeman, who then pointed out to her the "right" suspect; her subsequent perjury regarding her performance at the lineup; and evidence that, like David Harris, she had struck an implicit deal with Mulder—specifically, her testimony against Adams in exchange for the dismissal of an outstanding robbery charge against her daughter.

A week after the murder of Robert Wood, at which time a twenty-thousand-dollar reward was being offered for information leading to the arrest and conviction of the killer, Emily Miller had given a formal statement to the Dallas police. According to what she saw while driving the crime scene moments before the shooting, the suspect was "either a Mexican or a very light-skinned black man." That this description would divert suspicion from Adams, an auburn-haired Caucasian, perhaps explains why Mulder never showed the statement to Adams's attorneys. By the time of Adams's trial, Emily Miller's description of the killer had metamorphosed so that it matched the defendant. In Judge Baraka's courtroom, when Schaffer presented Emily Miller with a copy of her original statement she said that she had left her eyeglasses at home and couldn't read it. When Schaffer then read it to her and proceeded through a barbed interrogation, she said, "I don't remember nothing that happened back then. Specifics, I don't remember who asked me what or who said what or who did what. That was twelve years ago."

As far as the officer who had coached her at the police lineup was concerned, she said, "I didn't base nothing I said on anything anybody told me. It was what I seen. And I'm sorry I ever seen it."

"You're not the only one, I'm sure," Schaffer replied.

The subject of Errol Morris and his filmed interview with Emily Miller arose.

The witness turned to the judge and said, "May I get this clear on this videotape? This man [Morris] came to my house and told me that he was going to make a movie. . . . They were kicking it around in their heads about making a movie about the police shooting in Dallas. So I said okay. He said, well, it would be interesting because, he said, 'In the first place, you're married to a black man.' This was his exact words. And I said, 'Well.' And he said, 'Do you mind? We're not sure we're going to film or anything. We're just going to kick it around.' And I said, 'Well, I don't exactly remember how everything went down back then.' And he said, 'Well, what the heck, it's just a movie, you know?' He said, 'Anything you don't remember. . . . I'll remember for you.' Well, this went on. . . . The movie wasn't accurate. It wasn't, you know. . . . I went along because he said what the heck, it's a movie. . . . He tried to make me look like trash."

During a recess, several reporters approached Morris—the courtroom was filled to capacity most of the three days of the hearing—and asked about Emily Miller's accusations. He pointed out that she had described the precise antithesis of his well-established interviewing style—his let-'em-talk-until-the-truth-flows technique—and he offered to roll the tape of the full interview for anyone who was interested. "She spoke extemporaneously, at length, without coaching, prodding, or interruption by me," he said. "It's quite clear that Emily Miller has no credibility."

Nevertheless, Emily Miller had accomplished something oddly significant: she had introduced the idea that *The Thin Blue Line* was a corrupt document. Months earlier, a reporter for the *Dallas Morning News* had said to Morris, "You know, Errol, there are two sides to every story," and he had replied, "Yeah, the truth and falsehood." Much as he still believed that about the Adams case, he also understood the mythology that attaches to movies, and he understood that in the iconography of this courtroom proceeding *The Thin Blue Line* had acquired a taint, as if it were some soiled version of the truth. Errol Morris, seated in the front row of the spectator section, wearing a blue plaid jacket, chinos, a white shirt, and a red paisley necktie, repeatedly heard himself referred to as "a filmmaker from New York"—a phrase chock-full of unflattering connotations. The word "movie" was chock-full of connotations. Robert Wood was dead, and Randall Adams had spent twelve years behind bars—those were virtually the only remaining unassailable truths. Almost every intervening fact had been tampered with by the police or lawyers or mysteriously motivated witnesses. In the immediate context, Randall Adams, in his jumpsuit, handcuffs, and leg irons, seated mutely with his back to the spectators, seemed more relevant to the proceeding than Robert Wood but less relevant than Errol Morris.

Other witnesses went out of their way to impugn Morris—most notably Gus Rose, a former homicide detective, whom Adams described in *The Thin Blue Line* as having pulled a gun on him during one interrogation session. Rose had come to court as the District Attorney's witness. During the direct examination by Leslie McFarlane, the appellate lawyer assigned to represent the Dallas County District Attorney, he made several statements that had Morris squirming in his seat and, whispering to me things like " Don't these people get embarrassed lying? After all, this is only a man who was sentenced to death." Rose complained that Morris had misrepresented his intentions in soliciting an interview and then had been argumentative during the interview. "You should *hear* this interview," Morris said to me. "I'm barely present." When Rose testified that Adams had never denied murdering Robert Wood, Morris seethed, "That's a lie. He told me on film that Adams had denied it. This is all lies, lies, lies."

During cross-examination, Schaffer gave Rose reason to regret this particular portion of his testimony. Holding a transcript of *The Thin Blue Line*—proof of Rose's failure to keep his own story straight—Schaffer stood at the detective's side and read a passage in which Rose recalled that Adams, shortly after his arrest, "almost over-acted his innocence." A hubbub arose in the spectator section, not unlike the inevitable moment when Perry Mason's assistant, Paul Drake, shows up with a previously elusive piece of physical evidence. A bearded man seated two rows behind Morris suddenly produced a videocassette of *The Thin Blue Line*, and Morris relayed it to George Preston, who passed it to Schaffer, who was able to taunt Rose with it, asking whether he wanted to see a moving picture of himself uttering words directly at odds with the testimony he had just given.

Trapped, Rose turned to Judge Baraka and said, "Your Honor, if the question is do I want to see the film the answer is no, I do not want to see the film or anything Errol Morris has anything to do with."

Baraka called a recess for lunch. In the hallway, I passed Mildred Adams, Randall's mother. A tall, broad-shouldered woman with light-blue eyes, blue-gray hair, and a beauty-shop permanent, Mrs. Adams was standing in a bath of bright light, being interviewed by a television reporter, saying not for the first or the last time, "If Dallas County will just admit that they made a mistake and let that boy come home. . . ."

One evening, I went to the Dallas County jail to have a conversation with Randall Adams. I rode an elevator to the eighth floor of the courthouse building, signed in, presented a guard with a letter from Randy Schaffer authorizing my visit, and was directed to a pinkish-beige room about twice the size of a prison cell, along one wall of which was a row of telephone receivers and thick six-by-twelve-inch windows. Adams, standing on the opposite side of the wall and holding two adjacent receivers—one to each ear—was concluding a conversation with Nancy Bapst and Mary Baugess, his sisters. A black woman who had three children with her was talking on one of the other phones. When Nancy Bapst handed me her receiver, a wall clock said eight-forty-five—which meant that we didn't have long before the visiting hour would expire.

Adams and I discussed Randy Schaffer's aggressive style ("I need somebody who can intimidate. That's what you need") and Doug Mulder, who was scheduled to testify the next morning ("I know what those people did to me, but I have no personal animosity toward them"), and then I turned the subject to Errol Morris.

"If it wasn't for him . . . I sat down there in Huntsville and this man listened to me—I was pleading for somebody and this man listened," Adams began, in a flat voice, which, although it originated only a couple of feet away, sounded distant and disembodied, as if it had traveled through water. "Errol Morris, when I talked to him, I talked to him for one purpose and one purpose only: for the investigation of my case, whether good or bad. I told him, 'Whatever you want to do—you can dig into my closet if you will allow me to look at whatever you turn up.' I knew what these people had done to me, but I couldn't prove it. Randy Schaffer and Mel Bruder [another appellate lawyer], they didn't know. The only one who knew was Dennis White, but he was shook up entirely and he was devastated. I agreed to talk to Errol Morris on the condition that he would share with me what he found out. I like to call Errol the Easter Bunny. I needed somebody to gather up all these facts and put them in one basket. He went and did his investigative work, and everything we're doing now is because of what he did with his investigation of the facts. That is what *The Thin Blue Line* did for me."

The next morning, Doug Mulder gave a poised and self-assured courtroom performance. As Leslie McFarlane lobbed him across-the-letters questions, Mulder, a handsome man in his late forties with a squarish face, not much of a neck, and a stocky, athletic build, effortlessly swatted them out of the ballpark.

McFarlane: "Everything that you discovered and everything that you reviewed in preparation for this case indicates Adams's guilt, is that correct? . . . Did you find anything inconsistent with that?"
Mulder: "Nothing that comes to mind, no."

Schaffer, when his turn arrived, proved somewhat less ingratiating. His gambit, for instance, went "Well, I guess today you've returned to the scene of one of your greatest triumphs." Leslie McFarlane objected to the argumentative tone, and the judge agreed with her, telling Schaffer, "That's not the way to start." From there on, Schaffer and Mulder dueled for more than an hour—until it was apparent that the judge had had enough and that Mulder was not going to throw up his hands and declare, "Okay, ya got me, my legal career's a shambles, I'm finished in this town." The judge's impatience with Schaffer belied the fact that he had already made up his mind on the basic question. After a masterly summation by Schaffer—sufficient in its eloquence for McFarlane, when her turn came, to apologize, accurately, that her closing argument would be notably devoid of eloquence—Baraka said he was ready with his decision.

Of the thirteen grounds for relief cited in Adams's writ, Baraka agreed on six: that Metcalfe, the original trial judge, had erroneously denied the admissibility of David Harris's prior criminal record; that Teresa Turko's initial statement describing the killer had been illegally suppressed; that, similarly, Emily Miller's initial statement describing the killer had been illegally suppressed; that evidence of Emily Miller's failure to identify Adams in the police lineup and subsequent coaching by a police officer had been suppressed; that Emily Miller had later committed perjury regarding her performance at the lineup; and that Adams had been denied effective assistance of counsel.

It seemed that, because Baraka had rejected seven of the contentions cited in the writ, a final observation he made was designed to eliminate any remaining ambiguity: "I think over all, when we look at this trial, all the nuances that are involved, I think there's no question that the defendant did not get a fair opportunity to a trial. I would not go so far as to say that the defendant is innocent of this. I would go so far as to say that if the defendant were to be retried, considering all the testimony elicited and what would be presented to the jury or a court, that more likely than not the defendant would be found not guilty."

The ruling did not mean that Adams was now at liberty to walk out of the courtroom; it meant that one judge officially believed that Adams had yet to receive a fair trial. As a practical matter, Baraka's recommendation could languish with the Texas Court of Criminal Appeals for months before a final ruling came down. And the court could, of course, reject Baraka's recommendation. Imminent freedom for Adams, in other words, was by no means a foregone conclusion. Knowing that Baraka lacked the authority to grant Adams bail in the meantime, Schaffer asked for it anyway, and the motion was denied. On that note, the hearing ended.

There was applause, and a call for order from the court officers, and then the television and newspaper people were ready with their questions.

Adams, seated in a wooden armchair and still wearing handcuffs and leg irons, said he felt "numb"—the same word he had used in *The Thin Blue Line* to describe his frame of mind when, twelve years earlier, he heard himself sentenced to death.

A woman with a microphone asked Adams if he had anything to say to David Harris. No, he did not.

A reporter from *Newsday* asked, "Do you think you'd be here today if it hadn't been for Errol Morris?"

"Without the facts that came from the movie, no, I wouldn't be here in this courtroom today. We needed the facts, and the film helped. It helped immensely."

Roughly the same question was directed to Schaffer, who was standing nearby: "Do you consider that if the file that Errol Morris got out of Mr. Wade's office had not been found, we'd be here?"

In his summation, Schaffer had belittled the Dallas District Attorney, saying, "They'll give their file to a moviemaker, because he'll go out and make a movie and they'll be famous, but they won't give it to a defense attorney." Elaborating, he now said, "No, if Errol had not decided on his own that this was a story worth telling, Randall Adams would have been buried forever. Yes, that was the linchpin."

Mildred Adams, between bouts of crying for joy and kissing Morris and Schaffer and any willing members of the press, said she hoped people would remember Robert Wood and his family in their prayers. When the excitement had lasted close to half an hour, Morris suggested to Mrs. Adams that she and her daughters and sisters and brothers-in-law should join him for champagne at the Adolphus Hotel.

"Did I tell you what Randall Adams said to me about my movie?" Morris asked me as we headed for the hotel, a few blocks east of the courthouse. "He told me another inmate asked him, 'How come your case is being argued in the entertainment section of the newspaper?' And you know what Randall's response was? He said, 'I'll argue my case anywhere I can, any way I can.' "

The Thin Blue Line made dozens of critics' lists of the ten best films of 1988; according to a survey by the *Washington Post*, in fact, it turned up on more ten-best lists than any other film. Both the New York Film Critics Circle and the National Society of Film Critics chose it as best documentary of 1988. An Academy Award nomination is highly likely. Although its box-office receipts have not extended into the *Roger Rabbit*

(1988) or *Crocodile Dundee II* (1988) vicinity—at the end of the year, it was playing in fifteen theatres around the country—Morris no longer faces the prospect that he will soon again be working as a private detective or dodging collection agencies. Immediately before the writ hearing in Dallas, he was in Italy, where *The Thin Blue Line* was shown at a festival in Florence. On the same trip, he made stops in London—where he screened it for some people from the London Film Festival—and in Munich, where he met with Reinhold Messner, the legendary Alpine climber and the first man to have scaled all fourteen eight-thousand-metre peaks on earth (including Mt. Everest without oxygen). Messner was planning an ascent of Cerro del Toro, in Chile, and he wanted Morris—who happens to be an experienced rock climber—to accompany him and make a film. "I'm thinking of doing it," Morris said, in Dallas. "Messner's a terrifically interesting person. He told me he's been doing a lot of walking recently. You or I might assume he meant he was taking long strolls in his neighborhood. What he actually meant was that he had just walked across Tibet. And he's planning to walk across Antarctica. He told me some interesting stuff about meeting the yeti—you know, the abominable snowman. He's seen two—the red yeti and the black yeti. Messner was very reassuring. He said, 'The only thing you really have to be scared of is when you hear the black yeti whistling—whistling through his nose.'"

Heading off to South America with Messner would mean delaying a couple of other projects that Morris was eager to carry forward. He still had plans to complete *Dr. Death*—the movie he had intended to make before the Randall Adams case sidetracked him. He also hoped to direct *The Trial of King Boots*, a feature-length examination of how an Old English sheepdog named King Boots—the most highly decorated performer in the annals of show-dog competition—became the only canine in Michigan history to be prosecuted, in effect, for homicide. Morris already had a vision of what the film's publicity posters would say: "Only Two People Know What Happened. One Is Dead. The Other Is a Dog."

If Morris could find the time to finish *Dr. Death*, he might at last tie together an odd melange of material: interviews with Dr. Grigson himself; action shots of a lion tamer; scenes from lab research on a mammal called the African naked mole rat; archival footage from an Edison silent film called *Electrocuting an Elephant*; and a meditation on Zoar, an extinct Utopian community in Ohio. After a previous trip to Europe, Morris had told me with satisfaction about finding the right music to accompany the Zoar material. "It's called 'Yodeler Messen,'" he said. "I'd been hearing this stuff on the radio in Zurich, and then I went into a record store and asked whether they had any liturgical yodeling. They came up with 'Yodeler Messen.' It's, like, based on the idea that God might be hard of hearing."

One afternoon, in his office near Times Square, Morris patiently tried to walk me through the connections between the elements that would compose *Dr. Death*, an exercise that struck me as analogous to a journey along the scenic route from the right side of his brain to the left. He told me that his fascination with Dr. Grigson's disturbing theories of sociopathy and recidivism had aroused an interest in lion taming, and that in 1985 this led him to the eponymous ringleader of a circus act called Dave Hoover's Wild Animals. Of the three basic schools of lion taming—what Morris delineated as "the persuasive, mutual-respect school, the behaviorist school, and the chairs-whips-guns school"—Hoover subscribed to the third. Having filmed Hoover at work for several hours—the soundtrack consists mainly of scary roaring noises and the determined voice of Hoover saying, again and again, "Bongo! Come! Come to Daddy! Bad girl! Caesar! Get home, *Caesar*! Good boy!"—Morris was uncertain what to do with the footage.

"After I'd looked at this stuff awhile, I decided, Oh, no, I can't use this. It's too goofy," Morris said. "Then I got interested in the mole rats. What's the connection between the lion tamer and the mole rats? I don't know if there even is one. Mole rats spend their entire lives digging tunnels. They have a rigid social system. They're like wasps or bees—there's a queen and workers. Mole rats dig at random, looking for tubers. Maybe they find a tuber, or maybe they don't. They just dig away. At one point I had thought the mole rats addressed the Utopian ideal of what it would be like if there were no crime or criminals, if you could say hello to your neighbor and your neighbor would say hello in return and we'd all be assured that no one would attack us with an axe. Is aggression innate in mammals? Well, supposedly not in mole rats. The mole rat was thought to be the only mammal that lives in harmony with its fellow-mammals, its fellow mole rats. *The* only. But it turns out that mole rats are nonviolent only under certain circumstances—that, in fact, they can be really nasty critters after all, who at times really do seem to hate one another. When one colony of mole rats meets another, they can be extremely vicious. Anyway, that was my original idea—Dr. Grigson, lion tamers, mole rats. I then decided to add to this compote *Electrocuting an Elephant* (1903)—which was, if anything, a miscarriage-of-justice story."

When it became clear that I was unfamiliar with the once popular habit—practiced during the first half of this century—of systematically executing "bad" elephants, Morris eagerly took a book from a shelf next to his desk and handed it to me. It was a prolifically illustrated memoir titled *I Loved Rogues*, by George (Slim) Lewis and Byron Fish. Lewis was a passionate lover of elephants who spent most of his working life in the employ of zoos and circuses, and Fish was a newspaperman whose interest in elephants was that of an involved amateur. The book had chapter titles like "They Are Not House Pets" and "Ziggy Tries to Kill Me" and "How to Feed and Water Your Elephant." The foreword included a reproduction of a painting labeled "George Lewis and Tusko"—Tusko being a vast bull elephant who came close to being executed for doing something deemed bad. A photograph on the facing page, captioned "Byron Fish painting Wide Awake," showed Fish perched on an elephant's shoulder, giving the animal a cosmetic treatment with a bucket of oil made from horse fat. The phone rang. While Morris took the call, I wrote down some more interesting captions and passages:

> "Occasionally the victim of an elephant's attack is a man who was hated for reasons of the elephant's own" (p. 29).
>
> "Black Diamond seemed to know that he was taking his last walk" (p. 47).
>
> "After 170 shots by the firing squad, Diamond finally goes down" (p. 48).
>
> "Joe Metcalf was another man Slim often met in his travels. The man with his head in the elephant's mouth was Alonzo Dever" (p. 62).

"Isn't that a wonderful book?" Morris said after he hung up. "I'd very much like to show you *Electrocuting an Elephant*. This elephant, Topsy, was, if anything, a *good* elephant rather than a bad elephant. Topsy was being electrocuted because, as I understand it, some guy was smoking a cigarette and gave the cigarette to Topsy, burning the tip of her trunk. Now, the tip of an elephant's trunk is the most sensitive part of an elephant. Topsy picked this guy up, tossed him in the air a couple of times, and hurled him onto concrete. I ask you: Does Topsy deserve the juice for this? The film of Topsy's electrocution is a 1903 Edison short—one of the first times electricity was used in capital punishment. And, coincidentally, the equipment malfunctioned and the person who pulled the switch almost electrocuted himself while he was electrocuting Topsy."

Morris paused. We could hear the traffic on Broadway, two floors below, and from the editing room, ten feet away, we could hear a litany of "Come, Bongo!"s and "Home, Caesar!"s.

"My favorite line in *Dr. Death*, I think, will be when the last living Zoarite is quoted as saying, 'Think of it—all those religions. They can't all be right. But they could all be wrong,'" Morris said. He looked down at his hands, massaged the tips of his little fingers—a characteristic tic—and then looked up, smiling his asymmetrical smile. "My two remaining ambitions are to have my picture hung up in my local Chinese restaurant and to have a sandwich named after me at the Stage Deli. And I guess I'll still keep making films. I always felt film was a good medium for me to work in, because if you don't finish, the level of embarrassment is so high."

Trying to Get a Fact-Fiction Mix on the Air

SHAWN ROSENHEIM/1994

IT IS A FINE September day in the farmlands of Vermont, but Errol Morris is unhappy. Only a short drive away lives the Rat Man of Peru, an eccentric about to be evicted from his home for tending a colony of several hundred wild rats. It is a scene rife with possibility, yet Mr. Morris can do nothing about it. Instead, the filmmaker sits on the porch of his summer home, an old farmhouse outside Bennington, and muses on the difficulties of being an independent director. "If I had an ongoing television series," Mr. Morris said, "I'd go to see the Rat Man in a minute, no question. But I think it would be mildly frustrating to go up there to see all those rats running around without the wherewithal to do anything about it."

In fact, Mr. Morris *does* have a series. He just doesn't have a network to broadcast it. The director has produced three episodes of *Errol Morris: Interrotron Stories*. A half-hour blend of high-tech studio interviews, news footage, and stylized reenactments, Mr. Morris's hoped-for show is a new kind of "reality' programming: coolly sophisticated in its look but luridly tabloid in its content—rather like a David Lynch movie starring real people instead of actors.

What Mr. Morris has in mind is unusual tube fare, to say the least. And Deborah Leoni, vice president for dramatic series development at ABC, says that "the appetite for reality material has diminished." But as the man responsible for *The Thin Blue Line*, Mr. Morris knows a thing or two about real-life dramas. That film, a 1988 documentary about Randall

From the *New York Times*, 30 October 1994. © 1994 The New York Times. All Rights reserved. Used by permission and protected by the Copyright Laws of the United States. The printing, copying, redistribution, or retransmission of the Material without express written permission is prohibited.

Dale Adams, a man wrongfully sentenced to life in prison for the murder of a Dallas police officer, culminated with a chilling taped confession by the true killer. Thanks both to Mr. Morris's investigation and to the public outcry the film provoked, Mr. Adams was freed in 1989.

Interrotron Stories is not Mr. Morris's first brush with television. Years ago he proposed a series for public television called *Oddballs, One-Shots and Curiosities*, whose episodes were to include "Road," the story of a man building a private highway across northern Minnesota, and "Car Baby," about a New Jersey couple who sold their infant for a new Corvette. PBS declined. More recently, he has worked primarily as a director of commercials, for clients that include 7-11, American Express, and Ford. Mr. Morris—a 1989 winner of a "genius grant" from the MacArthur Foundation—regards advertising with undisguised affection. He calls commercials "my real MacArthur," since his fees subsidize his production offices in Cambridge, Massachusetts.

But Mr. Morris recently got a new agent, who pushed him to reconsider his prospects for a series. "He kept telling me, 'If you do *The Thin Blue Line* as a series, you'll become wealthy beyond your wildest fantasies.'" But, Mr. Morris says: "I didn't want to do it over and over again. I'd done it."

Instead, he pitched *Interrotron Stories*, whose weekly episodes would chiefly center on criminal trials still in progress. Though each episode is narrated by participants in the case, Mr. Morris's idea was "to create a format based around me and my perspective," treating "news stories ranging from major national events to far more obscure incidents" like the Rat Man's plight.

Like *The Thin Blue Line*, *Interrotron Stories* reveals its director's training as a former private investigator and as a graduate student of philosophy obsessed with issues of criminal evidence. One consequence is that Mr. Morris uses reenactments not to show "what really happened" in a case, but to illustrate the slipperiness of truth; to "call attention to the fact that what we see may be a lie," or only one of many possible interpretations of events. Central to the series is the Interrotron, a device that allows subjects to look directly into the camera lens while simultaneously looking at the interviewer. It bounces a live image of Mr. Morris onto a glass plate in front of the interview subject, just as the director— "off in a booth somewhere, like the Wizard of Oz"—addresses a video image of the person being interviewed.

The result, he says, is "the only true first-person film."

"Not that you always have to be looking into somebody's eyes," he adds. "But if there is eye contact, every look takes on a completely different significance. The inclination of the head suddenly takes on enormous dramatic power." As Mr. Morris's dramatically lighted, larger-than-life-size faces recount stories of violence and injustice, they stare from the television with an unnerving intimacy.

Having perfected his Interrotron technique in his commercials, Mr. Morris shopped his series to various networks. At ABC, he screened a rough cut of "Stalker," about a postal supervisor who was blamed when a former employee went on a murder spree at a Michigan post office. "People were just speechless," Mr. Morris recalled. "I don't think anybody knew what to make of it." ABC ordered a pilot. But just as Mr. Morris was about to begin filming the final scenes of "Stalker," ABC's office of Standards and Practices halted the production, citing a network policy not to film any subject about which litigation is pending.

With that episode blocked, Mr. Morris was asked to submit ten new episode ideas. ABC picked a tale of the deathbed confession of a Ku Klux Klansman to a 1963 Alabama murder. Set comfortably in the past, it was plainly less risky material. Yet while Ms. Leoni describes the results as "riveting," the series was still not picked up, partly because of a conflict with *Turning Point*, an ABC news-magazine, but partly for fear that future episodes would raise similar legal tangles.

Oddly, while Mr. Morris's films (including *Gates of Heaven, Vernon, Florida*, and *A Brief History of Time*) helped fuel the vogue for reality programming, the filmmaker found himself caught in a no man's land. *Interrotron Stories*—true stories filmed to feel neither exactly like fact nor exactly like fiction—was deemed too dramatic for news and too real for drama.

Mr. Morris took *Interrotron Stories* to Fox, which also ordered a pilot but ultimately did not pick up the series. (The episode that Fox liked was about a murder trial in which the defense called a parrot as a witness.)

Mr. Morris isn't beaten yet. Britain's Channel Four has offered to buy the existing pilots—which have been shown at the Telluride and New York Film Festivals—and is discussing financing the series with an American network. Fox wants to talk to him again. And so, Mr. Morris—who is now avidly pursued by commercial clients interested in the Interrotron's distinctive visual signature—decides after all to head for the nearby town of Peru and its Rat Man.

"I still can't tell whether the Interrotron is a joke or something truly wonderful," he concludes before leaving. "But I like it. It's one more technique in a whole arsenal of techniques that you can bring to bear on nonfiction."

A Need to Create Something Timeless

JOHN ANDERSON/1997

Q: *You've made some of the decade's more remarkable films—films conveniently classified as documentaries—including* The Thin Blue Line *and* A Brief History of Time. *In your latest,* Fast, Cheap and Out of Control, *you take four men from widely divergent walks of life—a lion tamer, a topiary gardener, a robot scientist, and a naked mole-rat researcher—and weave them together into a film of disturbing resonance. But what are the connections?*

A: I look at the movie as a kind of elegy, because in all four of these stories there's this edge of mortality. The gardener tells us that he's labored his entire life to build something, to produce something that can be destroyed in a day. And there's this very good chance that the garden will not outlive him, because there's no one to take his place.

There's this late Nathaniel Hawthorne—everyone talks about his novels; no one ever talks about his stories—called "The Artist of the Beautiful," which reminds me of my movie. It's about a man who labors his entire life to make this mechanical butterfly, which is then destroyed in an instant.

I'm not sure there is a moral. I think somehow there is this need to create something larger than ourselves, something that could possibly but just might not outlive us. I think it's a universal human need. I was told that I should be grateful: "You're an artist; the movie will live on after you." Maybe. Maybe not.

I took my son on this trip to the Canadian Rockies to meet this paleontologist, Jack Horner. We were down in the basement looking at fossils and I was sticking my finger in the brain cavity of a triceratops. I said, "You think somebody might be doing this to me someday?" And he said, 'You should be so lucky."

From *Newsday*, 1 October 1997. Reprinted with permission of *Newsday*.

So it may be that time erases everything. Or almost everything. Maybe there's just some nobility or dignity just in the doing of things. Who the hell knows? I characterize the movie in so many different ways. One version of that is the myth of Frankenstein. The need to create life and, having created it, to control it. And there's a kind of coda, and the coda is: The attempt fails horribly.

Parallels with my own filmmaking? Of course. Certainly, the gardener's line—"Cut and wait"—applies to my own editorial process. I guess the best excuse I have for the film is that they are themes that interest me. The themes of in control/out of control, for better or for worse, interest me.

I feel I've become a little bit too pedantic talking about this but I'll talk about it anyway. Since the beginning of photography, still photography or motion-picture photography, people have been fascinated by what they perceive as this close, causal connection between the photographic image and the real world. What part of photography is journalism, and what part is fantasy? I think both of those elements have been present in photography from the beginning.

A lot of people have been interested in this whole question because it seems to touch deeply on what attracts us to the photographic image itself. I think when documentary began, documentaries weren't just journalism, they weren't just reportage.

Films like Vertov's *Man with a Movie Camera* or Vigo's *A Propos de Nice* are expressionistic films to me, although in some sense, some very real sense, they're composed of what we would today take as documentary images. I like to think that my films in part are a return to part of that kind of idea: that documentary really isn't journalism at all, but can be a kind of pure filmmaking.

In every piece of filmmaking, whether it's documentary or fiction, there are elements that are out of control and in control. Our idea of a fiction film is that everything is controlled somehow—costuming, production design, script, casting, on and on and on—I guess, taken to its logical conclusion, a set of completely controlled images.

Whereas the *cinéma-vérité* idea came close to the exact opposite—a set of totally uncontrolled images where one does not even interact with what one is filming. What happens happens unconstrained. Available light. Hand-held cameras. So much has been written about this stuff, but in every piece of filmmaking what brings film alive is that it does capture the odd combination of the spontaneous and the contrived. And that's true of documentary films and that's true of fiction films.

There are all these ironies running through the movie. I mean, here's [lion tamer] Dave Hoover, a guy who can give you this long discourse on the lion mind, the philosophy of lion mind, what the lion has on his mind when he's looking at you in the ring—and what emerges is this paranoid world where the lion has dinner on his mind.

But he's talking about this stuff and at the same time you're looking at these lions and they have periodontal problems, mange, eczema, balding, weak-knees. These lions have trouble getting up in the morning and going to work much less mauling somebody. But it's this strange kind of mental world set against the reality of life. Which is what I like about the movie.

Planet of the Apes

CHRIS CHANG/1997

IF YOU STARE AT a word long enough, it turns into gibberish. If you stare at a human long enough—especially if it's given a chance to open its mouth—the human turns into gibberish. Errol Morris is a filmmaker who has based a career on this phenomenon. Although his technique and style has evolved with Darwinian efficiency, his vision remains unchanged; his subject matter will always be humans, and the contradictory stories they tell themselves, each other, and anyone else who cares to listen. Morris: "The thing that makes civilization possible is that people lie to one another routinely." Contradiction is the key to the universe.

To remain consistent with his own subject matter, Morris presents an immediate contradiction when you try to classify his work. Any time his name pops up, so, inevitably, does the term "documentary." As it turns out, "the 'D' word," as he calls it, is a term he's somewhat averse to; his preferred terminology is "nonfiction film." Part of the reaction is based on the limitations the "D" word seemingly signifies. Documentaries have rarely had the audience draw of feature films. Simply put, the real world prefers an escape into the world of the movies, rather than a circular escape back into the real world. As a participant in Morris's *Vernon, Florida* remarks, "Reality! You mean this is the real world?!? (Laughs) I never thought of that!" Although everyone knows truth is stranger than fiction, what we don't always realize is that Truth and Fiction can be outmoded concepts. The dissolution of the barrier separating the two and a subsequent assault on dichotomy in general—is at the heart of the Errol Morris project.

In a 1987 *New Yorker* profile by Mark Singer, Morris summarized his program: "I like the idea of making films about ostensibly absolutely

From *Film Comment*, September/October 1997. Reprinted by permission.

nothing. I like the irrelevant, the tangential, the sidebar excursion to nowhere that suddenly becomes revelatory. That's what all my movies are
about. That and the idea that we're in a position of certainty, truth, infallible knowledge, when actually we're just a bunch of apes running
around. My films are about people who think they're connected to something, although they're really not."

Since *Gates of Heaven*, the not-so-prolific but forever busy filmmaker
has made five nonfiction films, one fiction film (*The Dark Wind*, a 1992
Tony Hillerman adaptation taken away from him during the editing process), three episodes of a TV series that never went into syndication, and
a few ads. Along the way, a tantalizing array of thwarted projects have
passed through various stages of preparation. Since we know certain for-
mative predilections Morris admits to—including fascinations with casu-
alty statistics, mass murder, the insanity plea, and amateur taxidermy—a
slight pathology begins to emerge as we browse the catalogue of unmade
films: *King Boots*: an English sheep dog with the most successful show career in American history is put on trial in Michigan for the murder of his
owner's eighty-seven-year-old mother. *Car Baby*: a couple with a reversed
set of priorities trade their infant child for a brand new Corvette. *Insanity
Inside Out*: an adaptation of Kenneth Donaldson's book about the fifteen
years he spent in a mental institution after he was wrongly committed
by his own parents. *Ablaze!*: a study of spontaneous human combustion.
Whatever Happened to Einstein's Brain?: title tells it. *Weirdo*: a California
teenager breeds a giant (twenty-eight-pound) chicken. *Road*: portrait of a
man maniacally obsessed with building a highway across northern Minnesota that no one wants (an allegory for Morris himself). *The Wizard of
Wendover*: something to do with "laser-induced fireball experiments in
Utah." Etc. Needless to say, Morris, a 1989 recipient of a MacArthur Fellowship—the so-called "Genius Grant"—is fond of both the *National Enquirer* and the *Weekly World News*.

Gates of Heaven, Morris's first film, is a fully formed realization of his
trademark interview style. The film was inspired by a newspaper headline: "*450 Dead Pets Going to Napa Valley*." (Newspapers, pages from books,
legal documents, maps, diagrams, formulae, and other blocks of text are
common visual punctuation marks throughout his films.) It was a headline he couldn't refuse. The "story" unfolds in a series of interviews that
form the foundation of the film, and the core of Morris's filmmaking
strategy: He provides his subjects with a great deal of cinematic space,
and a significant amount of time to dwell therein. The director's presence, in terms of his own voice and questions, is less than minimal. "The

idea is to allow each character to create a world for themselves, a dream. I've always thought of my portraits as my own version of the Museum of Natural History, these very odd dioramas where you're trying to create some foreign exotic environment and place it on display."

Gates revolves around two California pet cemetery projects—one successful, one not. The failed version was the dream of Floyd McClure. Since the death of his childhood collie, McClure has been possessed by a vision—a self-proclaimed mission to create a memorial to comfort people grieving over their dead house pets. The film is composed of cinematic snapshots: Each individual sits in his or her own characteristic environment—home, office, living room, etc. The camera is locked down on the tripod; the participants appear locked down in their seats. Movement is scarce, and the composition of each frame remains onscreen long enough to leave almost painterly impressions in the viewers' memory banks.

Roland Barthes, in his perennially irritating book *Camera Lucida*, writes of the *punctum*, an innocuous aspect of a photograph that somehow manages to transcend its own mundane existence, puncture the surface of the commonplace, and arrest the eye. In *Gates*, all of the compositions have punctums. (As Barthes explains, the punctum is a subjective thing, so bear with me.) For Floyd, you can't help but notice the Scales of Justice knickknack on a piece of furniture behind him. You also can't help noticing the pen and pocket organizer in his shirt pocket—identically positioned even after he changes shirts. And then there's one of Floyd's pet cemetery investors who has polyester dress socks that all but drown out his interview. Or the chat with a cemetery groundskeeper with a can of Coors sitting disturbingly untouched on the table before him. Obviously, Morris chooses set and environment carefully, and he balances his choices with a discreet emphasis on the meaningless debris people surround themselves with, as if the two negatives of meaningless people and meaningless things canceled each other out and produced an ineffable profundity. Morris allows reality to basically let itself be, and take care of its own set-dressing. He captures moments when you can see people with their own production design strategies laid bare, as his film sets become analogues of, and vacillate with, the realities they represent.

Vernon, Florida opts for both looser image and freer organization. If Morris is aiming for the ultimate "film about nothing," this is getting pretty close. (Actually, amidst its obsessive cast of worm farmers, wild turkey hunters, and white trash philosophers, I think it's about God.) Even though he's switched from the West Coast to the South, the people he's found are carved from the same stone. The film's opening sequence sets the stage for the characters to come: As a quiet swamp town slumbers, a truck slowly plies its way through the streets, pumping clouds of what is most likely toxic insecticide in its wake. And as the town's various inhabitants are introduced, one can only speculate bleakly as to the health effects of the chemicals. Which raises a crucial point: A cursory reading of some of the "characters" Morris interviews begs the question of directorial condescension. Some of the people seem so out-there, and so damaged by their own reality, it becomes somewhat suspect for a director to prey on them for the benefit of filmgoing audiences. Invariably, people will laugh at some of the relatively grotesque lifeforms Morris parades before our eyes. But in carefully modulated ways, his revels in the realms of human oddity seem more akin to forms of identification, rather than patronization or satire. (Even though ultimately it's all three.) Morris readily admits that by placing people within his own films, he "uses" them. Addressing an audience at Harvard after screening his new film, *Fast, Cheap and Out of Control*, he explained how the four completely disparate subjects that comprise the film were chosen. In regard to the film's "shit-eating mammals who live in tunnels," Morris commented, "I've just always loved mole rats." The director finds a kindred spirit in the hapless rodent's absurdity. To take identification to a more physical—and human—level, and to get the shots he wanted of the insecticide truck fumigating the sleeping residents of Vernon, the camera was placed directly in the path of the oncoming clouds of poison. They drift over the frame, the camera, and presumably the director himself. Perhaps the ultimate statement of solidarity with the dispossessed occurred in the *New Yorker* article when Morris commented on a habit he'd picked up at the Ed Sullivan Theatre, the home of many fundraising telethons: "My favorite was the Stop Arthritis Telethon. When I would go to these things I would always see the same people in the audience, and I'd look upon them with some pity. And then I realized I was one of them."

Morris claims it's more effective to look as if you're a good listener than to actually listen well. The technique hit paydirt during the shooting of his groundbreaking *The Thin Blue Line*, a film that not only freed a wrongly convicted killer but also anticipated the renaissance of what we now call, in a zenith of TV phraseology, Reality Based Programming. Morris was acting as the perfect listener but not actually listening when he interviewed Emily Miller, "one of the whacko eyewitnesses" whose testimony eventually helped get Randall Adams off death row. (Adams was falsely accused of shooting a Dallas police officer in the spring of 1977.) After filming her interview, Morris was reviewing the footage back in the editing room. Much to his surprise, Miller, a key witness, had admitted that she failed to identify Adams in a police lineup, contradicting her original testimony and throwing the entire court decision into question. Morris, a man who takes obvious pleasure in both impossible-to-summarize films and films uniquely summarized, called *TTBL* "the only murder mystery film that actually solves a murder."

At times, an Errol Morris film acts as the cinematic equivalent of cosmological entropy. Hawking: "It is a matter of common experience that disorder tends to increase with time if things are left to themselves." On the other hand, the apparent disorder of an Errol Morris film can seemingly reverse the Second Law of Thermodynamics, and create intuitive forms of order out of chaos itself—much like the experience one has when watching the slowly evolving cohesion of the disparate stories of *Fast, Cheap and Out of Control*, or *Vernon, Florida*. Hawking didn't want his film to be about anything else but the science he was involved with. Morris, working for the first time on a film he hadn't initiated, expressed trepidation, but the result, as the director once again turns antagonized contradiction into art, is a surprisingly moving biographical meditation on a genius trapped in a broken body—and the possibility of using science as an interface with "the mind of God." And it's another example of Morris's mastery of the ironic, a tool that suddenly takes on mystical proportions in its explorations of human absurdity.

Since *TTBL*, Morris has followed two basic themes: True Crime, reflecting his lifelong interests and also an actual stint as a private detective; and Weird Science, reflecting his "failed" education in both the history of science and philosophy. (A poignant and ironic example of the two paths crossing occurred when Morris was assaulted by his own graduate advisor on the grounds of the Institute for Advanced Study in Princeton. The scuffle was instigated by a theoretical paper Morris had written.)

Morris gave True Crime a technological twist by designing a device called the Interrotron. Two cameras are linked by silvery projection screens; as Morris "listens" to his subjects, the image of his face appears onscreen so the subject can look at Morris—and vice versa—while also looking directly into the lens. The talking-head format gains greater visual veracity as you literally feel the subject making eye contact with you. "We're actually looking at each other down the central axis of the lens. It's the difference between faux first person and the true first person. There's an added intensity. The Interrotron inaugurates the birth of true first-person cinema." It's a subtle nuance, but once you're aware of the heightened degree of optically subjective penetration, especially when dealing with subjects who are probably lying through their teeth to protect themselves from implication in various criminal acts, the effect is mesmerizing. Morris, even though he'd be the first to rail against it, is putting the vérité back in cinéma. (He shot three segments of the proposed Interrotron series. The stories involved a parrot that *may* have witnessed a murder, a man who froze his mother's head, but *may* have removed it before she was dead, and a post office supervisor who was so fascistic in his methods, he *may* have been the final straw for an employee who went berserk with a shotgun. Maintaining his characteristic conceptual waffle, *may* is the primary operating principle of *The Interrotron Stories*.)

Morris has a favorite line from Jacques Tourneur's 1947 masterpiece *Out of the Past* (1947). Robert Mitchum—forever ensnared by the noir fatalism that surrounds him—mutters, "I could see the frame, but I couldn't see the picture." When Morris describes the apparently agonizing process he faces in the editing room, you can imagine him mouthing the words as a mantra. At Harvard, he described his work on *Fast, Cheap, & Out of Control*: "The movie was a nightmare to put together. It was a very, very difficult editorial process." He even admitted to a desire for a standard film element that he will probably never employ—at least "normally": "It occurred to me over and over again during the editing that movies really do have story lines." Although *FC&OC* was begun years ago, put on hold, and then resumed, Morris, in response to the death of his mother and stepfather in the interim, now calls the film "an elegy." And, indeed, the film amounts to a tremendously moving—not to mention entertaining—evocation of human finitude, and a documentation of various attempts to surmount it.

The four men whose various obsessions bind *FC&OC* together can be lumped into two fuzzy camps. Dave Toover, the liontamer, and George Mendonca, the aging topiary gardener (think geriatric Edward Scissorhands), have their minds and emotions firmly planted in the past. Toover has a severe case of nostalgia for both the late Clyde Beatty and the world he was a part of: "We lost part of the circus industry when we lost him. . . . And I don't know if there will be anyone of that stature left in this business." Mendonca's malaise is more abstract: "It's just cut and wait. . . . Cut and wait. . . ." (Morris describes the phrase as one that most closely resembles his experience with editing the film.) Ray Mendez, the naked-mole-rat enthusiast, and Rodney Brooks, an MIT scientist who builds robots and is intrigued by the possibility of silicon-based lifeforms as the next phase of earthly evolution, are clearly looking toward the future. All four men are extending themselves into their surrounding environment with the help of the "animals" of their trade. In a way, they are each somehow incomplete without these externalized obsessions, and it is surely the vector of obsession itself that landed them roles in Morris's film. (The animal analogue, not-so-incidentally, is where it all began. "The first interview I ever filmed was the Howards [from *Gates of Heaven*], and the very first line, which was probably the start of my film career, was when they said, "Trooper was the kind of dog that didn't have other dogs to relate to. He lived with adult human beings.")

FC&OC is the most visually sophisticated film Morris has ever made. Using a variety of grain and emulsion, found footage, Super-8, 16mm, Super 16, 35mm, video, color and black-and-white, 35mm transferred to video and then reshot on 35mm, etc., the director goes ballistic with a barrage of image and texture that suit the multivalent layering of obsession that drives the film. During the sequence of the topiary animal garden at night, he explains he achieved "some kind of documentary absurdity," a phrase that truly gets to the heart of his work. To achieve the shot, he brought in four rainmakers, three cranes, a fog generator, and a group of 16 and 18k HMIs to boost the light to five times the normal level, allowing the camera to capture the scene at the ultra-slow motion speed Morris and his DP, Robert Richardson, desired. (Richardson was responsible for shooting Oliver Stone's *Natural Born Killers*, the greatest rock video ever made.) In shots like these, you can truly feel Morris on the brink of something totally different. What that is, however, is beyond even his imagination. Temporarily.

Whether creating order out of chaos, or just adding more chaos to the existing chaos, the underlying thread tying all of Morris's work together is deep emotional realism. (That you can frequently laugh at.) After everything is said and done, and after "all the valiant human enterprises come to naught," Morris will continue to revel, cherish the moments, and interview the bystanders. When he speaks in public, his language is riddled with references to anything from Nabokov—whom he greatly admires for his use of the "self-deceived narrator"—to Yeats, to Shakespeare, to one of his favorite—and most hated—quotes from William Faulkner's Nobel acceptance speech. Faulkner said that not only should man endure, he should prevail. Morris, fueled by the powers of contradiction and his own creative angst, has his own variation: "Who said we should even endure? Let alone prevail?"

Genre Buster

MICHEL NEGROPONTE/1997

ERROL MORRIS'S quirky vision has created an impressive filmography that includes *A Brief History of Time* (1992), *The Thin Blue Line* (1988), *Vernon, Florida* (1987), and *Gates of Heaven* (1978). He describes his newest work, *Fast, Cheap and Out of Control*, as "four versions of the myth of Sisyphus." A lion tamer, a mole-rat photographer, a topiary gardener, and a robot scientist reflect on their life's work and create a memorable metaphysical journey. With its stunning visuals and haunting score, *Fast, Cheap and Out of Control* is a touching meditation on people creating worlds out of their fantasies.

Q: *I want to begin with a comment that Jean-Luc Godard made about how the Western world no longer knows what stories to tell or what fictions to invent. What is it about that thinning line between fact and fiction that fascinates you?*

A: Well, it's not altogether clear there is a thin line between fact and fiction, or whether there is any line at all. In fact, discriminating between the two could be called an elusive task. I often like to think of my movies as various attempts to examine that question in one way or another. The Dave Hoover story in *Fast, Cheap and Out of Control* is in part about his obsession with the legendary lion tamer, Clyde Beatty, who appeared in a whole number of Hollywood movies, serials, radio shows, and comic books. When I was digging through all this Clyde Beatty material, I found his first movie, *The Big Cage*. In it, there's a lion and tiger fight that's clearly crazy. The animals are just ripping each other to pieces. Well, in Clyde's autobiography, he tells the story at how this scene was produced, and it was very much a fight that got out of hand. The lion

From *The Independent*, October 1997. Reprinted by permission.

kills the tiger—if you like, it's a kind of snuff film—and the question I always ask myself about this piece of footage is: is it a documentary or is it a feature?

It appears, of course, in a feature film that's fiction, but it also is a documentary of this particular fight—a fight that was out of control, that ended in one animal killing the other. When you look at this footage, what is it that makes it a documentary in one instance and a piece of fiction filmmaking in the next? I think the answer is that there is nothing that makes it fiction or documentary, save how you look at that material. There's nothing inherent in the filmmaking itself.

Q: *There are tools and traditions from narrative filmmaking that have spilled over into nonfiction filmmaking that we don't immediately associate with documentary. For instance, your use of music scoring, production design, and photographic cinematography in* Fast, Cheap and Out of Control. *You use those elements in a very creative and unabashed way.*

A: But they're just simply conventions—conventions of how movies are really put together. We somehow think that documentary filmmaking is documentary filmmaking by virtue of the fact that you have a hand-held camera or you use available light or whatever. Whereas we might associate a completely different style with feature filming. But that's just stylistic stuff.

Q: *Yes, but you do choose to adorn the image, and that's a fascinating choice.*

A: I like to think what I've done in documentary film is just to introduce a lot of techniques that are more common to fiction filmmaking.

Q: *I wondered if you ever consult the pioneers of documentary like John Grierson or Robert Flaherty. There are very poetic and visual elements in films like* Night Mail *and* Louisiana Story *that seem to have inspired you. Do you like that work?*

A: I do like it, but my own affinity is for a completely different tradition in documentary filmmaking that comes out of Georges Franju, Jean Vigo, and Dziga Vertov. There are other kinds of documentary film that carry a lot of baggage with them, a sort of claim about truth-telling. They carry an almost scientific veneer, as if the camera were in the hands of a social scientist or anthropologist recording material for future study. Then there's a completely different tradition of documentary that's a kind of pure filmmaking, if you like, without that additional metaphysical baggage. Or maybe it has a more ironic relationship with the world.

Q: *Are the visual pyrotechnics of your film in some way a reflection of the demands of the marketplace?*

A: I actually don't think they are. Maybe I would be the last to know.

Q: *Well, more simply, most distributors run away from documentaries, but they don't run away from your work. Why?*

A: I don't know. Because they're free of that idea of adult education or deliberate pedagogy, and they're intended to be movies.

Q: *I felt throughout* Fast, Cheap and Out of Control *that you were documenting a state of mind—not only the subjects' state of mind but possibly your own as well. There was both a sense of loss and a sense of wonder.*

A: There's certainly the sense of loss. I often think of the movie as an elegy. An elegy for, among other things, my step-father and mother who died during the making of the movie.

These four stories are all about obsessive characters. In two instances, they're characters who are interested in preserving something of the past. A topiary gardener preserving this very odd privet against all those things that might destroy it—hurricanes, birds, blight, whatever. In the case of the lion tamer, it's this artificial jungle he's created in a circus ring, that he's inherited from one of the greatest lion tamers of all times, that he seeks to preserve, but at the same time realizes that it may be coming to an end, that whole circus world may be a world on the wane. Those two backward-looking characters and the two forward-looking characters— the mole rat guy, who imagines this odd unitarian society of vermin— and the robot guy, who actually, in true Frankenstein fashion, is creating his own life form that he believes will replace us. So there is that feeling of loss, that feeling of a world that has slipped from our grasp and a world of the future that may not even include us.

Q: *I found the film to be very tender. It's not a word one would associate with some of your earlier work.*

A: Well, I really like the characters in all my films, at least most of them. That's certainly true in *Vernon, Florida*, which I think has a kind of tender quality; it has an absurdist quality too, but I don't think those two are incompatible.

Q: *You describe* Fast, Cheap and Out of Control *as the ultimate low concept movie. What do you mean by that exactly?*

A: When selling a movie in Hollywood, people want a one-line description of what the movie is going to be about. That's a high concept idea. I use low concept in this instance because the movie, I believe, defies those kinds of descriptions. Certainly the last two movies I made are high concept in the extreme: "Innocent man in jail" and "World famous scientist confined to a wheelchair surveys the universe." *Fast, Cheap and Out of Control* isn't really that kind of movie. It works in a different way altogether, and it attempts—whether successfully or unsuccessfully—a different kind of storytelling.

Q: *Your film is a very textured landscape, and your concerns have become almost painterly. Talk a little about mixing film formats with video, home movies, and film clips. Also the use of severely canted frames, slow motion, and fast motion. I call it the Waring Blender palette.*

A: Well, it is a palette. Often films are put together without a palette, and there's just one style. This film really lends itself to a whole variety of approaches. A part of it certainly comes from my cinematographer. I've had the good fortune to work with a lot of great photographers, from Stefan Czapsky to John Bailey, and in this last movie, Robert Richardson. Richardson is unique. He's attempted a lot of things other people haven't. Certainly he does see filmmaking as a kind of painting with a very broad palette. In the old days, you would hear people talk about the lengths they would go to to get one emulsion batch, to make sure all of the raw stock they were using came from one run at Kodak.

The Richardson idea is just the opposite of that. When we were shooting *Fast, Cheap and Out of Control*, we were using almost every emulsion you can imagine. Not just black and white, color, and infrared, but every version of color and black and white that you can imagine, from reversal to negative, fine grained to high speed, and so on. Also different gauges: 35mm, Super 16, 16mm, Super 8, as well as video. The last day of shooting at the Philadelphia Zoo, we built mole rat stages and filmed the zoo's mole rats in them. We called in Roto-Rooter. They have a fiber-optic sewer camera that they send into drains to look for obstructions. And so we used their sewer cam in the movie.

Q: *A fiber-optic sewer cam? I really appreciate the spirit of "anything goes" which clearly drives your film. What about the use of slow and fast motion?*

A: Maybe it comes out of a certain perversity. Film always is in some ironic relationship with the world. I have my own variant of Godard's "film is truth at twenty-four frames per second." My variant is that film is life at twenty-four frames per second. The use of different camera speeds is just a way of heightening that irony, if you like. It was certainly used by Jean Vigo in *A Propos de Nice* as a way of creating a kind of surrealism, and I like to think that I've used it to similar effect in my own films. I know that often while shooting I keep saying to myself the one speed that we should avoid is twenty-four frames per second, because it seems to be the one speed that's inherently the most corrupted. It's a sleight of hand. You're trying to convince people that they're seeing something real. Even when they know better.

Mr. Death: The Executioner's Song

SCOTT MACAULAY/1999

IN 1988, FRED A. LEUCHTER, an engineer from Massachusetts who made a living designing more "humane" electric chairs, was hired by Ernst Zundel, the publisher of several pro-Hitler, Holocaust-denying tracts, to conduct a forensic investigation into the use of poison gas in Nazi concentration camps. On his honeymoon, Leuchter traveled to Auschwitz and, with his wife sitting in the car reading Agatha Christie novels, illegally chipped away at the brick, collecting mortar samples which he transported back to the States. Testing these samples for traces of cyanide gas, Leuchter "proved" that the Holocaust never occurred. Taking these findings, Zundel published *The Leuchter Report*, which sold millions of copies around the world, and was later tried, in Canada, of disseminating "false history." Leuchter, of course, was the main witness for the defense, and at the trial his callously sloppy science was thoroughly discredited. In the process, Leuchter lost his wife, his reputation, but not, as Errol Morris shows us in his philosophically probing and horrifyingly funny documentary *Mr. Death*, his plucky American "can-do" attitude.

Fred Leuchter is the latest in a long line of American originals framed by the amiably merciless camera of Errol Morris. His first film, *Gates of Heaven*, comprised heavily of talking head interviews, is a classic portrayal of two feuding pet cemetery owners that resonated on social, political, and economic levels. His 1988 film, *The Thin Blue Line*, blended a patented off-screen interview technique with dramatic reenactments and surreal visual flourishes to solve the mystery of a small town murder. And in 1997, Morris made *Fast, Cheap, and Out of Control*, a tremendously moving portrait of four obsessed individuals whose singular pursuits

From *Filmmaker Magazine*, Fall 1999. Reprinted by permission.

Morris merges into a visually stunning meditation on death and morality. His latest, *Mr. Death* is a worthy addition to the Morris canon, a startling, deceptively straightforward work in which Morris's engagement of his subject, Fred Leuchter, creates a knowing and cautionary cinematic portrait a man who is incapable of knowing himself.

Q: Mr. Death *deals with a lot of issues—epistemology, belief systems, how one forms one's own identity—and then there's the whole subject of Holocaust denial. Were you worried about making a film where a big part of the media is probably only going to deal with that one issue, the Holocaust, which to me is not really what the film is about?*
A: I agree with your assessment of the film, but it worries me that you're already predicting how people are going to respond to the film, as if it has to be that way.

Q: *Well, there certainly will be people who will view the film as being successful or unsuccessful in how it presents this controversial subject.*
A: I had similar problems with *The Thin Blue Line*. That film is an attempt to have your cake and eat it too. To paraphrase what you just said, it was an attempt to make a movie about how we see the world, various epistemic concerns, how believing is seeing for many people if not for all of us. And it told a story about a miscarriage of justice.

Without making any kind of exact comparison between *The Thin Blue Line* and *Mr. Death*, there are similar kinds of problems. In *The Thin Blue Line* it became absolutely imperative in telling the story to make it clear that there was a miscarriage of justice. That David Harris was in all likelihood the killer and Randall Adams was not. And in this movie it becomes absolutely necessary to make it clear that the Holocaust happened and that the Leuchter report is devoid of value. It would have been irresponsible not to.

Q: *There's a paradox at work here. As a subject matter, the Holocaust is capable of dwarfing all of the film's other philosophical concerns. But in a way the enormity of the Holocaust is exactly what causes these concerns to register on the deepest possible level.*
A: I agree. One person asked me: "Why this interest in murder in your films?" And to the extent that I know, I believe it's because we are deeply fascinated with why people do things. Asking the question of why someone crossed the road on a certain date at a certain time lacks drama. Murder is such a dramatic event that we feel compelled to provide an explanation for why it happened. We get drawn into all of these philo-

sophical issues about how we know things about the nature of explanation. Another tricky element of course is that I never at any time in the course of making this movie or *The Thin Blue Line* wanted to convey the idea that truth is subjective or that I believe that truth is subjective, that I'm some kind of post-modernist in that respect.

One thing I am fond of saying about Cambridge, Massachusetts, is that the name Baudrillard does not appear in the phone book. And this is not a film about how history and truth are up for grabs. This is far more old-fashioned in the sense that I believe in facts, knowable facts. Maybe the reasons people do what they do are more elusive, but the question of whether or not poison gas was used in Auschwitz is not something of conjecture. It's something that has been established overwhelmingly with historical evidence.

Q: *How do you find people like Fred for your films?*
A: People always ask me these questions as if there's some kind of algorithm that can be cited. I've come to realize that maybe it comes down to some kind of talent that I have, for better or for worse. I think I share with my mother, who died a number of years ago, the quality of being really interested in people. And I think what's interesting about interviewing is that it is a kind of model of human interaction on some kind of formal level—the relationship of one person to another person. Yes, the rules change. In some cases there's supposed to be a lot of interaction, and the drama derives from that fact. In say, a Mike Wallace interview, it's presupposed that part of the nature of the interview is an adversarial relationship between the subject and the interviewer.

Q: *How do you situate yourself on this continuum of interviewers?*
A: I think I'm almost the polar opposite [of Mike Wallace] because my intention is to create monologues, to remove myself from the interview process as much as possible even though I'm very much there.

Q: *But at the end of this particular movie,* Mr. Death, *we hear your off-screen voice asking a question to Leuchter.*
A: It's become a stylistic thing with me. I've done it now in *Fast, Cheap, and Out of Control,* and this movie, by choice, and in *The Thin Blue Line* I was there just by necessity because I needed to put that material in the movie. But I like it—it's this reminder that there is this other person out there, and I think that the question registers my puzzlement with Fred and maybe at the same time captures the audience's puzzlement with him.

Q: *Have you heard from Leuchter after the film was finished?*
A: I showed him the film. He liked it.

Q: *There's an irony here. People accuse Leuchter of being megalomaniacal, of naively believing that his own faculties can refute the historical evidence of the Holocaust. But that same kind of presumption is probably what motivated him to agree to do your movie and to perhaps believe that he would come off looking good.*
A: That's probably true. When I see Leuchter at the end of the movie on his rock pile, pounding away, it takes on this very sad significance because at that point in the movie, you realize how empty his enterprise really is. That image has a kind of existential awareness that I find interesting. It's one of the strongest metaphors that I've ever stumbled on to. The two central images in the movie are the Van der Graaf generator at the beginning which you see reprised at the end and the shots of Leuchter on the rock pile. In fact the rock pile was a reenactment done in the studio in Boston where we built a piece of Auschwitz, and where Fred is pounding away again.

Q: *Why is the Van der Graaf generator one of the central images for you?*
A: Well, let me ask you a question. What did that image do for you?

Q: *It connects to the tradition of the mad scientist—the '50s inventor doing homemade science in his basement.*
A: That's certainly intended. It's intended to invoke Frankenstein and a self-invented inventor. But I also saw the image as this man who sees himself in possession of certain knowledge, who sees himself almost as a version of God, as the arbiter of what is death and what is life. And putting it at the end of the movie in juxtaposition of Fred on the rock pile— it's like, "What is he doing?"

It's the quintessential picture of benighted humanity engaged in a totally quixotic, meaningless, and senseless—if it weren't also so deeply pernicious—enterprise. This is a story about a clueless narrator. Or is he a clueless narrator? I see the film as a kind of *Citizen Kane*, a movie where you have various characters speculating about [a subject's] underlying motivation. But we never really know for sure who he is and what he's doing, or, if you prefer, why he's doing what doing.

Q: *I was surprised throughout the movie at Leuchter's lack of interiority, his lack of any kind of philosophical introspection about what he was engaged in. His enterprise seemed purely mechanical, divorced from society, culture, or politics. And also, there seemed to be something truly hapless about his adventure.*

A: To me, certainly there is something hapless about his adventure—but don't forget I ask him in the movie "Fred, did you ever consider the possibility you might be wrong?" And he says, "I'm well past that." And to me, this is getting into a kind of crazy area of megalomania.

What's so interesting about how Leuchter tells his story is that he himself points out in the early part of the movie that prison officials were mistaken in assuming that because he had expertise in one area that it extended to other things as well. Because he could build electric chairs, that didn't mean he could build lethal injection systems, or gas chambers. He ridicules them for making the assumption. And then we learn a short time later that he has bought hook, line, and sinker into this whole Zündel-defined enterprise of going to Auschwitz on a fact-finding trip. He has no expertise, yet he manages to sell himself to himself as the final arbiter of these things. And to me that goes well beyond "hapless."

Q: *When you ask him that question at the end, most intelligent people could say, "Yeah, I've thought about it," or "Maybe I am wrong," but you get the sense that this guy is incapable of saying these words because that would shatter one of the few beliefs he has—in himself, and to do so would be to shatter his own conception of who he is.*

A: Yes. I think that's a fair description.

Q: *I might be giving him the benefit of the doubt.*

A: Likewise. I don't really have that firm a grasp of Fred even having spent years with him. There's something very slippery, something very elusive about him.

Q: *And the movie's quite canny in the way it plays with that, like the shots of him on the rock pile, oblivious to the ramifications of what he's done.*

A: Yes. I mean, I think that there's this idea that filmmakers are social workers—which they're not! At least I'm not. I'm grateful to Fred for participating in the film. Why he did it, I'm not altogether sure. Maybe he hoped for some kind of vindication, or maybe he just enjoyed the attention.

Q: *Is that an important question to you, something that figures into your filmmaking process—why someone would agree to be in one of your films? Once you have the conception of the film in your mind, is the scrutinizing of your subjects' motivations important or not?*

A: I would say it's inevitable. With Leuchter I thought about it often, because it was in a way a question of the whole movie: Why is he doing this? I believe that there's this whole question about people who do bad things—do they know they're bad, or do they think that they're good? Have they construed themselves to themselves in such a way that they have convinced themselves that they are good and not evil? And in Leuchter's case, he seems to me to be a person who believes in his own rectitude, in his own correctness.

Q: *There's something very American about that: the self-made man.*
A: There's something very human about it. Yes, I think there's an American aspect to this story: I would not disagree with that. The idea of a self-made man, or a self-invented inventor, or crazy entrepreneur who finds a need and fills it. He sees that executions are taking place in the United States and says, "Aha, I can cash in on this!" But I think the problem is not properly considered [as] an ethnic problem!

Q: *You screened an early version of the film at Sundance and now there is this revised version. Talk to me about your editing process in constructing a film like this because structurally the film seems very clear. The film tells a story quite methodically, it is arranged in coherent sections, and yet I know that you worked on it for some time and went through different versions of the movie.*
A: There are so many decisions being made when you're putting a movie together. In this case the major decision was whether to include voices other than Leuchter's? Should we just hear Leuchter talking or interview other people as well? And I actually edited a version of the movie with Leuchter alone and then felt the necessity of adding other voices in order to make two things absolutely clear: that he was wrong, and also to show the disparity of views about him, people's general puzzlement.

Q: *All of your films are funny to varying degrees. And there are moments in this film that are truly funny, but they are funny in their horrifyingness, like Leuchter stumbling into a concentration camp looking like some American tourist with his wife on her honeymoon. At the screening I was at, there was some nervous laughter, and some people laughing out loud, and other people incapable of laughing. Is humor an unintended by-product of your stories, or are you consciously using it as a storyteller?*
A: Humor is complicated, it's not an ingredient that you actually put in something, like you add salt.

Q: *Actually, in a lot of filmmaking, it is something you put in like adding salt. In a Hollywood film someone might say, "This scene doesn't play. We need a laugh here." And someone writes a joke.*

A: I think a lot of the humor in my movies is absurdist humor. These are absurdist, surreal films, among other things. And part of the humor, in this particular movie, derives from the utter disjunction between what Fred is talking about or what he thinks he is talking about, and the reality of what he is talking about. His crazy capital punishment stories, his botched executions, the honeymoon in Auschwitz—which is utterly surreal, absurd, and grotesque. And he is utterly unaware of this fact. Do I consciously make use of this sort of thing? Yes!

Q: *You spoke earlier about creating monologues, but in this film there is also the formal device of the blackouts which punctuate Leuchter's dialogue.*

A: It's something I started using in *A Brief History of Time*. In [that film] it had an odd metaphorical character to me, linked with that weird on/off clicking of Steven Hawking's own communication and the possibility of him being blacked out. There was something about it that I liked—information being parceled out. Here it seemed to sort of capture the fragmentary way in which we know people, or know anything.

Q: *Has there been feedback on this film from the revisionist history or neo-Nazi community?*

A: I believe the movie has already been attacked in several places. This movie is certainly not intended to convince Holocaust deniers that the Holocaust happened. I don't think anything could convince them. But I do think that it demolishes *The Leuchter Report* on its own terms.

Hapless Fred, as you call him, goes to Auschwitz. He takes these samples. He puts them in bags. He has them tested. Why doesn't he find cyanide? We learn that the chambers might have been covered in plaster. He may not have the surfaces [and testing for cyanide requires] surfaces tests. And he took the samples in such a way that they were horribly diluted. And [this is said by] the chemist who was hired by Leuchter to do the test. But why am I saying all of this? See, now I've been trapped into talking about [the film] in terms of the Holocaust! And that's all because of you!

A Hundred Million Years
of Equivocations

RON ROSENBAUM/1999

RR: *We've just watched* Stairway to Heaven, *your film about Temple Grandin, designer of abattoirs. Why did you choose not to show the execution of animals?*
EM: Temple didn't want me to. It's a pretty simple answer. I would have filmed it if she'd allowed it, though I don't know whether I would have used it. It's really not part of her story, or even my story about her story. As Temple tells her story, she takes the animal all the way up to the point of the bolt gun but no further.

I first became aware of Temple in an article that appeared in the *New Yorker* written by Oliver Sacks, called "An Anthropologist on Mars." And this was an article which, among other things, said how Temple was disconnected from the world, disconnected from other people. I remember feeling my first meeting with her, and many times subsequent to that, how deeply emotional Temple really is, how connected she is with the world. Not that she relates to things like everybody else. That's not quite right. Part of her problem is she seems so deeply—if this is a problem—so deeply ingenious and trusting. I felt that I was in the presence of someone with very powerful emotions and someone deeply connected. And one of the ironies of her own stories is that she talks about herself as though she's removed, even though she is not. I prefer to think of Temple as a person with very deep emotions. She makes more sense to me that way.

Apparently she's not as autistic as she was when she was a little girl. A lot of people wish they could function as well as Temple. She has a doctorate, a college teaching job. She runs her own company. She has writ-

From The Museum of Modern Art, Fall 1999. Reprinted with permission by Ron Rosenbaum, author of *Explaining Hitler* and *The Shakespeare Wars.*

ten several books and has functioned as a worldwide spokesperson for autistic people. In a conventional sense, Temple is very functional. My job was not to ask, "Is she in this category or that category of autism?"

RR: *What Temple Grandin seems to share with Fred Leuchter is that they both believe that humane execution is not an oxymoron. Are there any other similarities here?*

EM: Well, both of these stories are about killing machines, designers of death equipment. Very simple answer: I really admire Temple Grandin, and I really don't admire Fred Leuchter.

RR: *But haven't you at one point said that you loved Fred Leuchter?*

EM: Oh, I guess so. I get into trouble with this and then I have to endlessly qualify what I'm saying. How about this, and I hope it's not too smarmy or self-serving. Loving and admiring Fred are two very different things. When I say I *love* Fred, I *love* the *idea* of Fred—I'm *fascinated* by him. He has to be the most ingenuous person I have ever come across. Well, either ingenuous or absolutely insane.

For many, many years I have been in search of what I would call the absolutely clueless narrator, the narrator who has absolutely no perspective about himself, whatsoever. You've all heard about the examined life? Here's an example of a life, which has not been examined at all. That's right: the totally *unexamined* life.

RR: *If Temple Grandin is autistic, would you call Fred Leuchter morally autistic?*

EM: Beyond morally autistic. He's morally *idiotic*. What's so puzzling about Fred's story is how he sees himself, how he imagines himself in the story about himself that he narrates in the film. In *Mr. Death* Fred talks about designing humane execution equipment. Quite clearly he sees himself as the Florence Nightingale of Death Row, the guy who took the "ouch" out of the death penalty. He is positively bursting with enthusiasm. I almost hear him saying, "I never thought the death penalty could be so wonderful." So there you have it. Fred sees himself as a humanist and humanitarian, a seeker of truth, civil libertarian, champion of the underdog. At times, he even talks about himself as if he is some sort of Galileo figure, a guy pursuing truth despite the consequences. I watch this movie—and I'm assuming other people feel the same way—and I see Fred as deeply mistaken about who he is.

RR: *When you're introducing Fred's trip to Auschwitz to scrape away at the walls and his flight there, didn't you cut to some of Leni Riefenstahl's footage from* Triumph of the Will?

EM: I just love that footage. The opening sequence of *Triumph of the Will* is Hitler's plane coming through the clouds. Hitler as God. His plane as some kind of weird bird, I suppose, a vulture disguised as a phoenix. It's one of the grand delusions of all time, the Third Reich. And as Fred is flying off to Poland on his supposed fact-finding mission, it's nice to see a companion piece: Hitler on his way to Nuremburg.

RR: *Both of them deluded in the same way?*

EM: No, I can't quite say both of them deluded in the same way. But think of the *magnitude* of the delusion. Here is Fred, imagining himself as a hero, and in fact, he's involved in something totally despicable, something truly grotesque. I mean, there is some kind of disjunction between how Fred sees himself and how we see him, what he's doing. It's really quite amazing that we're capable of such things. You'd think there would be some kind of Fred inside of Fred that would leap out and smack him around and demand that he come to his senses and stop this nonsense. But of course, there isn't. There's just Fred. That's why there are people who have complaints about this movie. There's the view that a film about a Holocaust-denier shouldn't even be made, let alone seen. There is a need to have someone—say the second Fred, the good Fred—stand up and say, "Look at yourself. Look at what you're doing. This is nasty. This is despicable."

RR: *You succeeded in your film, I think, in exploding Fred's alleged science and his botched historical research. But in conversations with me you always felt resentful that you had to do that. You kept saying, "I feel like I'm engaged in proving the obvious. Maybe the next film I'll make will be proving the sky is blue." Do you still feel resentful?*

EM: Yes. I could do a whole series. I could take a camera to the airport and show that there are heavier-than-air flying machines. I didn't want to make a film showing that Fred was wrong. It has always been quite obvious to me that Fred is wrong. And furthermore, the story is *not* about whether he is right or wrong. It's about how he *thinks* he's right when he's wrong.

RR: *But when you first showed the Leuchter film to an audience—I think it was to a Harvard film class—they bought it, or half of them bought it. And the other half thought that you were a Holocaust-denier. So you somehow felt the need to counter-balance that, to investigate and explode Fred's obvious fraudulent science that's still out there, right?*

EM: Well, it shocked me. I guess it's little bit like the Stockholm syndrome. You're trapped in a room with this one man—namely Leuchter. He's talking and talking and talking. There's no one in the movie to grab you by the shoulders and say, "You know, this is, of course, nonsense." It's a scary thought. What if there is no one in a society to say a man like Leuchter is crazy or wrong or evil. Isn't there something like an insanity detector inside us all? Well, in this Harvard class, there wasn't. One of the professors got up and took me to task. "How could the same filmmaker who made *The Thin Blue Line* not investigate Fred's claims and call him to account." In the end, I decided he was right.

There are people who would argue that answering Fred is playing into the hands of anti-Semites, neo-Nazis, you name it. But there is no belief so sacred that it should be beyond scrutiny, no canon of historical knowledge so buttressed by evidence that it can not be challenged, that it can not be examined, including the Holocaust. Looking at Fred's claims— and I am speaking now as a Jew—reconnected me with the history of World War II, particularly looking at the Nazi documents in the Auschwitz archives.

But I also very much wanted to have my cake and eat it, too. I wanted to make a movie that had a strong *factual* element, but at its heart told a story about an *interior* world. I'm very interested about how people see themselves. When we think about documentary, we think about documentary as being some species of journalism, as if we're engaged in providing a picture of the *reality*. From my first film, *Gates of Heaven*, I believe I've been involved in a somewhat different enterprise: revealing an interior world, a *mental landscape*, how people see themselves as revealed through how they use language. If you listen to what people say, that gives you a route into how they see themselves. It's a different kind of enterprise.

RR: *Let me ask you about the lightning show at the start of* Mr. Death. *Is there some suggestion in this use of electricity and electrocution that maybe film itself is some Faustian device? Are you fascinated with the Frankenstein concept, that we've created something in film that is, in some way, monstrous?*
EM: Maybe. But if film is monstrous, it's because *we* are monstrous. In film we've created a way of capturing not only the world, but our dreams as well. That may be a truly monstrous thing. Actually I think it's a good thing. Perhaps monstrous *and* good.

About the lightning show, I wanted to put Fred in the Van de Graff generator from early on, from when I first heard about his story. It's the world's largest lightning machine. From very early on this image came into my head: Fred and the lightning machine, Fred as God, Fred as Zeus or Thor, hurling lightning bolts. It seemed to capture how Fred saw himself, Fred as the arbiter of life and death. Actually Fred denies that there's really any difference between the two. One of my very favorite lines in the movie is when he explains to us very patiently, "There is no difference between a life support system and an execution system." He goes on to qualify that "If a life support system fails, you die. If an execution system fails, you live. That's the difference between the two." Subtle, very subtle. But yet, a difference. The two central images in the movie is Fred in that infernal machine, and Fred chipping away endlessly at the rock in Auschwitz.

We spent a good part of the day filming Fred in this machine at the Boston Museum of Science. And I've often thought about the whole experience of being with him that day. Not once did he ever ask me, "Why are you doing this? What is this for? How is this going to be used in the movie? What are you thinking, Errol?" He just enjoyed this whole process of being in that cage, riding up and down, and firing bolts of lightning at his command. It's very much like we built a lethal injection system, a *faux* lethal injection system for the purposes of photographing a scene. When we put Fred on the set, he suddenly came alive. It became unclear whether he realized this was a set, that this was a fantasy, or did he see himself as somehow really there, in that place, doing that thing? I think it's a big problem for all of us: what's real and what's been fabricated in our mind.

RR: *Do you believe in "the banality of evil," or Fred as an instance of that?*
EM: This is definitely a leading question, because Ron has written a polemic that appeared in the *New York Observer* against the phrase "the banality of evil." He has taken Hannah Arendt to task. I'm glad you mentioned this. The line I remember from the article is, "Hannah Arendt: good philosopher, bad court reporter."

RR: *I think I said, "world's worst court reporter."*
EM: And I went back to Arendt's *Eichmann in Jerusalem* and re-read sections of it. I guess I was looking for a clue as to what she herself had meant by the phrase. And the line I came up with was: "Banality of evil as a kind of thoughtlessness." That phrase struck me as resonant, particularly in light of the story of Fred Leuchter. If his life is truly the unreflective life, it moves the question beyond, "What was he thinking?" to the question, "Was he thinking? Was there an ethical dimension present?" I guess I think of evil as in some way connected with self-deception. I don't think

Arendt was saying that evil is banal. Evil is evil, and people commit evil acts for many different reasons, including truly banal ones.

RR: *As a coffee drinker, what I loved was your beautiful shots of perking coffee in* Mr. Death. *I'm in awe of his forty cups a day.*

EM: When I first heard that Fred drank more than forty cups of coffee a day, I thought, "This is very, very important. Though I'm not sure why." It just seemed, to me, a significant detail, important enough to put in the movie. Maybe it's Fred's claim to be immortal, or to be *invulnerable.* You know, "I build electric chairs, I drink forty cups of coffee a day, I smoke six packs of cigarettes, and I feel just great."

I first filmed Fred in 1992. We had gone down to Nashville, Tennessee, to film in a death chamber which he had designed. He had built their execution system, he had built their chair. He had designed their execution room. And I went down there to film at the scene of what was for him one of his greatest triumphs. Fred was already in trouble. Stories had come out about his involvement with Ernst Zündel and his role as a Holocaust denier. The warden in Tennessee didn't want to be seen with Fred. Fred had become a hot potato, so to speak. And to ensure that we couldn't photograph Fred with any prison personnel, the warden locked us in the death chamber with Fred for the entire day. We had lots of coffee, sandwiches. Fred was smoking at that time, I don't know how many packs of cigarettes a day, but he was smoking a lot. But he declined to be photographed smoking a cigarette. And I said, "Well, how come?" And he said, "Because I'm a role model to children."

RR: *Let me ask you a question about heaven. You've got heaven in the title of your first movie, and then we've got* Stairway to Heaven. *And you explore with Stephen Hawking his view of the heavens and whether or not God exists. Do you believe that there is an afterlife, and will I be reunited with my cat, Stumpy, in it?*

EM: These are two separate questions. No, I don't believe in heaven. But yes, I do believe that you will be reunited with Stumpy.

RR: *Thank you. That's reassuring. So you don't believe in an afterlife?*

EM: I'm not sure what that would even mean. I think this life really is quite enough without having to imagine yet more. And then again, more of *what?* I have enormous trouble getting anything done. What if I could live for a hundred million years? The usual refrain is: with all that time I might really get something accomplished. But what if it turned out to be a hundred million years of telling myself I was going to accomplish something tomorrow—a hundred million years of equivocations, eva-sions, vacillations, procrastinations. What a nightmare. It's a great bless-ing that it all does come to an end. You know the old saying—I guess I should attribute it to myself: "Where there's death, there's hope."

RR: *Let me ask you another theological question. You've said that your inter-view machine, the Interrotron, is a way of getting at truth. Putting someone on the Interrotron, you can look him or her in the eyes. Continuing to see a logical theme, if you had God on the Interrotron, what would you ask Him?*
EM: If He was really capable of self-knowledge.

RR: *What does that mean?*
EM: Does God know Himself?

RR: *Or is God a self-deceiver, like all of us?*
EM: Yeah. After all, in Genesis, God starts creating stuff, pauses and then sees that it's "good." Good, eh? It's a little self-serving, don't you think? You know, I have this version of the expulsion from the Garden of Eden. God, in expelling Adam and Eve, felt kind of bad. He had got-ten very angry, right? You know, you get angry and then you feel, "Well, maybe I overreacted." So God was in that kind of mood when he ex-pelled Adam and Eve from the garden. But His hands were tied—He had to go through with it. He had made the decision. God doesn't want to constantly second-guess himself. But He thought, "I know. I'll give them self-deception. Things are going to be truly horrendous out there, but they'll never notice."

RR: *Are you able to tell when you're deceiving yourself?*
EM: Probably not. I don't think I'm in any better position than anyone else, certainly not the people I put on film. I don't feel I'm in any way different from them. I have something of a suspicion about people who claim absolute knowledge of any kind, including absolute knowledge of themselves. Dr. Grigson, the psychiatrist from *The Thin Blue Line*, is a perfect example of this. There's a phase in every capital trial in Texas where a decision has to be made about whether the defendant should live or die, whether he should be given a life sentence or be sent to the elec-tric chair. To help the jury make this decision, prosecutors would bring in a psychiatrist who would testify about the defendant's "future danger-ousness." Grigson played this role in many trials and always said the same thing, that the defendant would kill and kill again unless he, in turn, was killed by the state. Of course, I don't believe that you can predict human

behavior, except in one instance: what Dr. Grigson will say in the penalty phase of a capital murder trial.

RR: *Are you fascinated by him because he's someone who claims to know what's inside someone else's head?*
EM: That's the essence of it. In my first interview with Grigson he made this claim, a very surprising and ambitious claim: he could tell whether someone was lying or telling the truth. So, essentially, he claimed to have solved the Cartesian riddle of whether we can know for certain what's out there, whether we can have certain knowledge. His solution: "Just ask me what's out there, what's true or false! I'll tell you!"

He offered an example: the story of Big Chief Greenfield. This defendant came into his office one day and claimed to be accompanied by Big Chief Greenfield. No one else was there. Just Grigson and this defendant guy. No Big Chief Greenfield. Or at least, no *visible* Big Chief Greenfield. Grigson started by asking him a number of questions. "I asked him, 'How tall is Big Chief Greenfield?'" This is Grigson now telling me the story. "And the guy said, 'Well, he's about so-tall.'" He motions with his hand. And then Grigson says, "At that instant, I knew he was lying." Grigson looks right at me and says, "Do you want to know how I knew?" And I said, "Sure, of course I do." And he says, "If Big Chief Greenfield had actually been there, or if the defendant had thought that Big Chief Greenfield had actually been there, he would have just pointed to him and said, 'Just see for yourself.'"

Although I didn't voice these sentiments out loud, I remember thinking, "Well, what if Big Chief Greenfield was sitting down?" And then, of course, I became involved in this investigation which later became *The Thin Blue Line*, and in the course of the investigation, I learned that Grigson had made two predictions about the murder case of Dallas Police Officer Robert Wood. He made a prediction about the defendant, Randall Adams, and he made a prediction about the chief prosecution witness, David Harris, this kid who turned out to be the real killer. So let's look at Grigson's scorecard. He predicted that Randall Adams, the guy who had been convicted of the crime, would kill and kill and kill again. I don't believe he has ever killed anybody. And since he has been released from prison, he has lived an ordinary life, no violence, no felonies, no nothing. And he predicted that David Harris, the kid who had really killed the police officer and who committed God knows how many other murders and felonies, would never kill. So, there you go. In one fell swoop he provided two predictions, a false negative and a false positive. Or if you want to think of it in a slightly different way, in this one case, he was 200 percent wrong.

RR: *I want to ask you a little bit about private-eye techniques, because I envy your private-eye training. You were telling me various distinctions I found fascinating, like pretext and heavy pretext and various FBI techniques. Do you want to talk a little bit about what you learned as a private-eye?*

EM: Ron said to me, just before this screening, that he always wanted to be a private detective, that he was envious of my former employment. But in fact, he is one of the great private detectives already. A private detective working in service of his own stories and an extraordinary one at that. When you remove all of the hype about being a private detective, really, what is it? It's the ability to sit and talk to people. And have people, even more importantly, talk to you. It comes down to an interest in finding out things. So, I learned quickly that what I did as a filmmaker was not so different from what I was doing as a private investigator.

RR: *What was that thing you told me about the FBI guy who would arrive at someone's house and just show his badge?*

EM: Ron likes this story, quite clearly. I used to work with a lot of FBI guys. One of them, Harry, told me he quit the FBI because of his partner. He just couldn't deal with his style of investigation any longer. It went like this. His partner would knock on a door, flip open his wallet, show his FBI badge, and say, "I guess we don't have tell you why we're here today." He wouldn't even be talking to the target of an investigation. It might be just background work. Someone down the block, someone who lived around the corner, someone who had nothing to do with anything. The guy at the door would invariably break down and start sobbing. Then one day they were at this one door. The partner goes through his routine. Flips open the wallet. Delivers the line. The whole bit. And the guy starts bawling like an infant, "How did you find out? How did you know?" Then he confessed to being a World War II deserter. I asked Harry, "Well, what did you do?" And Harry told me, "We had to turn him in, of course." After that, he couldn't take it any more.

My work, when I was a private detective was really exciting. I had the opportunity to work for one of the best private detectives in America. But I was embarrassed a lot of the times because often I had to pose as a filmmaker in order to get people to talk to me. Which is, when you come to think of it, rather sad.

RR: *Returning to film then, I want to ask you about your visual style, which really changed, it seemed to me, in* The Thin Blue Line, *when you began to use these extreme almost fetishistic close-ups of coffee cups, of a footstep splashing on the concrete, in a kind of almost mock-*film noir *sort of atmosphere. You were sending it up, but in some ways you were also embracing it. Did you have to send it up in order to embrace it? What was going on with that?*

EM: I became obsessed by the details of this particular case and how it was so easy to misread these details. Minor details, you might even think, insignificant details, that nevertheless made a very crucial difference in how you saw the entire crime. And I tried to abstract those. My obsession with various elements, whether it was the tossed milkshake or the number plate of the car, led me to try and capture them in the movie. They become metaphorical and fetishistic at the same time.

RR: *I wanted to ask you an epistemological question. A film like* The Thin Blue Line *suggests that reality is just a series of perspectives. But on the other hand, you believe that Randall Adams was innocent and the other guy did it. It's the same with Holocaust denial. Do you believe that there is such a thing as real, historical truth? Or is it all socially constructed or a matter of perspective?*

EM: Yes, I believe there is such a thing as real, historical truth. I am no post-modernist. I live in Cambridge, Massachusetts. And one of the nice things about Cambridge, Massachusetts, is that "Baudrillard" isn't in the phone book. To me, there's a physical world out there, pure and simple. There's a world where things actually happen. In *The Thin Blue Line*, it was of all-consuming importance to figure out who was driving that car; who pulled the gun out from underneath the seat, who shot the cop. Questions like these are not up for grabs. There's a real world in which real things happen. And in some small way, my job is to look at that world and to try to figure out what those things might be.

RR: *But you've also said that rather than "seeing is believing," you think "believing is seeing." In other words, we see what we want to see. Is that right?*

EM: I believe we face incredible obstacles in our attempts to see the world. Everything in our nature tries to deny the world around us, to re-fabricate it in our own image, to reinvent it for our own benefit. And so it becomes something of a challenge, a task, to recover—or at least attempt to recover—the real world, despite all the impediments to that end. I often think that when people talk about truth, they have this idea that truth is just sort of handed over to you, like on a truth combo platter. But it doesn't work that way. It's difficult to come by, and properly speaking, it's a *quest*, the pursuit of an ideal. It's the business both of us are in: an attempt to get at truth and at the same time to provide a chronicle of evasions of the truth. The fact that there is a *knowable* world out there informs everything that I do. To me, it's impossible to even think of the Leuchter story without calling attention to the fact that he is investigating and denying something that *really* happened.

RR: *Are you interested in the question of what is the nature of evil? Do serial killers open up that question for you?*

EM: There's something truly fascinating about murder because it brings you to that fundamental question about why people do things. I suppose we could devote ourselves to asking questions about why someone crosses a road on a certain day at a certain time, the chicken-crossing-the-road question. But murder raises the stakes. It makes it important— even essential—for us to come up with answers. I suppose you could consider it a dramatic device that raises the stakes and draws us in. I don't think evil is the specific province of murderers. I think that we all share a capacity for it. But murderers do allow for the possibility of examining evil in a highly charged and possibly less ambiguous context. But I think that we are all truly capable of doing really bad things.

RR: *I wanted to ask you a question about* Gates of Heaven, *which I could watch it over and over again. I actually got into an argument with someone a couple of days ago about the swerve* Gates of Heaven *takes at the end, when you get into the successful pet cemetery run by disciples of W. Clement Stone's success theory. There seems to be some sort of discourse about love in the film. Am I right about that?*

EM: Yes. I was struck again and again while making that film that what was important was the fact of love, not what it was directed towards. The fact that these people were in love with their dead animals seemed quite wonderful and respectable. But it also seemed to speak about our tremendous capacity for abstraction. I think, for example, our ability to communicate with live people is questionable at best. When they're dead, I think it becomes even harder to communicate with them. And when they're dead pets, even harder. But yet there was this strange dialogue going on which I found magnificent. We didn't put it in the movie, but I made lots of recordings of people grieving. There were people that were wandering around in Bubbling Well Pet Memorial Park who were sobbing. There was a couple standing at the grave of their dog, who said, between sobs, "It's a sad day for us every time we come up here." And then he added, "We come up often."

RR: *So many of your films involve animals. You've got an Interrotron story about a parrot who was a key witness in a murder story. You've got, of course, the Temple Grandin story. You've got* Gates of Heaven *where some guy says, "The difference between a dog and a human is you turn your back on a dog, and you turn around again, and the dog will be the same. You turn your back on a human, and you never know."*

EM: Somebody, evidently, with a pessimistic view of human nature.

RR: *Well, that's what I wonder. Is that your view of human nature?*

EM: No, no. Good people, bad people, good dogs, bad dogs. . . . There are dogs that when you turn your back on them, they bite you.

RR: *Tell me about the Interrotron Stories. Weren't you originally commissioned to do them by an American network?*

EM: I went through a number of pilots with ABC and with Fox Broadcasting. At that time, Fox was going through a change of regimes. When *The Parrot* was completed, I couldn't find anyone at Fox even to admit that they had seen the program.

The Parrot was a story of a parrot that was a witness to a murder. This woman was strangled to death, suffocated to death in her mansion in Napa county, Northern California, and her African Gray parrot was a witness to this murder. The parrot was found at the crime scene in a state of extreme distress, something obvious to the law enforcement officials that found him. Max, who by all accounts, had an extensive vocabulary, a vocabulary of something like 300 or 350 words, probably larger than my own, Max was reduced to saying the same thing over and over again and nothing else, namely, "Richard, no, no, no," followed by these gasping strangling sounds. And so it was conjectured, not without reason, I might add, that the parrot might be repeating what it heard the moment its owner died. So I made a movie about this. And I couldn't get anyone even to say they had seen it. It could have been at a dead letter office. No executives would, in fact, say they had seen it.

Later, an executive explained to me—I think he was trying to be helpful—he said, "Errol, when I first got in this business . . ." and he mentioned the name of someone I was supposed to know, but who I actually had never heard of. He said, "When I first got in this business, so-and-so told me that people really, really like *new*. People love new. But at most, they want 20 or 30 percent *new*. Not, say, 40 or 50 percent *new*. And quite frankly speaking, Errol, I think what you have here is probably 50, 60, maybe even 70 percent *new*. You've overdone it. The problem is, I think this is just too *new*."

Truth Is Not Subjective

ROY GRUNDMANN AND
CYNTHIA ROCKWELL/2000

F I L M M A K E R S   L I K E Errol Morris are the reason the definition of
the term "documentary" is so contentious. Morris is generally lumped
into the catch-all category of "nonfiction film," though even the broader
term seems a bit of a stretch. Morris's films are as far from documentary
as they can be without taking the leap into fictional narrative; he so consciously and consistently blurs the lines between fact and fiction, reality
and fantasy, objectivity and subjectivity that the use of real-life subjects
and lack of a pre-written script seem to be the only thread by which hangs
his documentary classification. But Morris has no loyalty to the nonfiction world—if his reality-bending films weren't evidence enough, he
is planning for his next project to be a fictional feature film.

It's no surprise, then, to hear Morris say that he was as influenced by
masters of Hollywood artifice such as Douglas Sirk and Billy Wilder as he
was by documentarian Fred Wiseman. And these influences are clearly
evident in his films, which punctuate so-called documentary interview
episodes with clips from old Hollywood films, creative enactments of
interviewees' stories, fantasy sequences, and highly stylized images of the
films' real-life subjects. Even the most documentary aspect of his films—
the interview—is intricately shaped by Morris and his "Megatron," the
next generation of his Interrotron interviewing device that, rather than
sitting interviewer and interviewee face-to-face, creates a technical distance between Morris and his subjects by placing each of them in front of
cameras with attached monitors that display their respective images. The
Megatron advances on this concept with the addition of ten to twenty

From *Cineaste Magazine*, vol. 25, no. 3 (Fall 2000). Reprinted with permission.

more cameras, and the objectives of this approach are threefold: the distancing, Morris says, helps his subjects to speak more freely than they might face-to-face; the technical setup allows the subject to make eye contact with Morris while at the same time speaking directly into the camera, giving the impression of first-person monologue; and the use of multiple cameras allows Morris many more opportunities to manipulate and stylize his images.

And manipulate he does. By using different camera angles, interrupting the image with black leader, and other stylistic effects, Morris shapes the interviews—the closest ties to "reality" in his films—and ultimately deconstructs every aspect of journalistic objectivity his films may contain. This is not to say, however, that his films reject reality. He uses the cinematic medium to seek realism in a philosophical rather than objective sense, by exploring the intersections of the "fictional" and "real" worlds we create and inhabit. In Morris's world-view, people live inside personal story worlds that they construct for themselves about who they are and what they're doing, worlds that may be divorced from reality and which are revealed through a person's language, through the stories they tell about themselves.

His subjects tend to be unusual people with unusual stories, but underlying his bizarre portraits is the suggestion that everyone, even so-called "normal" people, live, to some degree, in their own personal dreamscapes. Morris's first feature, the 1978 *Gates of Heaven*, tells the story of two pet cemeteries, one that fails and one that flourishes after adopting savvy marketing techniques. From there Morris went on to make a film originally titled *Nub City*, about a phenomenon in a small Florida town where people amputate their limbs to collect insurance money. Morris had to drop the project, however, when his subjects threatened his life. He moved on to complete *Vernon, Florida* (1981), a film about the eccentric residents of a Florida swamp town, and then in 1988 he released his landmark *The Thin Blue Line*, for which Morris is credited with overturning the conviction of Randall Dale Adams, who was wrongly accused of murdering Dallas police officer Robert Wood. But sensational storyline aside, the film is as much about the personal story worlds of Randall Adams and his accusers as it is about a gross miscarriage of justice in the American criminal justice system. In 1992 Morris released *A Brief History of Time*, a film about Stephen Hawking, the physicist who is often compared to Einstein and who has spent much of his life in a wheelchair. In 1997 Morris completed *Fast, Cheap and Out of Control*, a film that somehow links the disparate stories and obsessions of a lion tamer, an expert on the African mole-rat, a topiary gardener who shapes hedges into giant animal shapes, and an MIT scientist who designs robots.

Morris's latest film, *Mr. Death* (1999), tells the story of Fred Leuchter, a self-styled execution technologist who worked as a consultant on the design and maintenance of execution equipment and who, because of his "expertise" in execution technology, was hired by Holocaust revisionist Ernst Zündel to find evidence that the Holocaust never happened. Zündel sent Leuchter to Auschwitz, where he illegally (and shockingly, as depicted in video footage of his trip) sampled the walls of various structures, sent the samples to a lab to test for cyanide, and, when he found none, concluded that the Holocaust is a myth. His now infamous Leuchter Report has been embraced by Holocaust revisionists, neo-Nazis, and anti-Semites worldwide as "proof" that the Holocaust is a lie. But *Mr. Death* is as much about the dreamscape constructed and inhabited by Fred Leuchter as it is about the Holocaust itself. And this is also what makes the film so controversial.

The Fred Leuchter that Morris serves up is not an evil man. He is a nice man. A pathetic man. Endearingly pathetic, in fact, so that when his fortunes take a turn for the worse, we actually sympathize with him. Morris humanizes him, this man who has been demonized by the public, and in so doing creates a portrait even more disturbing than the persona created for him by his critics. Through Morris's lens, Fred is a lonely, middle-aged man who saw his chance to become somebody when he was asked to take a chisel and hammer to Auschwitz and challenge the veracity of the most incomprehensible human tragedy in history. In his own dream world, Leuchter is a scientist conducting important, authentic research. In reality, he is a history major practicing as an engineer with no scientific background and conducting a grossly inadequate and flawed series of unsound, unscientific tests. And from these, Leuchter convinces himself— and a legion of anti-Semites, neo-Nazis, and Holocaust revisionists—that history is wrong. Leuchter makes the mistake of plunging his private dreamscape into the public arena to challenge twentieth-century history, which triggers his down-fall. Years later, after losing his job and his wife, after being jailed and villainized by the public, Leuchter is still convinced he's right. So divorced is he from reality, so important to him is his story world, that he remains inside it despite all negative and "real" consequences. In this sense, Leuchter becomes the quintessential embodiment of the Morris "dreamscape," and *Mr. Death*, Morris's deepest and most sophisticated examination of the theme. The film is also the most heavily stylized and visually sophisticated of Morris's films, filled with expressionistic, metaphoric visual imagery that takes Morris even further from the realm of documentary.

Morris is now working on *First Person*, a series of half-hour interviews for Bravo. Part of the Bravo Network's "Counter Culture Wednesdays" (a title Morris says he had nothing to do with), the show features first-person interviews with an array of unusual subjects ranging from Lorry Greenberg, pen pal and would-be biographer of the Unabomber, to Temple Grandin, a university professor and diagnosed autistic who has designed one-third of the slaughterhouses in the United States. The interviews are similar to Morris's films in that they contain his characteristic use of old film clips and other creative manipulations of reality, but, as the episodes progress, Morris's presence becomes increasingly explicit, both through the sound of his voice questioning the subject and his own image framed in the Megatron's monitor.

But the dreamscape theme continues into the series. Morris's world-view is exemplified in the "Spy" episode of *First Person*, in which a former CIA agent, in describing his lifestyle, literalizes and externalizes precisely what Morris reveals his other subjects to be doing subconsciously. Always speaking in the third person and using the pronoun "you" rather than "I," the subject describes the life of what sounds like a professional dreamscape-dweller. As a spy it is his job to construct stories about himself, to create personas and live inside them self-consciously—to the point of forgetting who the "real" person is behind all the constructed alter-egos. He admits to often having trouble remembering which person he's supposed to be at any given moment. Such a state, Morris says in the interview, ultimately begs questions such as, "If I were me, what would I be doing right now?" A question Morris would say lies subconsciously under everything we, ourselves, do.

Q: *Looking at* First Person, *Mr. Death, and even some of your earlier films, it becomes clear that your interviewees are not exactly ordinary people.*

A: First of all, maybe there are no ordinary people. Maybe the whole idea of ordinary people is just some kind of fantasy picture that we have of people that does not truly square with what's to be found out there in real life. That is certainly a possibility.

Q: *Would you say, then, that anyone could become one of your subjects? Or is there something special about them?*

A: There is something special about them. They interest me. They have stories to tell which interest me. I knew at the beginning of this series that

I was very busy with advertising—I was doing a number of commercials—and so people were trying to find stories for me. It may be just something I have to do myself, something I just can't depend on other people to do. If the idea is simply that I like bizarre stories, that's not quite right—although I do like bizarre stories. I like there to be some emotional content, something engaging, real, emotionally powerful about the people who I interview. I also like the stories to be about something. It's not enough that they should be bizarre, quirky, unusual. They have to be about some issue or set of issues. Someone who worked here once said, perhaps uncharitably, that I was not interested in a story unless it contained a first-semester philosophy question. There is definitely some truth to that.

Q: *How do you find your interviewees? Do you have a standard method or is every story found in its own unique way?*
A: No magic dumpster, no secret place that I sneak out to where I can find this repository of stories. For the most part, they come from very standard places. The expected, if you like. When *Mr. Death* was first shown at Sundance, which is now over a year ago, Janet Maslin asked me where the story of Fred Leuchter came from. And I told her, page one of the *New York Times*.

Q: *So newspapers are an important source for you?*
A: Newspapers, magazines, books, television, but there's nothing unusual about where I find these stories. Nothing at all. Leuchter would have been hard to miss. He wasn't on the top half of the page, you had to turn the paper over in order to see the story, but it was page one. Very easy to find.

Q: *We find that a lot of your interviewees either crave attention or, when they happen to get attention—for better or worse—they realize how much they now want it. We see it with Leuchter's induction into the Nazi community, and with Greenberg's relationship with the Unabomber. But your films, too, give them attention. You often help make your subjects sort of famous or, at least, notorious, given the often kooky or controversial nature of their stories. Do you see an ethical issue in that? Are you tapping into the same kind of desire for attention?*
A: Yes and no. There are several answers to that. There's something about the way you've put the question that suggests that giving people attention because they want it is a bad thing, inherently. I don't agree. People in general want attention, want to feel important, want to feel as if

they are somebody, as opposed to nobody. I try to get people to tell their stories in a dramatic way. I try to energize the people I interview. I try to communicate my excitement about their stories to them. Of course, in any interview situation, you are making use of many such things—people's desire to get attention, people's desire to be important, people's desire to tell their own story to someone else—and to themselves. I think it's a deep, inherent human need.

Q: *You said that's one answer. Is there another?*

A: Well, the example that seems to sit in the wings, the example which hasn't been explicitly stated behind the question—correct me if I'm wrong—is Fred Leuchter. Because part of the story is about how Fred the nobody became Fred the somebody by virtue of going to Auschwitz, testifying on behalf of Ernst Zündel, appearing at the conferences, and so on. And clearly, in this instance, giving this man attention has enabled him to state pernicious ideas—falsehoods—but to me it's important to remember the problem here is not the fact that he was given attention. If you were going to eliminate vanity from how people see themselves and others, the world would be an impossibility, at least as we know it. So the problem here is not the attention per se, the problem is that the views are bad. Then you get into this whole knotty set of issues and arguments about whether it's a bad thing to give someone who is expressing pernicious ideas a platform on which he can continue to do so. That is another discussion in and of itself.

Q: *When you interviewed Leuchter for the first time in 1992, was the interview just about his execution expertise or was it also about* The Leuchter Report?

A: It was both. He'd already appeared in the Zündel case in 1988, and the *New York Times* article came out in 1990, and my interview with him was in the summer of 1992. So I was already completely aware of all of that.

Q: Mr. Death *uses some footage from the videotape Zündel's team shot of Leuchter in Auschwitz. How did you obtain that tape?*

A: Zündel's party gave us permission to use it.

Q: *What was Leuchter's motivation to do the film with you after you located him many years later?*

A: I'm not sure. I don't mean to be coy, but I find Fred puzzling, even after having spent a considerable amount of time with him. I think it ultimately comes down to his need to tell this story about himself, his need to provide an account of himself, to justify himself.

Q: *What was his reaction to the film?*
A: He liked it a lot.

Q: *We've read that he cooperated with you in making* Mr. Death *but that he also had some misgivings. What were they?*
A: I think he was worried about his mother, how she would view his co-operating with the film and how she would view the film itself.

Q: *But she knew about his story, right?*
A: Yes. Maybe it's that trade-off between competing desires—one, to talk about yourself and the other to retain a certain anonymity or privacy.

Q: *Overall, if you look at the film now, do you feel that you've been fair to your goals and to Leuchter? Did it come out the way you wanted it to?*
A: I like the film. I'm sick of talking about it, but I do like it. I always worry about everything that I do, and this film is no exception. I feel that I gave Leuchter more of a hearing than anybody else would have done. I don't feel that I've been unfair to him in any way. I wanted to make a movie about the Holocaust. Or about people. "People Do Bad Things," I guess would be the heading, the category. People doing bad things and as a result touching on the issue of the Holocaust itself, of how such a thing could have happened. I think the movie is very different from almost anything else that I have seen on the subject.

Q: *You have said that you wanted to make a Holocaust film without refer-ence to what other people have done—were you thinking of other films?*
A: I wasn't just thinking of other films but a lot of what I'd read. There are certain works that have influenced me enormously, Hannah Arendt's *Eichmann in Jerusalem* being one of them. But it's an opportunity to look at these issues in a investigative way, not just simply to put on seal of approval—because there is a correct and incorrect way of telling these stories—but to really be investigative in nature, to look at Leuchter as an object of inquiry rather than as something that was an expression of some received, already existing view. It would be very, very easy to por-tray Leuchter as a bad man, even as en evil man. I think it misses the point. It misses many points.

To me the real task is to look at him and try to figure out what is going on here. I've heard again and again that this is a movie about the banality of evil. It's a term that has been used far too much and in such a vague way that I shudder to make that kind of connection. What was interesting about Hannah Arendt's book, and one of the reasons that she got into so much trouble over it, was that Eichmann was supposed to be the quintessential monster, and in her examination of him, she found something different. That fact alone was troublesome. And I think that fact alone is troublesome in *Mr. Death* as well. I found something different.

Q: *That's also what makes the film interesting.*

A: Yes, it's finding something that is different from what you're supposed to find. It's finding something that may, in fact, be more disturbing. I mean, after all, there is this one view of evil, that evil was invented so that we wouldn't really have to deal with it ourselves, we could just project it onto others, that we would remove it from where we sit. I myself find the idea that evil can come out of very familiar kinds of things to be far more frightening and disturbing.

This is certainly a part of *The Thin Blue Line* as much as it is a part of *Mr. Death*. It's hard for me after so many years to say that it's even part of the movie. I believe it's part of the movie, but the issue that we discussed endlessly while editing *The Thin Blue Line* was, given that Randall Adams didn't do it, given that he was innocent, that he was unfairly, unjustly convicted of capital murder, murder that he did not commit, how could such a thing happen? How did this miscarriage of justice come to pass? Was he deliberately, intentionally, knowingly framed by the Dallas police, did they set him up for the fall, and convict him of a crime which they knew he had not committed? Or did they somehow convince themselves he was guilty, even though the evidence did perhaps not warrant such a belief, and everything that followed was a result of this belief? Put very simply and crudely, do people commit evil acts knowingly, or do they do it thinking that they're doing good?

Q: *I guess our culture, too, needs to attribute a certain metaphysical origin to evil, and if that's not the case, then where is it? The culture wants to picture the devil with two horns and a tail, and if you can't do that, how can you comprehend evil?*

A: Yes, where is this evil? Also, to me the key line in the movie is the line about denial. Ultimately, it is a movie about denial. Denial about the obvious, denial of self, denial of death, denial of the Holocaust. But at its center, it is a failure to see the world, to see reality. Living in a cocoon of one's own devising. Fabricating a universe that one occupies, that may in fact be divorced from the real world. Do I believe Leuchter was motivated by hatred of Jews, some virulent kind of anti-Semitism? I don't. I really don't. And if you ask me, does that make it better? No, it makes it worse.

Q: *You said it would have been easy to portray Leuchter as evil but that you found something different. By humanizing him it tends to make his detractors, especially Shelley Shapiro, sound as rhetorical and out of touch with reality as Zündel and Leuchter. Is that a dangeous byproduct of your approach or was it your intention to link them in their extremity?*

A: People told me to take the two Jewish women out of the movie. I heard that from a whole number of people when we were editing the film, but I left them in because I thought that it was important for someone at least to voice that sentiment, that I was not shirking at least that possibility—expressing it, if not agreeing with the fact, that this guy was an anti-Semite, that this was a bad guy, that he's pernicious, that this guy was, yes, evil. I think by virtue of the fact that they appear in the film and Fred is not treated as out and out evil, they do seem extreme, but that was not the intention. I think it's the byproduct of needing them to be in it to express that view.

Q: Mr. Death *quite deliberately links Fred Leuchter's expertise with execution devices with the Holocaust. But what, apart from this individual, Fred Leuchter, links these two areas?*

A: I had an angry question following a screening of the film, where someone said, "How dare you equate American capital punishment with the Holocaust?" And my answer—I'd like to give you a slightly different answer—but my answer on this occasion was that it was not me equating American capital punishment with the Holocaust, it was Leuchter, and that for me there is an enormous difference between the two. There's a difference between trial by due process, conviction, and execution, and murder. Our whole system of jurisprudence is based on just such a distinction. Putting men, women, and children in boxcars and shipping them a thousand miles across Europe to murder them in gas chambers is not the same thing as executions in the United States. But there is one theme that they share, and that is the idea of killing-as-solution.

The world leaves a trail, and it is our job as investigators—or, specifically my job as an investigator—to try to lead myself back to the world. It's not something that you just grab hold of. I spent three years sifting through evidence in the Randall Adams murder case. Maybe I can't say with absolute certainty that Randall Adams is innocent, but I can say that in the vast amount of material that I collected, almost everything points to his innocence, and nothing points to his guilt. Just like there was this confusion in *Mr. Death*—am I trying to prove the Holocaust really happened? No. The movie is set against a sea of information about the Holocaust, and about Auschwitz and Birkenau in particular. But there is material about how Fred led himself, or was led, or a combination of both, into error. That was the problem with *The Leuchter Report*. There was something disarmingly simple, naïve, almost childlike about it. "I went over to Auschwitz—I! Yes, illegally and surreptitiously, but I had no other choice—I collected the samples, I sent them to a reputable lab, the analysis came back: no trace cyanide!" And the question of course lingers, why not? Why no trace cyanide? How come? And the answer provided by the Cornell chemist is very important, because it tells you why: because this disarmingly simple test was no test at all. That's why.

Q: *Why did you decide to go to Auschwitz and shoot there?*

A: Because it seemed to be the center of the Leuchter story. I think, in part, I was drawn to that place. I've often thought that two people completely obsessed with death in their own way—Fred Leuchter and myself—found themselves in the epicentre of twentieth-century death: Crema II at Birkenau. It's about this place, it's about this point on the map. And we're removed from it now by some close to sixty years.

Q: *You had said there are two stories, two emphases in working on this movie.*

A: Yes, the need to go back to that place now removed from us in time. Two stories, and they almost become confused, conflated, as if they're the same thing, and, of course, they're two radically different things. I would call one the subjectivity of history, namely that we can never know historical truth—a view that I do not believe in. Then there's another theme, which I would call the perishability of history. The idea that we know our history, through the things that history has cast off, whether it's pieces of evidence, documents, the testimony of people who have lived through those times. If you think about it for a moment, there is that really sad realization that it could all be lost. It's not like science, where the world replicates itself again and again. History comes by only once, and the residue of history can be lost.

What I found so powerful about [Auschwitz historian] Van Pelt in the movie was that due to this odd circumstance, the Nazis overlooked the Auschwitz-Birkenau archive. Just by happenstance. After all, the Nazis were destroying all traces, all records, all evidence of what they had done—but they forgot this archive. Auschwitz-Birkenau was such a massive place, a massive building, construction, enterprise, that they had a separate archive for all of the architectural material, and that survived intact. They burned the main archive, they left the manuscripts dealing with the construction of the place intact. They were overlooked. And that is something about the perishability of history. We're lucky in this instance that we have a record, and the record is unambiguous. It tells us what happened there.

Q: *One could do a movie about Van Pelt alone.*
A: Yes, and Van Pelt and I remain friends. He comes and visits. He was an expert witness at the Irving/Lipstadt trial in London. Irving, the British Holocaust revisionist who is interviewed in the film, lost his case today. He sued Deborah Lipstadt for libel, and under British law it became her problem to prove that she had not libeled or defamed him.

Q: *In addition to going to Auschwitz, you reenacted, using actors, some of Leuchter's activities from the videotape.*
A: Well, people use this term "reenactment" and I think that it's horribly misleading. I've been accused of having created reenactment television, that somehow *The Thin Blue Line* spawned a hundred reality programs on Fox and elsewhere. What's interesting is that there were no reenactments per se in *The Thin Blue Line*. Reenactment to me suggests that you are showing people what really happened, that you're showing them some picture of the world. I have done something very different. I have shown people pictures of belief, untruth, falsehood, confusion. I have taken people back into what they thought they might have seen, thought might have been out there, but it's clear they were wrong or delusional.

Q: *In* Mr. Death, *the reenactments of the Leuchter videotape seem similar to what he actually did. Are they different from what you did in* The Thin Blue Line?
A: Well, in *The Thin Blue Line* it's also similar. You're out on a roadway. Similar, yes, in some crude sense that you are dealing with a scene. In *The Thin Blue Line* it's a roadway out there with a cop car, a blue Comet, and drivers. Similarly, in *Mr. Death* there is a chisel and a hammer and people walking around this ruined landscape. But not reenactments. There's nothing being reenacted in either movie. In some cases it's just so obvious as to make me wonder what people could even mean. For example, the Van de Graaf generator at the beginning of the movie is not a reenactment of anything. It's just a complete image generated out of

whole cloth. To me, when I hear the term reenactment, what I think is the intention to tell people. "This is what it looked like." There is none of that in my filmmaking.

Q: *Then what would you say is the function of the footage of the chiseling that you shot and the footage of the lab analysis?*

A: It's to take you into the mystery and the drama of what people are saying and thinking. It's expressionistic rather than realistic. It works in service of ideas rather than facts. Why the laboratory? There are lots of things I like about it, as I like the Van de Graaf in the beginning, the connection with Frankenstein, the whole play about life and death, the whole pseudoscientific apparatus of *The Leuchter Report* that somehow gives it the faux imprimatur of respectability. That because we were doing all of these things with Erlenmeyer flasks and test tubes and balance pans, it somehow had to be right is, of course, ridiculous. It's all ironic. It's all infected with my, I guess, horrible, unending sense of irony.

Q: *Thereby you're also saying we don't need a lab to prove that the gassing took place?*

A: I'm saying that this lab is proving nothing. Here we have all the visual accoutrements of laboratory work, but the end result is nothing. I like the line spoken by James Roth, the chemist, saying that the problem of what Leuchter did was that he went more than skin deep. There are so many visual metaphors in the film. No one ever writes about this—I think the movie gets so overwhelmed by questions of what it must be about or how it must function that the actual movie gets lost. I think in a way it's the most visually sophisticated thing that I have ever done.

Q: *It is, absolutely.*

A: I hate to go on about this but I think I've put some of my most interesting images in the film. The shot of Fred Leuchter walking along the roadway, for example. I don't know if you've been on sets but when you have a 600mm lens on the camera, which is the case there, the focus puller or camera assistant marks off all of the lines as the subject walks toward the camera, because it's so difficult when you have a long lens to keep the subject in focus. It becomes this big deal. You get out a tape measure, you measure off where they're going to be at time X, so that you know how to hit your marks. Well, it occurred to me to leave the focus on the background and have Leuchter disappear as he walks toward the camera. He would go more and more and more out of focus the closer he comes, until he, in fact, just vanishes. I've never seen a shot like that. Somehow it powerfully underlines what Irving is saying—the voice-over on that shot comes from Irving. He calls what Leuchter did an act of criminal simplicity. He came from nothing and he went back to nothing.

Q: *One of the most interesting scenes, for several reasons, is when you rewind the Zündel team videotape on camera with Van Pelt's voice-over. One reason is that, of course, Leuchter is a person who doesn't see the forest for the trees.*

A: Someone once made that comparison, that he's someone who doesn't see the forest for the trees, and I said he's a person who actually sees neither the forest nor the trees.

Q: *Yes, he's so obsessed with the minutiae and you, of course, are also expressing this at that moment. You're also very much concerned with minutiae. Van Pelt says, "Let's look at this again, in the spirit of 'we've got to see this to believe it.'" It also reminded me of David Hemmings's scrutinizing of photographs in Antonioni's* Blowup.

A: Well, certainly the idea of scrutinizing reality through images is part of my stories. There are so many things packed into that scene or, at least, I like to think that there are. Part of it is that here you are in this one piece of geography, Crema II at Birkenau. You might quibble about the exact number of people who were murdered there, but we know that it was a lot of people. Somewhere between half a million and eight-hundred thousand. A lot of people died there. Probably more people in one place than in any one place on earth. Place—an idea of geography, and there is Van Pelt and there is Leuchter in that very same place. What does Leuchter see? He sees a Hardy Boys mystery. *Mystery on Skull Mountain.* He sees God knows what—maybe there are animals down there. He's caught up in his own kind of dreamscape of who he is and what he's doing and where he is. Van Pelt is looking at that same piece of geography and is seeing something radically different. But in rewinding it, it's like walking back into the past, which is a part of the movie as well. So yes, that kind of surreal disconnection between these two men and that place is very powerful.

Q: *You have talked about death as an art object—some shots of the electric chair in the early section of* Mr. Death *are reminiscent of Andy Warhol's silkscreens of the electric chair. As an image-maker, do you feel you've been influenced by Warhol at all?*

A: Certainly I'm aware of the images, but my fascination with execution devices preceded Warhol. I think Warhol just tapped into a general interest shared by many people—the iconography of American death machines, the electric chair being such a machine which, perhaps, seems more than any other quintessentially American. It's never been used anywhere else. It's an American icon.

Q: Mr. Death *is a funny film. People laugh a lot. Did the subject demand humor or did this happen coincidentally? The film takes on the ironic humor of Vonnegut's* Mother Night *and Kafka's* In the Penal Colony. *Were you thinking of these works when making the film?*
A: Leuchter is very, very funny . . . unintentionally so. I would call it a kind of absurdist funny, rather than the usual "ha, ha" variety. Kafka, yes. Vonnegut, no, although I am familiar with *Mother Night.* Years ago I talked with the producer Robert Chartoff about a film adaptation of the Vonnegut novel.

Q: *Much has been made of your interviewing machine, the Interrotron, but one reads conflicting accounts of it. For the record, could you explain exactly how it works?*
A: Sure, although the Interrotron has now been replaced by the Megatron, which uses many more cameras—one segment of *First Person* was shot with seventeen cameras. The basic concept is that the subject sits in front of a camera with an attached monitor, which is projecting my image. I sit in the same room, though behind a curtain, like the Wizard of Oz. I'm also seated in front of a camera with a monitor that is projecting the subject's image to me. This way we are both speaking directly to the camera, but also making eye contact with each other.

Q: *You've said this technological distance helps your subjects drop their inhibitions and become more talkative.*
A: Yes. I've always thought that, for example, the distance involved with a telephone conversation in an odd way makes it much more intimate than anything that happens face-to-face.

Q: *In* First Person, *you actually show the Interrotron in a few reverse shots interspersed with a closeup of the interviewee. Why did you decide to do this?*
A: Why not? I have been using the Interrotron for a while now. I hate repeating myself, and the use of the Megatron, the twenty cameras, allows me to scrutinize the interview process at the same time as I am scrutinizing the interviewee.

Q: *You've said that the Interrotron helps you to make your kind of movie, the "typical" Errol Morris film, in that the subjects drop their inhibitions and become more talkative, allowing you to depict them as first person monologues rather than the ordinary talking-head format. What appeals to you about this format? Why is first-person narration so important to you?*

A: It de-emphasizes the relationship between interviewer and interviewee and focuses attention on the interviewee—how he or she sees themselves, rather than on how we see them.

Q: *What do you think is the effect of hearing your voice at the end of* The Thin Blue Line *compared to the effect of your voice at the end of* Mr. Death? *Your voice is also present in some segments* First Person. *Is this becoming a standard strategy?*

A: It is a simple reminder that I am there, lurking somewhere in the woodwork.

Q: *Do you ever meet with your subjects before filming?*

A: No, never. I think that's the best way to ruin an interview. It needs to be spontaneous. You can't go into an interview already knowing where you're headed. I need to explore and investigate and discover as I go along.

Q: *Another technique common in your interviews is to interrupt the image with black leader, while the soundtrack remains continuous. Why do you do this?*

A: I find the effect to be very powerful.

Q: *You also cut into the talking-head footage of interviewees, whereby the image continues at a slightly different camera angle. It is easy to see how this happens with the multiple cameras of the Megatron, but the technique is evident in your earlier work with the two-camera Interrotron as well. How is this accomplished?*

A: The camera is constantly being dutched, or tilted, constantly moving, so that when the moving image is interrupted for a moment, the camera has moved to a different position.

Q: *There seems to be a strong connection to Orson Welles in your work, especially in* First Person, *what with excerpts of* Othello *in the Greenberg segment and* The Lady from Shanghai *in the final episode about the spy. Welles is often referred to as "The Magician," and some people call you a magician as well. Do you feel an affinity with Welles?*

A: Well, I like the idea of the magician, because it's an admission that we do not completely understand our world, that there is an element out there that we can't or don't understand. That idea is very powerful. It fits in with what I'm trying to do. But I've never thought of Welles as the ideal of filmmaking. I just like playing with ironic images, and it's fun to use old movies. But I also like Bresson and Wiseman.

Q: *You've told us that you've been very busy in recent years shooting commercials. Can you name some of the products?*
A: I've done a whole line of commercials for Miller High Life, I've done commercials for Levis and Volkswagen—for both of which I used the Interrotron—and I've also done commercials for Adidas, Honda, Dell, and Datek.

Q: *You are rarely asked about your commercials, which is obviously a major source of income for you. Do you like commercials?*
A: I love commercials, unreservedly. The haiku of the West. And I like to think of consumerism as the most effective preventative to genocide yet devised. When someone shows up at your door and asks you to hack your neighbor to death with a machete, you're less likely to do it, if you have prior plans, say, to go and buy a DVD player.

Errol Morris: Megatron, Son of Interrotron

ROGER EBERT/2001

PARK CITY, UTAH — There is a tall curtain at one end of the room, and from time to time, Errol Morris peeks out from behind it like the Wizard of Oz. All of the seats are taken in the House of Docs for his demonstration of his latest interviewing device—Megatron, Son of Interrotron—at this year's Sundance Film Festival. Technicians scurry about, wearing ski parkas instead of white lab coats, but nevertheless looking like the minions of a James Bond villain, about to demonstrate a device that will (cackle) gain control of mankind.

In the audience, other famous documentarians have gathered like scientists about to see their sacred theories overthrown. I see Freida Lee Mock, who won the Oscar for *Maya Lin: A Strong Clear Vision* (1996); George Nierenberg, who made *Say Amen, Somebody* (1983); Kate Davis, who is here with *Southern Comfort* (2001); Anne Makepeace of *Baby, It's You* (1998), and Mark Lewis of *Cane Toads* (1988) and *Natural History of the Chicken* (2000) fame. Reid Rosefelt, Morris's publicist, presides like a Vatican protocol chief.

I grab a reserved seat in the front row. It is not reserved for me, but I do not stand on ceremony. I would want to be up front for Einstein, too. "It is time to begin," says Rosefelt, and from the loudspeakers we hear Errol Morris's disembodied voice: "Yes, I think so, too."

Rosefelt sits in a straight chair in front of the curtain. He looks into what appears to be a TelePrompTer. On a screen high and to the right, we see the face of Errol Morris. Another screen, to the left, is split into four segments, all showing different views of Morris.

"When Reid is looking into the camera in front of him, he is look-

---

From the *Chicago Sun-Times*, January 30, 2001. Reprinted with permission.

ing straight into my eyes," says the voice of Morris. "And I am looking straight into his."

I am ready for him to start swinging a gold watch on its chain, while Rosefelt goes into a trance and promises never to send out another press release. Instead, Morris explains the theory of the Megatron, a revolutionary improvement on the Interrotron.

But let's back up a second. Morris is perhaps the most famous and successful documentary filmmaker in America. He will soon re-launch his TV program *First Person* on cable's Independent Film Channel. An earlier incarnation on Bravo was described by *Time* magazine as one of the year's ten best TV shows.

Morris's credits include *Gates of Heaven*, a pet cemetery documentary, which I regard as one of the ten best films of all time, as well as *The Thin Blue Line*, which freed an innocent man from Death Row in Texas; *A Brief History of Time*, starring physicist Stephen Hawking; *Fast, Cheap and Out of Control*, which was about intelligent robots, lion tamers, topiary gardeners, and naked mole rats; and *Mr. Death*, the story of a Holocaust denier whose dream is to invent more humane execution devices. Morris's TV show has featured films on Temple Grandin, the world's leading designer of cattle-handling systems, even though she is autistic; and a parrot that was an eyewitness to a murder (but can its testimony be believed?).

On many of these films, Morris used the Interrotron, his own invention. "I like the name," he explains, "because it combines the words interview and terror." It also reminds him of alien devices in fifties sciencefiction movies. Instead of sitting face to face with his interview subjects, he has them look into a TV camera. They see Morris's face reflected on a screen. Morris looks into another camera and sees the subject. One is somehow not surprised to learn that two-way mirrors are involved.

Morris likes this approach because (a) "This way the subject is looking straight into the eyes of the audience, instead of off to the side of the camera," (b) "I can maintain unbroken eye contact," (c) "People will say things to a TV camera they won't say to a human being," and (d) "Sometimes if I just pause and wait, people feel compelled to say something because the Interrotron is waiting, and so they speak, even if they don't mean to."

Reason (d) is buttressed by Morris's Twenty-Minute Rule. This is his theory that if you let people talk for twenty minutes without interrupting them, they will start spilling the beans whether they want to or not.

How does the Megatron differ from the Interrotron? It can use twenty cameras instead of one. The split screen behind Rosefelt was showing the views from four of them. This capability doesn't change the eye-to-eye interview experience, but does allow Morris a greater selection of different kinds of shots when he is editing.

Morris had his technicians turn the camera from Rosefelt to the audience for questions. He could see his interrogators, and they could see him—a spectral black-and-white presence inside the camera. He said he had toyed with marketing the Megatron, but for now prefers to keep it proprietary. To be sure, there didn't seem to be an enormous demand; Mock, Davis, and Makepeace were not jostling for a look behind the curtain, and Lewis and Nierenberg had adjourned to the House of Docs Cafe for coffee and oatmeal muffins. So for the foreseeable future, Morris may have the Megatron all to himself.

He likes it that way. "I am toying with the idea," he said, "of an Inter-robot, which I could send to your house while I stay in the studio."

Truth Is a Linguistic Thing

NUBAR ALEXANIAN/2002

NA: *Do you orchestrate for the ear independent of the eye?*
EM: This is a difficult question. When you're putting a film together you're so much aware of both it's hard to extract them independently.

NA: *But you're a classical pianist and a cellist. Your knowledge of music is very deep and plays an important big part in your films.*
EM: I don't know if it's more important in my movies than it is in anyone else's. I do think that the kind of strange language that comes out of people talking is the bedrock of everything I do. It's heavily edited spoken language as opposed to written language. But the music, obviously, has to work with the spoken language. It can't be independent of it. Just getting music to work with my films has been the cause of I don't know how much trouble. Often, when you have a sequence that's purely visual, without dialogue, music takes on almost a dominant role. But it can't in my movies. I first started using music with *The Thin Blue Line*, and we had terrible difficulties finding music that wouldn't undermine or interfere with what the people were saying, that would enhance but not overwhelm or efface the spoken words. So I would say that the music in my films has always taken a back seat to the spoken word.

NA: *You often conduct long interviews. When I shoot a portrait of someone, I have a three-role minimum because I don't feel people can sustain their own view of how they're supposed to look for a camera for three rolls of film.*
EM: Oh, you mean they lose control.

NA: *Right. Is that what the twelve-hour interview is about?*
EM: Yes, loss of control. That's when things start to happen. The marathon

From *The Transom Review*, October 2002. Reprinted by permission, transom.org, the public radio storytelling website.

interviewing style started in 1973 when I was interviewing people with just audiotape, before I became a filmmaker. I would do these lengthy interviews with murderers and their families in California and in Wisconsin. I started with killers and graduated to serial killers and mass murderers.

NA: *How did you make the leap into film from that?*

EM: It was the idea that I could create something even more complex with pictures. But since then all of my work, regardless of what I've done, has been driven by the spoken word. The interviews are the script and precede everything. I'm planning to do a number of features with actors but oddly enough am basing these ideas for drama on interviews.

NA: *Years ago you were interviewing people with a tape recorder but you ended up in film, not radio.*

EM: I could have very easily ended up in radio if I had thought that was an option, but I never thought of Studs Terkel as a model and never looked at these interviews as radio. I saw them as books and then as movies. I still have all of these tapes, and it might be very interesting to do something with them as just audio tapes. You know, I've never even thought of it until you mentioned it right now.

Everything I've done has its origin in the spoken word. The interview fragments in my films give you a perspective on how these people see the world and what they are thinking. A friend of mine says you can never trust people who don't talk a lot because how else would you know what they're thinking? My art is based on that principle and on people's willingness to talk a lot. My belief is that we invented language so we could lie more effectively, that language is a vehicle of self-deception and evasion. I used to transcribe all of my audiotapes myself and there were these exciting moments where you would become aware of patterns of speech, the way people talk, the way they use language, the way they express themselves, the way they don't express themselves. When you sit and transcribe interviews, you become aware of things that you would never ordinarily notice. As you actually put these words down on the page you're listening to them in a completely different way. How much can you actually learn about a person and how do they communicate just from their patterns of speech? It goes well beyond the surface content of what they're saying.

I've always been amazed by the fact that you sit and transcribe and transcribe and end up with this huge pile of material. You transcribe an interview that goes on for eight, nine, ten hours, and end up with a small book. When you read it, you realize just how different it is from the film material. It's quite remarkable how the content of something changes once you see it associated with pictures. It's like being in this weird laboratory of language where you get to isolate various aspects of communication. You get to hear the audio for the first time when you're actually conducting the interview. You get to transform the audio into the written word. And then you get to see it once again as film. The difference between each of these elements is endlessly fascinating. When you read something, you can always imagine a voice. You imagine the words as being spoken by some ideal speaker that you have in your head, or as being spoken by yourself, or meaning certain things depending on how the words are delivered. It's always interesting to contrast that reading experience with looking at the person, once again, speaking the words on film.

NA: *I'm so taken by the visual elements in your films, but now that I hear you say that they're about language, it makes perfect sense to me.*

EM: Don't get me wrong: images interest me. You often hear this idea that voice-over is a failing of the screenwriter. Well, I started to think about doing interviews and using them as voice-over and constructing a completely fictional movie with actors based on it. I can preserve what really interests me, which is the linguistic element as a foundation, and can move my film-making in a completely different direction. The problem devolves to one basic difference between a standard feature and whatever it is that I do. Exposition is usually integrated into dialogue and becomes part of the scene but in my films there is almost always an ironic distance—even detachment—between what the characters are saying and what we are seeing.

We talk about feature filmmaking and documentary filmmaking as if there is this rigid line of demarcation between the two, that we can say, "This fits into category one and this fits into category two, and it's clear what the differences are." Well, the differences are important but they're different than what most people imagine them to be. People love to talk about truth. Truth-telling. Truth in advertising—try that oxymoron on for size. Most of the time I have no idea what people are talking about when they talk about truth. They somehow imagine that truth-telling is connected with style or presentation, that if it's *cinéma-vérité* or it appears in the *New York Times* it must be true. And look at the nonsense over the Rodney King videotape where people agree it was a videotape of a real event but they can't agree what that real event was.

Truth is not guaranteed by style or presentation. It's not handed over on a tray like a Happy Meal. It's a quest, and often it's as interesting to chronicle people's persistent avoidance of the truth as their pursuit of it. But in any event, whatever truth is, it's a linguistic and not a visual thing. I do not believe that the truth is subjective, that the truth is contextual, or that the truth is up for grabs. To me the real story behind *The Thin Blue Line*—and I think this is an important story to be told in general about the world—is not that truth is unknowable but that often people are uninterested in the truth. They don't seek the truth but rather some series of answers that make them feel comfortable or answer to certain needs that they might have.

To talk about a photograph being true or false is utterly meaningless. Words give you a picture of the world and visuals take you into the mystery of what is out there and whether language has captured it or not. When the characters in *The Thin Blue Line* are talking about the events on that roadway in Dallas and then you see images of that roadway, you start to think about the mystery of what happened, the mystery of our attempt to really grab a hold of the world with words and images. *The Thin Blue Line* is involved in two separate enterprises. One is to show you what the underlying truth most likely was, and the other is to show you how people came up with conclusions that were at such variance with the truth.

NA: *And then you do those re-creations on the road.*
EM: Yes, in a whole number of ways. I did it with reenactments and also with just the individual stories of the people who were supposed to be witnesses to the event, the people who testified at the trial. It becomes clear as the movie unfolds that the stories these witnesses are telling are not so much stories about what they saw but about what they wanted to see. My belief is that believing is seeing, not the other way around. That's one of the very strong themes for me in *The Thin Blue Line*. If there's enough pressure, if there's enough reason to believe something, then people will believe it no matter what the underlying truth might be, no matter what the evidence against their believing it might be.

The crime detailed in *The Thin Blue Line* went unsolved for a month. They didn't even have any suspects. A Dallas police officer is shot in cold blood and someone has to pay the price, so when David Harris pointed the finger at Randall Adams, here is something the police can jump on. We have the perfect witness to the crime because he claims he was seated next to the perpetrator. Finally there is a case which can be built around these claims, even though a moment of reflection tells us that this guy's testimony is unreliable because he might be the killer himself. At the center of the film is the question of how it happened that the guy who committed all of these crimes walked away scot-free so that he could commit other murders and other crimes, and the guy who hadn't done anything wrong ended up sentenced to death. Isn't our system of justice designed to prevent outcomes like this?

A lot of what I do as a filmmaker is about this concern with conspiracy versus human incompetence, confusion and infallibility. *The Thin Blue Line* is very much a story not of conspiracy but of just how incompetent and easily seduced we are into believing anything. That is the heart of the movie, and some of my other movies as well. I like to think of these films as stories about belief, about what people believe and how they see the world, set against what the world might actually be. *The Thin Blue Line* is very much a have-your-cake-and-eat-it-too movie. It wants to tell two stories. It wants to tell an investigative story in plain language, a story about what really happens, but it also wants to tell a story about the massive confusion and error that produced this incredible miscarriage of justice. I'm very proud of the film because I think it works on both levels.

NA: *You do these interviews and the tapes are transcribed. You edit from there?*

EM: No, I don't edit from the transcripts, I edit from the film. Transcribing the material is a way of creating an index for the material. While editing we can quickly find material in the transcript. In my first two films I was very much involved in creating the transcripts of the material but no longer do this myself. Paper edits—essentially taking the transcript and cutting and pasting together the sections you like—give you a very false idea. They never really work. You need to see the piece of film and cut it against another piece of film, and by doing so something happens that is lost on the page. All editing that's not done on film is a waste of time and is going to have to be redone.

NA: *When you go into an interview, have you done lots of research?*

EM: Yes. I never talk to the people in advance, but I prepare heavily. I used to think that if I ever had a tattoo it would say "Born to Babble." People have a need to talk, and if they've already told you that story, that need has been dissipated. I want it to happen on camera, and over the years I've found from painful experience that talking to somebody off-camera about what you want to talk about with them on-camera is counterproductive. There's also a tendency—it's a natural human tendency—that when you hear something good you want them to repeat it. "Oh! That thing you said was really good. Could you please repeat it for me." Well, that's not how it works. We're all familiar with the phenomena where you try to do something again and it's never as good as when it just happened the first time, when it happened spontaneously.

NA: *Do you want them to get to know you before they talk to you? Is that important?*

EM: No. They'll get to know me soon enough, in the process of actually doing the interview. It's not about them knowing me, it's about their need to tell me something and my interest in hearing it.

NA: *At one point, you made a living as a private investigator.*

EM: Yes. There's such mystery connected to detective work. There's this image of what I must have been: Errol Morris, comma, P.I., the guy who's sitting in a car late at night looking at the entrance or exit to some building. Or a person watching someone, tracking them, following them. In fact almost everything that I did as a detective is stuff that I do as a filmmaker. If you were to do the Venn diagram of the two, there was an enormous overlap.

NA: *You're a storyteller, and yet you use investigation as the way to tell a story.*

EM: I think there's a very strong investigative element in all of my movies. Investigation and storytelling work in opposite directions from each other. Stories, by their very nature, have to be tremendously simplified versions of reality. Reality is too complex, it's too chaotic. We tell ourselves stories so we don't have to deal with reality. We create stories out of the mess of reality by eliminating material, by reinterpreting material, by rearranging material. But the investigative element is what connects the stories to the world. It's what makes stories interesting to me.

The only way people can make sense of experience, of the world, of history, is by picking and choosing from a myriad of details and facts. When you make a movie, you need something to carry the audience through. You are telling a story as a means of taking people through a series of events. *The Thin Blue Line* is very much a story, but it's a story also dotted with these absurd, picky little details that fascinate me and which inform the story. But I spent two plus years in Texas investigating this crime, and one of the saddest things for me is that 99 percent of my investigative work in connection with this case is invisible. It's not in the

movie. You see the tip of the iceberg, you see the results of all of this effort that I put in over the years, but it's not really in the movie. The reasons are pretty straightforward: if you put them all in the movie, it would
be confusing and no one would watch it.

NA: *Tell me about your McNamara film.*

EM: For years and years I had talked about interviewing Robert McNamara but kept putting it off. Part of it was that I couldn't think of any
reason why he would want to talk to me.

NA: *But why him?*

EM: Because of his involvement in the war in Vietnam and because of
the three books that he's written since the mid-nineties: *In Retrospect, Argument Without End,* and *Wilson's Ghost.* McNamara is the quintessential American figure, a Zelig-like man who found himself at amazing
century-defining moments in the history of the twentieth century. From
Berlin on the day of the Nazi invasion of Poland, Shanghai on the day of
the Japanese invasion—part of their war to conquer China—and the firebombing of Tokyo in 1945, to his leadership role in the postwar economic
recovery, his ascendancy to the presidency of the Ford Motor Company
in 1960, his seven years as secretary of defense for Kennedy, Johnson, and
then his role as president of the World Bank. It's an amazing story, but it's
not just a story of these events, it's a story of one man's attempt to understand these events and his role in them.

NA: *And you interviewed only McNamara, no one else.*

EM: The traditional idea of how documentaries are to be put together
is that you talk to some twenty people and you inter-cut the interviews.
"A" says such-and-such, and then "B" contradicts "A" and then "C" says
something else altogether. Supposedly you gain perspective on an issue
by listening to this interplay of characters, in effect, arguing with each
other. Well, what if you tried something completely different? What if
you created a movie about one character's perception of history, about
one character's attempt to understand himself through history? I have
been playing with the idea for several years now, creating things around
one single interview, no other people. I tried that with Fred Leuchter in
Mr. Death but failed for a whole number of reasons.

NA: *You feel that film failed?*

EM: I don't feel the film failed, but it was to be based on Fred Leuchter's interview alone but in the end didn't work out that way. I had to

supplement the Leuchter interview with additional interviews, so in the end it wasn't this one voice, this first-person story that I had envisioned when I set out to make it. It had evolved into something quite different. What was so appealing about the McNamara project was this opportunity to try that same thing again with just one person: Robert S. McNamara alone. No other interviews. No other voice.

NA: *What are your own views on McNamara?*

EM: I remember going into the film knowing full well that there are millions of people who have very strong views about who McNamara is and what his role was in the American government in the 1960s. My goal, notwithstanding, was to try to learn something about him, to be interested in him in the sense that this is a person who has something very important to tell and that I should be willing to listen to him.

I demonstrated against McNamara years and years ago. I was at the University of Wisconsin and I graduated in June 1969. McNamara was already out of the Defense Department by early 1968 so I probably wasn't demonstrating against him, I was demonstrating against Clark Clifford and then, later, various officials in the Nixon administration. But I was certainly aware of him. I remember when I was in Wisconsin reading several essays by I. F. Stone that had appeared in the *New York Review of Books*. They were essays about the Gulf of Tonkin Bay incidents and the Congressional Resolution which followed: the incidents on August 2 and 4, 1964, and the resolution that immediately followed that essentially authorized the expansion of the war in Vietnam. There were these allegations that these incidents were trumped up, they were manufactured in order to insure acceptance of this resolution and acceptance of the escalation of the war. It's a serious charge, that the Johnson administration manufactured an international incident in order to wage war in Southeast Asia. I really admire I. F. Stone. He is for me an American hero, a real American hero.

I think there's something of a mystery surrounding McNamara, and whether I can answer this mystery or not is unclear to me. In fact, I doubt that I can. But I'd like to try. Go back to the Gulf of Tonkin Bay incident, which interests me because it's very much like the story of *The Thin Blue Line*. How did we imagine things that never happened? That was the center of the Gulf of Tonkin question. Did people somehow convince themselves that this was an act of communist aggression? Did they somehow imagine incidents that didn't occur? Not deliberately, but just because they were in the appropriate state of mind where they could easily imagine and believe that kind of thing.

NA: *How can you even resolve those kinds of questions?*

EM: Well, you can start by asking them. We're now privy to these amazing conversations that occurred between Johnson and his advisors. We can actually hear audio recordings of Johnson from the Oval Office talking to McNamara, to Dean Rusk, to Bundy, and so on and so forth. Some of these conversations with McNamara are in the movie. They shine light on this whole issue of what was going on the week we deliberated on these incidents [August 1–6, 1964], and then bombed North Vietnam.

NA: *Are documentaries defined by their subject matter?*

EM: I used to rail against what I called The Mother Theresa Principle: that any movie about Mother Theresa has to be a good movie because Mother Theresa is such a good person. It's the flip side of the same reasoning that tells us *Triumph of the Will* is a bad movie because it was made in service of the Third Reich. Are documentaries to be evaluated on the basis of their social content? Is there such a thing as a bad movie about a good person? Are there good movies about bad people? Do good things happen to bad movies? And what about movies that appear to be about good things but aren't really? One of my favorite examples of this sort of thing is *Scared Straight!*, which won an Academy Award for best documentary. It's about sending youthful offenders to a maximum security prison for a day. They spent a day with serial killers, pedophiles, and God knows what else. And guess what happened? They got "scared straight." I despised this movie. Okay. I more than despised it. I loathed it. Really, really loathed it. The movie claims to be presenting this social benefit, but it's deeply corrupt at its heart. It pontificates. "We turned these youthful offenders into law abiding citizens. Look at us. We did good." Well, it turns out that the kids in the movie came from an upper middle class neighborhood where the recidivism rate was nil, so the argument in the film that they were turned away from crime was vacuous, if not specious. Also the level of craft in the movie was beyond execrable, and even if there had been a real social benefit, which in fact there wasn't, is that the way we want to run our society, namely by scaring people into submission? Why not go and live in North Korea? "Do-good-art" often gives me the willies. Another abomination is *Night and Fog* (1955).

Yet there is great art that tries to capture something real about the world, something that we might not be aware of, even something that we do not want to be aware of, something disturbing, alarming. Something that does not play into what we want to hear, but something we might like to avoid hearing. Something that produces uneasiness.

NA: *But shouldn't documentaries strive to make the world a better place?*

EM: You seem to imply that documentary filmmakers should be social workers and that I should be protecting my subjects from themselves, from me, from real or imagined audiences who might look at them critically at some unspecified time in the future. Well, I have a confession to make: I'm not a social worker nor do I ever want to become one.

When I was speaking about *The Thin Blue Line*, shortly after its release, a Dallas journalist asked me if I had mirandized my interview subjects. Yeah. I told them that they had a right to remain silent, they had a right to have an attorney present, and they should know that anything they said could and would be used against them in a court of law. Or public opinion. Okay, no I didn't. However, I did point out to this journalist that I was a filmmaker and not a cop, not an agent of the State, and hence was not required to issue Miranda warnings. When you talk to a journalist—or to another person for that matter—you are taking a risk. Perhaps before every conversation a warning should be issued, and I don't mean just in journalism. I mean every conversation. "Warning: I might think ill of you. I might twist the things you say and use them to make you look like a complete idiot. Be on your toes. That's right. Watch out, buster."

In *The Journalist and the Murderer*, Janet Malcolm correctly pointed out that there is a power imbalance between a journalist and a subject. But she incorrectly imagines that that this is particularly true of journalists and their subjects. Well, I've got a secret. It's true of all relationships. She also imagines that the journalist always has the upper hand. Maybe yes, maybe no. Sometimes a journalist is more powerful than the subject, sometimes vice versa. It's the same in "real" life. Sometimes "A" is more powerful than "B," and vice versa. Journalistic relationships exhibit certain familiar features: abusiveness, betrayal, smarminess, protectiveness, kindliness, and so on. Is this so surprising? But I have to object vociferously to the idea that there are limits to what the journalist can show or express. Who decides? Martha Stewart?

NA: *Claude Lanzman was criticized for the techniques he used in filming* Shoah *(1985).*

EM: Yes. When Lanzman was interviewing Nazis, he surreptitiously filmed and recorded them. Of course, this became controversial. Is such a thing ethical? After two years of investigating I finally put David Harris on film. During the interview he confessed to the murder. Parts of the confession did not have an audio counterpart, for example I asked him, "Were you alone in the car when you were stopped by the Dallas police officer?" He smiled and nodded his head. Should I use his confession? Maybe I should be "protecting" him. Is that the nature of our relationship? He incriminates himself and I protect him by keeping it to myself?

NA: *Do you ever feel guilty about how you have conducted an interview?*
EM: Yes, just as I sometimes feel guilty about relationships that don't involve interviews. One thing should always be kept in mind: there is no such thing as a straight interview, though I would admit that there are good and bad interviews.

Interviews are human relationships in a laboratory setting. They allow us to scrutinize the nature of how one person relates to another, and vice versa. As such all the things that are common features of "ordinary" relationships appear in the interviews: deceit, coyness, misdirection, sincerity, honesty, dishonesty, confusion. In some instances—I dare say—there is the powerful impulse to protect a subject from himself or show him in the best possible light. I have a lot of these kinds of impulses. I actually like people to look good, and I attempt—even if I don't succeed—to capture their complexity in the interview and in the film I eventually produce.

Let me provide a couple of definitions of a good interview. A good interview captures the complexity of the subject. A good interview captures the complexity of the relationship between the interviewer and the subject. Sometimes it's a matter of discretion, sometimes it's Let the Best Man Win. But usually it's more complex than that. Anybody who says that they have never felt guilty about their own work is either (a) incapable of guilt, (b) self-deceived, or (c) lying. Gitta Sereny wrote an entire book about trying to convince her subject—Albert Speer—that he knew about the Holocaust. By the end, she clearly believes that Speer has admitted to her that he knew about the Holocaust. But I don't think Speer ever admits anything of the sort, to Sereny or anyone else, including himself. After all, Speer's "defense" is to admit responsibility for things he claims to know nothing about. It's an idea he developed at Nuremberg and never had occasion to modify. So whose self-deception are we talking about here? Sereny's? Speer's? Mine?

There is the wonderful assumption that we are in control of our relationships with other people, in interview situations or otherwise, that we know what we're doing much of the time and have a clear idea of our motivations and purpose. It's a wonderful assumption. It suffers, however, from one minor infirmity. It's false.

I don't want to get into the business of attacking or defending Janet Malcolm. Although I must confess I am an admirer, even a fan. She is the only true Chekovian journalist. She has been endlessly criticized because it is assumed she is talking about conscious mendacity, conscious journalistic ill-will. In such a view, the journalist imagines himself—or we imagine the journalist—to be in control of an interview and can manipulate it to his own advantage. The point I wish to make is that we often have the idea that we are in control of what we're doing when we are not. This kind of control is an illusion. Perhaps consciousness itself is nothing more than a crude device that allows us to deceive ourselves about our own motivations.

NA: *What's the best thing a filmmaker can do?*
EM: Perhaps create something that is unusual and unique, that has emotional power, that says something unexpected. My tendency as a filmmaker is to keep going, to keep gnawing at some bone until I finally come to a conclusion that satisfies me.

NA: *What kind of things would you do on your films if you had an unlimited budget?*
EM: Creating visuals. It's part of the problem of being in this no-man's land, or gray zone of filmmaking. Yes, I make documentaries, but no I don't make documentaries like other people. I'm not a documentary filmmaker who runs around shooting with handheld camera and available light. I do that on occasion but it's not the whole deal. Much of what I do just can't be accommodated on a documentary budget, and even though I have been very fortunate—I get not insubstantial budgets—the budgets are never enough to cover the cost of the film. All this may sound very boring but on some simple level it does inform my work as a filmmaker. I'm not a 16mm handheld guy, I'm some different kind of animal. And a more expensive, needy kind of animal.

There's this worry in filmmaking: who is going to watch the film I'm making? I would like my movies to be seen by more than half a dozen people. I've never been able to attract as large an audience as I might like, which is depressing. There could be lots of reasons for that. I tell myself that my movies haven't been marketed well, but it could be just simply the way that I put them together or the nature of the films themselves that restricts their audience. Or maybe I'm not that good, that could be another possibility. But the goal is to reach a larger number of people.

The idea of making films for half a dozen people is not an appealing notion, and even if it were, it's not a viable financial model because no one would ever give you the money to make them. Making a film is so complex and expensive that you can't do it without at least some idea of an audience in mind. Unless you're independently wealthy and can just pay for these things on your own accord, you have to have some kind of audience. That's true of all art. You can't make it without some real or imagined audience.

I remember someone asking me if *Fast, Cheap* was a cold calculation on my part to make something that was commercial. And I thought: are you insane? What? Oh, right, yeah, that commercial model: mole rats, topiary animals, lion taming, and the robotic scientist. Proving once again that people can say anything.

The Anti-Postmodern Postmodernist

ERROL MORRIS / 2003

HOMI BHABAHA: Growing up as I did in Bombay, some miles south
of the gaudy and glitzy world of Bollywood, you may well imagine that
my relation to the topic of truth in cinema is somewhat skewed, perhaps
even a little bit dubious. Song and dance routines aside, Bombay was also
the home of a pioneering documentary film tradition, rather like Errol
Morris's nonfiction features, committed to an invigorating aesthetic of
social inquiry. These documentarians distrusted the information that
was liberally disseminated in the public sphere. They tirelessly sought an
aesthetic form in film that initiated an interlocutory relationship with
the themes of their films and their audiences. The investigative genre assumes a more unidirectional search for truth. What I'm calling the interlocutory form, however, reveals what appears to be true only when the
subject—good, bad, or indifferent—talks back and the viewer, like the director, is empowered to read between the lines.

It gives me the greatest pleasure to introduce Errol Morris in the company of Bombay's interlocutory filmmakers, because he belongs to a public sphere of cultural citizenship, in which the truth of historical events
is not luminous. It emerges from the murky shadows, the twilight ter-
rain, from which we come to learn what really happened and what was
truly done. When *The Thin Blue Line* was released in 1988, a review at this
time wrote, "Errol Morris's film has built an investigation of a murder
and a nightmarish meditation on the difference between truth and fiction." When Randall Adams was released after more than twelve years
in prison, first on death row, the Dallas assistant district attorney complained that the mind of the judge who ordered Adams's release had been

---

Harvard University Lecture, 2003. Permission granted by Errol Morris.

warped by that New York underground cult movie-maker who was down here. The truth of Morris's film set Randall Adams free.

Morris himself describes *The Thin Blue Line* as a "nonfiction feature" instead of a documentary because like Truman Capote in *In Cold Blood*, he calls attention to the tension between reporting and trying to create a work of art. As Morris brings out one kind of truth from the human subjects of historical events that he records, he also sketches out the aesthetic sensorium, color, light, sound, shapes, music, and metaphors—the universe where both the subjects and his audiences live through a fog of vanity, habit, and circumstance even as they strive towards a kind of clarity.

In *The Fog of War*, we see and hear Robert McNamara try or not try to come to grips with his managerial arrogance and the hyper-rationality that led to tragically clouded judgment about Vietnam.

Writing in the *New York Times*, in response to the videotape of a U.S. Marine shooting an Iraqi prisoner in Fallujah, Morris suggested, "If you want to believe things, then you often find a way to do so, regardless of evidence to the contrary. Believing is seeing and not the other way around." In the best sense, Errol Morris's films are disturbing works of truth, history, and art. They renew our hope that new ways of seeing can unsettle old ways of believing. (Applause)

ERROL MORRIS: This is very kind. I should point out that the use of the term "nonfiction feature" so kindly described a moment ago was really a marketing tool. Probably the same could be said for Truman Capote's "nonfiction novel"—the desire to get your work before a larger audience is at least part of the motivation for making movies.

I picked this subject because when I started work as a filmmaker, I was concerned—and I still am concerned—with issues of truth and self-deception. I never liked Jean-Luc Godard's idea that film is truth twenty-four times a second. I have a slightly different version: film is lies twenty-four times a second.

The first film I made, *Gates of Heaven*, was very much in reaction to a prevailing idea about how documentaries should be made: the idea of *cinéma-vérité*, truth cinema. There was this idea that if you follow certain rules, if you shoot things in a certain way, then out pops the truth. The rules are fairly straightforward. Shoot with a hand-held camera. Shoot with available light. Become a fly-on-the-wall, observing but not observed in turn. And of course, try to be as unobtrusive as possible. It's one of those meat-grinders: you put in the appropriate ingredients, and magically, truth results.

To me, that's utter nonsense. Who could have ever made such a claim, and on the basis of what? I think not. My guess is the preponderant number of people in this room get a certain comfort from reading the *New York Times*. It's that familiar set of fonts that we're used to seeing every day, fonts which give us a certain level of comfort, a belief that what we're reading is true. I would submit that style doesn't guarantee truth. How could it possibly ever do such a thing? We may feel that the fonts are truth-telling fonts, but that's our uncritical reliance on a whole constellation of beliefs.

So, from the very first film I made, *Gates of Heaven*, I decided to break all of the rules. Instead of using lightweight equipment, we tried to use the heaviest equipment that we could afford. I tried to be always as obtrusive as possible. Fortunately, my budget was limited in those days, or I would have used even heavier equipment! You're told that people are not supposed to look at the camera. They're supposed to look anywhere but at the camera; face the other way, face to the left or the right or whatever, but *never, never, never, never look at the camera, pretend that the camera isn't there*. Well, I had people looking directly at the camera, talking directly to the camera. *Don't change things*. We changed almost everything. *Don't light things, use available light*. Everything was lit.

Now, was what I did, any less, any more truthful than *cinéma-vérité*? I would say no more, no less truthful. Very shortly after that, I made a film in northwest Florida, named after the town in which it was shot, Vernon, Florida. A town that I can honestly say is in the middle of nowhere, equidistant from Tallahassee and Pensacola. A place where no one in his right mind would go, let alone spend a great deal of time.

I went down there because of a story that I read in the *New York Times* about an insurance investigator who was chronicling the worst cases he had encountered in his thirty-year career of insurance investigations. It was just a couple of lines in the article, it was mentioned in passing, a town called "Nub City," so named because of this extraordinary history of self-mutilation, people taking out insurance policies on themselves and then cutting off their arms and legs in order to collect the insurance.

It's hard to know what I was thinking, or if in fact I was thinking at all. It was impossible to make this film. It's not as if you can actually walk up to an amputee and ask them to start explaining in great detail how they lost a leg or an arm or, in some instances, both an arm *and* a leg—

after taking out insurance policies on themselves. They have committed a crime. They're not going to talk about it.

So that movie never got made. Although I did get beaten up by the son of a nubbie in Quincy, Florida. This is the only time that I was really beaten up, and I have to say it was unpleasant. It hurt.

I ended up making a vastly different film. Someone once described it as "philosophy in the swamp," and that might be more or less true. I discovered all of this unexpected material from the people that I found down there, and one of the themes that fascinated me was truth or, more specifically, self-deception and the avoidance of truth. The truth is knowable, but often we have a vested interest in not knowing it, not seeing it, disregarding it, avoiding it. Consequently, my interest in truth had two parts: an interest in the pursuit of truth and an interest in examining how people manage to avoid the truth.

Who is the one truly self-deceived? This is a question, I think, very difficult to answer. But at least you should always entertain the possibility that it is yourself.

I finished that film and was out of work for a long, long, long time. I couldn't get anybody to give me money to make another movie, and the only job I could get was as a private detective in New York City. A friend of a friend had been looking for a detective, and recommended me. Of course, you need some kind of pretext when you're talking to people. My pretext, which I found really humiliating at the time, was—filmmaking. I pretended to be a filmmaker. Which I was, sort of, and which I also wasn't, sort of. At the time I was very much an *unemployed* filmmaker.

I finally got money to make another film, *The Thin Blue Line*. Actually, I got money to make a film that had really nothing whatsoever to do with *The Thin Blue Line*. I was so desperate that I submitted a proposal that I hoped would interest television executives at public broadcasting, even though it didn't interest me—about future dangerousness, about a Dallas psychiatrist nicknamed "Dr. Death." Well, his real name was Dr. James Grigson, but he was given the nickname Dr. Death because of the role he played in capital murder trials in Texas. (It's very nice that we have a governor, as I speak, pursuing a similar course. Thank you, Governor Romney, for proposing doubt-free executions.)

But in those days, which of course might be very similar to these days, in order to sentence someone to death, you had to make a prediction about his or her future behavior. In some states, they have mitigating circumstances in the penalty phase, but this is Texas, so they have exacerbating circumstances. (Laughter) The prosecutors in Texas were very enthusiastic about this one; they bring in a psychiatrist to make a prediction about the defendant. I am profoundly skeptical about our abilities to predict the future except what Dr. Grigson will say in the penalty phase of a capital murder trial. This can be predicted with 100 percent certainty: he will take the stand and say that the defendant should be executed.

In this scheme, you can think of executions as preventive murder. Like killings in a preventive war. There, of course, is a similarity between war and the death penalty. You could even think of war as the death penalty writ large.

I spent a lot of time with Dr. Grigson. He had a lot of time on his hands. He had lost all his private patients. He explained to me, he said, "You know, after I got that name, they just stopped coming." Evidently, it's not so easy to reveal some of your deepest and darkest secrets to someone known as Dr. Death. It's a sad story, but all too believable. It had an inherent plausibility to it, hard to deny.

At his suggestion, I went to various Texas prisons and interviewed people Dr. Grigson had helped sentence to die. And I had these prisoner auditions—I must have interviewed some fifteen, sixteen, seventeen inmates—and one of them turned out to be innocent. He initially interested me not because I thought he was innocent, but because he seemed odd. He had a singsong way of talking, as if he was convinced that no one really was listening to anything he had to say, like he felt compelled to go through some kind of formal recitation again and again although he somehow knew that it would fall on deaf ears. I became obsessed with this case for three years. Three years of investigating a murder making the film *The Thin Blue Line*, which resulted in this man's release from prison.

I looked at it as a triumph of sorts, for many, many reasons. I thought that it was proof that I was inherently a good person, something that I could trade off of for years. But I also liked the idea that in the process of doing everything wrong, I had accumulated real evidence, and sections of the movie were submitted as evidence in federal and state court. There are moments in these interviews that made the difference between this man spending the rest of his life in prison and his release from prison.

I don't think pictures have any truth-value. I'm always mystified when people talk about the truth and falsity of pictures. Correct me if I'm wrong here, but truth is something that arises out of the relationship between language and the world. If I look at a picture alone, it tells me nothing. If you look at a picture of the *Titanic* and the *Lusitania*, they look very, very similar, almost identical, with four smokestacks. You look at either picture, true or false? Neither. Put a caption at the bottom of one of them, that changes everything. If you put in the caption, "This is the *Lusitania*," and the picture is a picture of the *Lusitania*, then the caption is true. However, the picture itself is neither true nor false. It's just a picture. There were five witnesses against this man when he was convicted of capital murder. One of them actually turned out to be the real killer. Always an interesting irony. I think you could describe it that way. Three of them were wacko eyewitnesses that had appeared on the roadway that night and claimed that they had seen everything. And the fifth was a policewoman who was a partner of the police officer who was shot and killed. I always think about how I would like to be sentenced to death because of her testimony. (Laughter) I mean, probably it doesn't feel very good to be sentenced to death on anybody's testimony, but I think this would be particularly irritating. (Laughter)

This has become part and parcel of what I do, and it's certainly a very, very big part of *The Fog of War*. You could say it's an interest how people reveal themselves through language. A friend of mine has said, "You can never trust someone who doesn't talk a lot, because how else could you know what they're thinking?" This could be true. There's a belief that if you sit people down and you let them talk that they will reveal who they are. And then this also contrary to the whole idea about how you're supposed to investigate stuff. After all, you're supposed to ask difficult questions, particularly if you want to find something out, you're supposed to back the subject against the wall, press them hard, and get them to 'fess up in some way or another. This is one of many of the criticisms that I heard about my film of Robert S. McNamara, that he should have been subjected to much tougher questions.

Now this is very self-serving of me to say, but my silence during the interviews for *The Thin Blue Line* produced information that led to the conviction being overturned. At the very beginning of the interviews are some of my very favorite lines I ever put on film. "Everywhere I go there's murders. Even around my house." (Laughter) This could be another instance of self-deception on my part, but I concluded that she is confused, she is confabulating, she is a fantasist living in some crazy world of her own device. In all likelihood, people aren't being bludgeoned to death in the kitchen; they aren't being immolated in the living room; they aren't being stabbed to death in the bedroom. In all likelihood, none of that stuff is going on, even though she might like to think it is. After all, she wants to be a detective or the wife of a detective. (I guess I wanted to be a detective or the husband of a detective.)

In the middle of this interview—and it was not in response to any question, because quite honestly, I'm not that good—she started to talk about how she had failed to pick out Randall Adams in a police lineup. Having forgotten that she testified to the exact opposite in this trial. She was quite defensive. "I failed to pick him out because he was looking at me funny, and he changed the way he was dressed, his hair was different," blah blah blah blah blah. Near the end of the interview, when the interview was, for all intents and purposes, over, I said, "Emily, you say you failed to pick out the defendant in the police lineup. How do you know you failed?" And she said, "I know because the policeman sitting next to me told me I picked out the wrong person, and then pointed out the right person so I wouldn't make that mistake again." It's a good line, particularly when it's presented as evidence in a court of law. And believe it or not, she actually repeated it in a court of law. Go figure. That, probably more than anything, led to Randall Adams's conviction being overturned. I mean, there was enormous—and by enormous, I mean *enormous*—evidence supporting his innocence. Also at the very end of the movie, *The Thin Blue Line*, the real murderer confesses to me; there's that as well.

Making *The Thin Blue Line*, I spent a lot of time in Vidor, Texas; hometown of the KKK. I stopped wearing glasses in east Texas. I was wearing glasses at the time. And I started to become convinced that the glasses secretly said J-E-W, and that I would do much, much better without them. In one bizarre conversation, a police officer in Vidor asked me if I lived in New York. I was living in New York City at the time. And then he said, "There are a lot of deli restaurants, aren't there, in New York?" I thought, "Is this going where I think it's going?" I said, "There are a lot of deli restaurants in New York." And then he looked at me and he said, "I bet you really like deli food, don't you?" (Laughter)

When *The Thin Blue Line* came out, the movie was criticized by many reviewers. One of the complaints was that I had used reenactments in the film. And actually, one reviewer even suggested that I had been remiss, because clearly, I had been out on the roadway that night, and I should have tried to stop the crime. (Laughter)

The reenactments in *The Thin Blue Line* were never used to make you think you were looking at the real world. In fact, there were reenactments that were in conflict with each other, reenactments that were demonstrations of falsehood, reenactments of beliefs, reenactments of what people claimed that they had seen rather than what I thought they had seen. Their purpose was to bring you deeper and deeper and deeper into the mystery of what actually happened, and heighten the conflict between the claims made by the various witnesses and the reality of the real world, in which things either do or don't happen.

I like to think of myself as the ultimate anti-postmodernist post-modernist. Notwithstanding the unusual narrative or visual devices that appear in many of the films, what kept me going for the three years of investigating this story was the belief that there were answers to questions such as: *Adams did it, didn't he?* Or *Harris did it, didn't he?* That it's not just up for grabs. Today, I believe there's a kind of frisson of ambiguity. People think that ambiguity is somehow wonderful in its own right, an excuse for failing to investigate. I think this view is wrong; at best, misguided, and maybe even reprehensible.

Over the course of making *The Fog of War*, I had a lot of trouble with McNamara. Horrible disagreements about stuff I had put in the movie that he did not want in there. One of the major disagreements concerned the lessons in the film. There are eleven lessons. And he repeatedly said, "You know, Errol, those are not my lessons; they are your lessons." And I said, "Yeah, they are. But they're extracted from things that you've said." Perhaps they were not the lessons that McNamara would have chosen, but then, he was not directing the movie. I think that the lessons are ironic. It's very odd to me that people talk about the lessons without pointing out that there might be intended ironies with each and every one of them.

McNamara's batting average seemed better than Grigson's: 50 percent in the Gulf of Tonkin. As he put it in *The Fog of War*, "We were right once and wrong once." Of course, after he and LBJ took our country to war and more than three million people died, his 50 percent batting average provides limited consolation.

The Fog of War was based on this belief that I could tell history from the inside out. That I could start with a subjective account, a deeply subjective account—you can't imagine an account being more subjective—and learn something important about history.

There was a reporter at the New York Film Festival, at one of the very first screenings of the movie, who asked me, "Are you aware of the fact you interviewed only one person?" (Laughter) Yes, I was aware I had interviewed one person. Again, breaking all of those rules, this time, the rule of balance. You often here that in journalism you're supposed to have balance—whatever that might be. No one has every really described balance to me in any way that makes sense. Balance, it seems to me, is often no more than the appearance of balance, fairness, whatever. You're supposed to give the appearance of balance, whatever that might be.

Well, *The Fog of War* is a movie that eschews balance. It has no interest in balance, as such. It takes a subjective account of one man and examines it. Often it is set it off against the historical record. Set it off against evidence—documents, presidential recordings—with the hope of creating a kind of tension between how McNamara and the viewer experienced history.

Again, not truth with a capital "T," but an attempt to investigate and to learn about things in some unexpected way. Cinema is no more a vehicle for truth than a magazine or a book. It's just another one of those devices that we use to tell stories. But I think underneath all of it, on the part of the person actually making the films, there can be an interest in truth and in the pursuit of truth that can be captured and talked about in a movie. And I hope that, at least in part, that's what my career has been about. (Applause) We have some time for audience questions. I like abusive questions, so please be cruel.

Q: *What do you say to people who criticize you for making fun of the people who you interview?*
EM: It hasn't come up in the case of *The Fog of War*, because the criticisms have come from the opposite side—that I've been far, far, far too kind to McNamara. But in many of my earlier films, I was told that I was setting people up for ridicule. I used to defend myself by denying it. Now, I am less excited about doing so. Properly considered, filmmakers in general and documentary filmmakers in particular should not be creating ads for humanity. Wow. Look how great the human race is. I never thought that being human could be so wonderful. Nor should I be protecting my subjects from themselves. If they are ridiculous, why can't I show that? Does it make the other humans nervous? Am I writing ad copy for some kind of television program on Neptune on why the human race should be allowed to continue, and have to show us to our best advantage?

I make enough commercials without having to turn my movies into them. I make my living from directing television commercials and have probably directed over a thousand ads in the last ten years.

The important thing is to capture the complexity of your characters on film. One of the very kindest things that anyone has said about *The Fog of War* came from McNamara's son, Craig McNamara, who said that he thought that the movie had been successful in capturing the complexity of his father. And if that's true, then I've done my job.

Q: *Why would you have McNamara view your film—couldn't he potentially want you to change things you've done that you think are important?*
EM: The film was a collaboration. Legally, he could not force me to do anything, but I saw the movie as a collaboration between the two of us. I never saw the movie as my attempt to "get" Robert S. McNamara. I saw it as an attempt to try to understand McNamara, and to answer questions about McNamara. To me, McNamara's a mystery. In fact, people, to me, are mysteries.

The movie really has two endings. There is the ending that McNamara would like to have had where he is quoting from the last of the *Four Quartets*, "Little Gidding," by T. S. Eliot. Through Eliot's poetry, he's talking about how at the end of our lives, we can return to the place from where we started and can come to know it for the first time. It's optimistic. Oddly enough, it's not optimistic if you read the whole poem, but in that snippet that McNamara has chosen and often repeated, it is optimistic. It tells you that you can learn from experience. You can review the circumstances of your life and derive lessons, and perhaps others can profit from these lessons as well. There's something to be gained, something to be learned. Life has some benefit.

But then there's the epilogue, my epilogue, where I ask McNamara a series of questions that linger on: Do you feel responsible? Do you feel guilty? How do you live with the weight of all of this? And the final line, "Do you think you're damned if you do and damned if you—?" He interrupts and says, "Yes, and I'd rather be damned if I don't." I like the line. It's the essence of McNamara, and I feel that the line can be given many different readings.

People have asked me, "Does he feel sorry? More than three million people died in southeast Asia; does he feel guilty?"

I asked myself the question: Do I actually want to hear McNamara say he's sorry? And I decided: No. I don't. I think there would be something obscene about an apology. Sorry for the death of 58,000 Americans and 3 million-plus Vietnamese? Is that the kind of thing where you say sorry?

I have my own theory of apologies. We love apologies because they empower us. You can say, "I'm sorry, will you forgive me?" and then the ball is on our court. We can say, "No, I don't forgive you. Fuck you." Or we could say, "I accept your apology. Apology accepted. You are forgiven."

I don't want the ball to be in my court. I know what I feel about the war in Vietnam. I demonstrated against the war as a young student at the University of Wisconsin and at Princeton. The war was abhorrent to me then, and my feelings about it have not changed one little bit over the years.

Q: *When you were an anti-Vietnam War protester, were you actively rooting for the communists to win and defeat us? Recently, I heard you draw a parallel between Iraq and Vietnam. Are you pulling for us—the United States and our allies—to defeat the bad guys in Iraq, or are you pulling for the bad guys to defeat us militarily, like in the war in Vietnam?*

EM: This seems to be a question of whether I'm on the side of good or evil. Maybe I'm on the side of evil in this instance. And no, I was not rooting for anybody in the war in Vietnam. I wasn't rooting for the communists. I wasn't rooting for the U.S. military or for my country either. I don't see international affairs as a football game, I'm terribly sorry. I don't see it as a situation where I am called upon as a citizen to decide whether I belong to the Blue Team or the Red Team or the Green Team or the White Team or any other team for that matter. It seemed to me that people were dying for no good reason in Southeast Asia, and that someone should find a way to stop it.

My feelings about Iraq are not terribly dissimilar. No, I don't think that if you were to set up a simple mathematical equation, that Vietnam equals Iraq. Every historical situation is different. That there's only one thing that remains the same in history, and that's human idiocy. That's a constant. Our capacity for self-deception, our capacity for ignoring history, our capacity for turning evidence into a form that's palatable to us, even if it means accepting untruth remains constant.

Q: *It sounds like you would have gotten a different story if you started with different questions. Perhaps he would have clammed up. How do you plan the sequence of questions that you are going to ask?*

EM: I don't. I don't know what questions I'm going to ask. But, of course, there is this psychiatric problem: how do you keep the patient coming back week after week? It's also a problem with an extended interview. Why should McNamara want to talk to me? Curiosity, at first? Okay. But why should he want to continue talking to me? Did I avoid asking certain things because I thought he would get up and leave? Absolutely. I wanted him to continue with our conversations.

I like to think that I successfully tread a line between being completely uncritical and being too confrontational. Certainly in the years following the release of the movie, I have continued to talk to him and to press him about various details. It has been an ongoing discussion. We have had a number of extended discussions on the provocation and the Gulf of Tonkin incidents and, also, on the Cuban Missile Crisis.

One thing is true about every movie that I've made, and it's certainly true of *The Fog of War*: there has been an element of caprice, of chance, of happenstance. I set out to do one thing and ended up doing something quite different.

My first interview with Robert McNamara was pre-9/11. It was in May of 2001. It was simply an accident. I don't know how better to describe it. He came on a Tuesday, that Sunday, the *Times* had published an article on Bob Kerrey, his Congressional Medal of Honor and his possible war crimes in Southeast Asia. It had also been the subject of a report on *60 Minutes*. McNamara came into the studio and I started talking to him about that article. It was on my mind, and I believe it was on his mind as well. He vigorously defended Bob Kerrey, saying, "How can you hold him responsible for those things that his superiors did?"

And then I mentioned to him I had read an article by Richard Rhodes about Curtis LeMay that had appeared in the *New Yorker* years ago. In the article LeMay had said, "Our side won, or I would have been tried as a war criminal." He was referring to World War II, the firebombing of Japan, and the use of the two atomic weapons. That was an extraordinary comment on LeMay's part. Very, very early in the interview, within the first twenty minutes, when we had just started to talk about the Lemay quote, McNamara said that he considered himself, as well as LeMay, a possible war criminal with respect to the firebombing of Tokyo and the sixty-six cities that followed. (This, of course, is separate from the nuclear bombing of Hiroshima and Nagasaki which followed the firebombing.)

Q: *Why did you use jump cuts in* The Fog of War?
EM: Well, I have always heavily edited my interviews. The tracks have been cut up, almost as if they were worked over with a Vegematic. Chop, chop, chop, chop. The idea is to clarify what people are saying. McNamara has a way of talking where he endlessly qualifies what he's saying. He says X, and then he stops and he qualifies X, and then he qualifies the qualification, and then often qualifies the qualification of the qualification, and so on in some infinite regress. Not quite infinite, but often confusing, and also long-winded. Of course, it could be argued that it is precisely these extended qualifications that give us a deeper understanding of McNamara's personality. Yet, I think that's there's enough of them left

in the movie to give the general idea. I wanted to hear him talk, but I also wanted the essence of what he was saying. In all of my previous films, I have tried to cover my tracks. I've tried to, no pun intended—although, have you noticed when people say, "no pun intended," a pun is almost always intended? (Laughter) So that may be a lie—but I always try to cover my tracks. I put images over the cuts in the soundtrack, and I hide all of the cuts. In this film, for whatever reason, I liked leaving them raw. But, you know, one man's manipulation is another man's non-manipulation and on and on and on it goes.

I was on *Charlie Rose* with McNamara. It was a sixty-minute program, and McNamara talked for sixty minutes and then he looked at Charlie Rose and said, "You're just going to put this on as it is—you're not going to cut anything! Because I used sixty minutes and the show is sixty minutes and I've timed it out!" (Laughter)

Q: *Could you describe working with Philip Glass?*

EM: Yeah. Working with Philip Glass is very difficult. (Laughter) We've done three movies together: *The Thin Blue Line, A Brief History of Time,* and now *The Fog of War.* I remember complaining to him while we were working on our first movie collaboration, "You know, this music just isn't repetitive enough." And he gave me this very strange look and said, "That's a new one." (Laughter) Somehow we have managed to get along. He keeps working with me, and complaining constantly about me at the same time. In one interview, he called me a "benevolent maniac." Which was kind of nice. Music has been essential to these three movies. I can't imagine them without his music. Recently, someone asked me why I used Philip Glass for *The Fog of War* and I said, quite truthfully, "He does existential dread better than anybody."

One last, brief story. I've always wanted to make a movie about the Utopian community of Zoar, a failed Utopian community in south central Ohio. The Zoars fascinated me, because unlike the Shakers, they really had very little going for them. The architecture was execrable, the food bad, the dress appalling, and not too surprisingly, they and their community became extinct. But I found in an archive in Ohio a record of the last words of the last inhabitant of Zoar. She said, on her deathbed, "Think of it, all those religions. They can't all be right, but they can all be wrong."

Clearing the Fog

LIVIA BLOOM/2003

QUESTIONS OF PERSONAL responsibility and public account-
ability lie at the heart of *The Fog of War*, the latest work from celebrated
documentary filmmaker Errol Morris. In the film, Morris uses his satiric
wit, his multi-lensed Interrotron, and his fascination with morality, intelligence, power, and politics to profile former Secretary of Defense Robert
S. McNamara. (The Interrotron is the "teleprompter/ camera" Morris designed to capture direct eye contact with a subject on film. Etymology:
"terror" plus "interview.")

Once the icon of American corporate and military might, McNamara,
now eighty-six, discusses America's military action and policy during his
career in an effort to finally set the record straight.

The result is layered and complex, deftly revealing the violence, power,
and scope of McNamara's experience. *The Fog of War* exposes shades of
meaning underneath McNamara's words—their implications, subtext,
idiosyncrasy, and their shocking relevance today.

Lesson Plan

LB: *Mr. Morris, I'm delighted to talk to you about your film* The Fog of War.
Can you tell us how you got involved with . . .
EM: Why did you like it? Let *me* ask *you*.

LB: *Why did* I *like it? Well, hmm . . . can I tell you at the end?*
EM: No!

LB: *No? I have to tell you now?*
EM: Yeah. I'm curious. (Laughs)

From *The Independent*, April 2003. Permission granted by Livia Bloom and *The Independent*.

LB: *Okay, okay I'll talk. I thought* Fog of War*'s organization around "Mc-Namara's Eleven Lessons" was appropriate. A more traditional documentary might be structured chronologically but here, inter-titles periodically give numerical "Lessons," which in turn are detailed by footage from McNamara's interviews. For me, it fits the way that McNamara corrects himself throughout the film, saying, "Oh wait, let me go back. . . ." Did you structure the film to suit the often revisionist nature of history?*

EM: The lessons came into the movie very late in the game. In this movie, like every movie that I've done, the deck has been shuffled and reshuffled. McNamara himself at the very beginning of the film says, "Learn the lessons and pass them on." So, as a way of focusing the film, I started to think, "What are the lessons?"

People have complained that the Lesson structure is somehow a simplification of McNamara's ideas and experience. I don't look at it that way at all because I don't think that the lessons in any way summarize the film. They have, if anything, an ironic, absurdist quality that leads you from one step to the other. At Lesson Eleven, you end up with: "You can't change human nature," the lesson that tells you that all the other lessons don't matter. We can't help but repeat what we do no matter what!

LB: *One of McNamara's lessons is: "Never answer the question asked of you, answer the question you wish you had been asked." Did you find it difficult to get him to give you straight answers?*

EM: It's never clear what a "straight answer" might be. Questions and answers are very peculiar. They're often most interesting when the answer actually has nothing whatsoever to do with the question.

LB: *So if he didn't answer, did you look at that from almost an anthropological perspective?*

EM: McNamara is a person who's been interviewed by literally, I would imagine, tens of thousands of journalists over the years, so not everything is original to the film. But I've never really believed in that style of interviewing where you're supposed to coax some kind of answer out of your subject—particularly the answer that someone doesn't want to give. People will tell you interesting things no matter what, if you give them the opportunity to do so. And that was certainly true in this case. I was told many surprising things by McNamara, and as usual, he told me things that I could never have asked questions about, simply because I didn't know enough to ask them.

The firebombing of Japan is a perfect example of McNamara telling me a story that *no one* really knows about. There have been several full-length biographies of him—he has appeared in countless books as a major character, if not the central character. Yet there is no mention in any of those of the firebombing of Japan, or the role he played with General Curtis LeMay both in Europe and in the Marianas. So that was something altogether unexpected and really, really interesting.

Also, it was within five or ten minutes of the beginning of my first interview with him that he said: "Our side won . . . or else we would have been considered war criminals." This is the kind of thing you expect to hear after the twenty hours of interviewing, not the first five minutes— but there it was.

LB: *McNamara says in the film that his earliest memory from the end of World War I is of "a city exploding with joy," and at the same time Woodrow Wilson believed we had "won the war to end all wars." I found that McNamara had told that story, in the same words, in at least seven different places . . .*
EM: Really? You know it's interesting that you researched those lines. I think it's a good thing to do, and an interesting thing to do, and most people don't do that sort of thing.

LB: *Among the times he told that story were two ECAAR (Economists Allied for Arms): Japan symposia. He said the same thing in 1995, and then again in 1998—to the same group of people!*
EM: (Laughs) You know, James and Janet Blyte, who have written two books now with McNamara, actually had the phrase: "It was a city exploding with joy" printed on a cup!

LB: *McNamara has been called "Mr. I Have All the Answers," and he certainly has an amazing understanding of how to draw significant conclusions from statistical data, among other things. How did you prepare yourself to speak his language?*
EM: Well, I tried to do my homework. He told me that I was one of the very, very few people who he had talked to that had actually read his books—and I *had* read them. I researched lots of stuff he talked to me about. On the firebombing of Japan—we actually went to various archives and found his work product from World War II—I think we're actually the first people to look at this stuff in sixty years! We found the actual documents that he wrote advising that the accuracy of the B29s bombing from high altitudes was such that the bombing was ineffective. [These documents led directly to an increase in the "efficiency" of the campaign, i.e. the use of *firebombs* dropped from *lower* altitudes, and had what McNamara considers a "disproportionately devastating" effect on Japan.]

I also was able to give McNamara the transcripts of several telephone conversations between he and Johnson—or even the actual recordings—and ask him: "What was Johnson really saying here? What were you really saying here? What was going on between you two?"

LB: *Had McNamara heard the tapes before?*

EM: A few of them he had accessed with Ladybird's permission while he was in the process of writing the book *In Retrospect*, but most of them he had not heard, and many of them have still not been released by the Lyndon Johnson Library.

LB: *Many Americans, in describing McNamara, mention* In Retrospect *as the place where he admits regret for some of the decisions he made as Secretary of Defense. Why does* The Fog of War *not mention his decision to write* In Retrospect, *or what some see as his "change of heart"?*

EM: Hmm, *that* is a very complex question. I got interested in interviewing McNamara after I read *In Retrospect*, which came out in 1995. I read the book, and it struck me as very strange—it still strikes me as very strange. Then I read reviews of the book, and I remember feeling that almost all of the reviews got it wrong. There was only one review—it was Christopher Lehman-Haupt's in the *New York Times*—which said something to the effect of: "You know, this book really isn't a *mea culpa*." Which it isn't. It was written about endlessly as a *mea culpa*. Instead, Lehman-Haupt said, "This book is far crazier than that." And it is.

A *mea culpa* is: You say, "I did something wrong," "It was my fault," and "I'm sorry." To be a *mea culpa* as I understand it, you have to have all three of these basic ingredients.

But McNamara does not say "I'm sorry"; McNamara does not say, "I did something wrong." Instead, he says, "*The war was wrong.*" And you could call it an evasion . . . I don't even think that that is quite right. I think it's someone really tortured by his own past. As if by going through a detailed recitation of what happened, somehow he could figure it out.

I actually find that more powerful than a *mea culpa*. I once told my son that when you say, "Excuse me" and "I'm sorry," it doesn't give you license to do anything you want. You can cut someone's head off with a battleaxe and then you say, "Excuse me" and "I'm sorry," and supposedly it's okay? I think what [McNamara has] done is far more interesting. *It's not about redemption*. I think it's one of the things that disturbs and infuriates people. It's about trying to understand, what the hell happened? Or, what the hell happened *to me?*

It's very easy, to sort of imagine the David Halberstam view of McNamara: Best and the Brightest, Number-Cruncher, Statistician, Guy Who Couldn't

Relate To People, Devoid of Human Values, Ethical Sensibility, tra-la-la-la-la-la-la-la-la-la. I don't think it's true of McNamara. I think the disturbing thing is that this was a man with real ethical dimension who did something terrible—something that *never* will be redeemed.

I'm not a great believer in redemption. I mean, part of the ugly truth is that you do bad things and they remain bad things forever! No matter what you do.

The Grand Illusion

EM: It goes back to my lessons again. There was an element of my favorite writer, Nabokov, in structuring the film around those lessons—an element of his circularity, of ending up where you started, where Lesson #11 tells you to ignore all the other lessons. And what is his first lesson? Well, it's not enumerated in the film as such, there's not a Lesson #1, but the "city exploding with joy" is McNamara's first memory. It's this memory of people cheering in the streets . . . but the memory is clouded by the memory of a flu epidemic in which millions of people were dying! So you see the people cheering in the streets, wearing these gauze masks. And then, as if that's not enough of a harbinger of things to come, he tells you that it was Wilson's "War to end all wars." The war that ushered in the worst violence in human history! I think that's at the center of the story. If at the end McNamara tells you that he's come back to where he started, that's where he started.

This would be the sad element for me. McNamara started with what Renoir called "The Grand Illusion"—that there ever could be an end to war, that human behavior in some sense is tractable, and can *ever* be ameliorated. A very simple theme: We're fucked.

You know, today, we have the new version. It's not called "The War to End All Wars" anymore, it's called, "Preventive War: The War to Prevent All Wars." A lovely thought, don't you agree?

LB: *Since you ask, I disagree. War may not be inherent to human nature. I believe war occurs when we allow our creativity and ingenuity to fail.*

EM: Really? Hmm. Well, there's always the Three Guineas Approach.

LB: *I'm sorry?*

EM: Blame the men.

History Lessons

JASON ANDERSON/2003

IN HIS NEW DOCUMENTARY *The Fog of War*, Errol Morris sets up his fabled Interrotron recording device in front of his most controversial subject to date. As Secretary of Defense under John F. Kennedy and Lyndon Johnson, Robert S. McNamara was vilified as the architect of the Vietnam War. In the image of McNamara most commonly portrayed in the press—an image that was not much corrected by McNamara's frank 1995 memoir, *In Retrospect*—he was a heartless, arrogant, rationally calculating bureaucrat who bullied Johnson into continuing a war that Kennedy hoped to dismantle, and who had no misgivings over the concept of overkill. After all, he had been a key adviser to General Curtis LeMay during World War II, helping orchestrate the bombing campaigns that ravaged Japan even before Hiroshima and Nagasaki. In one night, American bombs killed 100,000 Tokyo civilians. The war's capacity for carnage was unprecedented.

Yet the horror of those times—and the times that would follow in Southeast Asia—is not lost on McNamara. "LeMay and I behaved as war criminals," he says in one of many revealing comments in the film, which Morris constructed from nearly twenty hours of interviews with McNamara, who had originally agreed only to do two. Besides the odd question from Morris, McNamara is the only speaker in *The Fog of War*, which gives the film a much tighter focus than more free-ranging Morris works like *Gates of Heaven* or *Fast, Cheap and Out of Control*. These conversations are combined with a typically dense and cunningly deployed array of archival material and accompanied by a requisite score from Morris's long-time collaborator Philip Glass. (Or, rather, most of a score—Glass hadn't finished it in time for the film's Cannes premiere, so Morris filled out the soundtrack with familiar stretches of Glass's music for *The Thin Blue Line*.)

From *Cinema Scope*, Summer 2003. Reprinted with permission by Jason Anderson.

Constructed as a series of eleven lessons abstracted from McNamara's life—e.g., "Rationality will not save us," "Belief and seeing are both often wrong," "Never answer the question that is asked of you"—Morris's film is not a history of the Cold War and Vietnam, or a biography of McNamara, or a defense of a man whose actions were long regarded as indefensible, even if it is all of those things at times. Instead, *The Fog of War* is a masterful survey of several decades' worth of American politics as seen through the eyes of a pivotal figure, one who turns out to be forthright and unusually forthcoming. Whether or not you are inclined to take McNamara's statements at face value—after a while, even his most ardent denials start to feel like admissions, at least of his feelings if not the facts—it's hard to deny that the film is anything less than a richly detailed and fair-minded portrait.

"A lot of people think I'm a son of a bitch," says McNamara near the end of the film. And he doesn't say that those people aren't right. But in his view, he acted according to the wishes of his bosses and the information at hand—information which, in the cases of the Cuban Missile Crisis and the Gulf of Tonkin incident that refuelled the Johnson administration's commitment to war, was highly spurious or flat-out wrong. The film also incorporates startling evidence that supports McNamara's version of events: in two newly released White House phone conversations, McNamara counsels his first president to remove military advisers from Vietnam, and then listens to his second president tell him they'll do nothing of the sort.

As Morris notes during a conversation at Cannes—where the film debuted out of competition—parallels between the political climate described by McNamara and the current situation are so clear, the film does not need to emphasize them. For one thing, the McNamara phrase that serves as the title of the film quickly became a piece of lingua franca in coverage of the latest Gulf War. But in McNamara's estimation, the impossibility of being able to clearly assess one's actions during wartime does not excuse oneself from being responsible for those decisions after historians have determined the body count. Ultimately, *The Fog of War* depicts him as a man who, years after finding himself in a pivotal and unenviable position during some of the most volatile years in American history, continues to wrestle with his conscience: he's yet to find his way out of the fog.

JA: *Robert S. McNamara is one of the most vilified figures in American history—was this film at all an attempt to rehabilitate him?*

EM: No. This was not an attempt to create a new version of the Robert

McNamara story. It's not why I made the movie. But in the course of making the movie, and much to my surprise, I started to think very different things about him. That was in part based on my interviews with him and in part based on what I would call new evidence, evidence that was unknown until very, very recently. Those are the White House tapes. This material is still being released—it was being released as the movie was being made. It's really quite remarkable. When the Johnson library released bits and pieces of it, it has been transcribed in part by Michael Beschloss and published in a series of books. But if you choose—and, of course, I did choose—you can get the actual tape recordings from the Johnson library. And now they've released 1963, 1964, 1965, and a very little bit of 1966.

One thing I like to emphasize, and I don't know if this is me talking to the McNamara of recent years as opposed to the McNamara of the sixties, is that there's a story that everyone knows, or thinks they know about McNamara. It's if you like the perceived view about McNamara, the King James version of McNamara—the Best and the Brightest, the number cruncher, the statistician, the logic guy, who somehow was devoid of ethical and moral sensibility, and then belatedly came to the view that the war was wrong, and then cried alligator tears, "Boo hoo, I've seen the error of my ways, I'm so terribly sorry." It's the perceived view, the only problem I have with it is I don't think it's right. I think it's wrong.

JA: *What do these White House tapes reveal?*
EM: I recently watched John Frankenheimer's last film, *Path to War*, in which Alec Baldwin plays Robert S. McNamara. I didn't care for the film for many, many reasons, but what was interesting to me was that this was a film that purports to tell you the "inside story," and yet it rehashes that same view of the events leading up to the escalation of the war in the same way we have heard again and again and again. And what is the version? The version is that an indecisive Johnson was pressured by a bellicose McNamara to escalate the war in Vietnam. McNamara was the chief architect of the war—if you like, the author of the war in Vietnam.

Well, there are two very powerful conversations on the tapes, one from Kennedy and one from Johnson. One conversation has McNamara urging Kennedy to remove advisers from Vietnam—he's just returned from Vietnam, and he tells Kennedy, who is reluctant, "We need to find a way to get out of Vietnam and this is a way of doing it," this being pulling advisers out of South Vietnam. Then President Diem is assassinated and Kennedy is assassinated, and we hear Johnson in the Oval Office, talking to McNamara on the phone, saying, "I sat silently while you and the president"—he's still calling him the president—"spoke about taking advisers out of Vietnam. How in the hell do you think you're gonna win a war by pulling advisers out?" This is not the HBO version, this is not the received version of McNamara that I have read about in countless different places.

JA: *Wasn't this material also in McNamara's book?*

EM: Yes. However, there is more stuff in the movie than in the book, and there's a big difference between having McNamara tell you, "I told Kennedy such and such, I told Johnson such and such," and hearing the conversation itself. It's a powerful difference. It connects you to history in some very, very real sense.

JA: *Could you talk about how this project came about and what the extent of McNamara's involvement with the final cut would be?*

EM: I told him from early on that I couldn't make the movie without him—I didn't plan to interview other people. I'm not sure if the project began when I was demonstrating about the Vietnam War forty years ago, but it probably began when I read *In Retrospect.* I found it to be a very strange book; in many ways a crazy book, a tortured book. And from that point on, I always wanted to do something.

JA: *How did the film come about? Did you approach him?*

EM: Yes, I approached him. I've only been approached by really one person that I can think of. Jack Kervorkian. Kervorkian and his lawyer called me and I was told that I was Kervorkian's favourite filmmaker. And this was actually well before *Mr. Death.*

JA: *Did McNamara know your work?*

EM: I'm not sure McNamara has gone to more than two or three movies his entire life.

JA: *What does that tell you about him?*

EM: Not an avid cinephile.

JA: *Why did he trust you not to chop him up into little pieces on the big screen?*

EM: I'm not sure he did trust me. He had just published his third book—*Wilson's Ghost*—and he had been on a speaking tour, speaking around the country about the book, and part of me thinks that this was just another thing to do as part of promoting the book.

JA: *Was there much talk of ground rules before the interviews began?*

EM: It's pretty clear without ever setting ground rules that there are things McNamara doesn't really want to talk about. He doesn't want to talk about his family, although he did talk about his family. He obviously does not like talking about Vietnam and yet he talked extensively about Vietnam, though maybe not about everything I'd have liked him to talk about. But take, for example, the Gulf of Tonkin incidents in 1964: he talked at enormous length about these two attacks and the resolution that followed, and about the mistakes that were made at the time. So a lot of things that ostensibly he refused to talk about, he did talk about. There is also a lot of "I don't want to talk about that," "I said I wasn't gonna talk about that," "I'm not gonna say anything farther," so on and so forth. I put some of that at the end of the movie—if I included it all, that would be an hour-long movie in and of itself.

JA: *Do you think McNamara regarded this as a chance to make a confession?*
EM: I dislike the word "confession" because it already loads the gun against him. It's saying that he's somehow guilty of a crime. He is unique, at least unusual among major American political figures from that time, to actually attempt to delve into what he'd done, what it means, why he did it. It's not true of the Bundys, the Rusks . . . but it is very much true of him. When McNamara published *In Retrospect*, Howell Raines wrote an editorial in the *New York Times* entitled "McNamara's War." And at that time, people were fond of referring to McNamara's "confession" in *In Retrospect*. To people who didn't read the book, there was this feeling that somehow here is a man who knows he is a criminal and is now revealing that fact to us. This was supposedly the nature of the book he wrote. It was not. There's a difference between a man desperately trying to assess his past and confessing to a crime. Having said that, does McNamara feel guilty? My two cents' worth of opinion is yes.

JA: *In the film, McNamara is quite emotional when he refers to rumours of a breakdown that he suffered during his tenure with Johnson. What do you make of his denial?*
EM: I have my own theory of language which applies in this instance. Language came into existence to allow people to lie more effectively. For example, when someone says something like, "People say I almost had a nervous breakdown and that wasn't true," the fact that he's saying it is a suggestion that in fact he did.

There's another very strong moment for me in the movie. I ask people about this, and it seems that people do take this away from this moment. It's when McNamara breaks down upon receiving the Medal of Freedom. In the ceremony he's unable to speak, overcome by emotion. Then he says what he would have said about Johnson. He says, "I know what you're thinking, you're thinking that this man was duplicitous, you're thinking that he withheld things, you're thinking that he wasn't always honest." Well, I think that, in part, McNamara is speaking of himself. It's a very, very powerful moment.

JA: *What could a man of his age be thinking about when agreeing to be part of a film like this?*

EM: The same that a man of any age could be thinking about: his sense of self-esteem, of self-worth. He would be exposing himself to someone he doesn't know while still knowing that there's a public out there predisposed to dislike him—not everybody, but a lot of people. Has McNamara ever been the subject of attempts on his life? Yes. Has he found himself in violent demonstrations against him? Yes. Has he been accosted at various events by Vietnam vets who want to go after him either physically or verbally or both? Yes. So the fact of his age to me is not entirely relevant. Two days before he was to come to Boston to make the film, he calls me and says, "I don't know what I was thinking, I shouldn't be doing this, this makes no sense. People are telling me this makes no sense. I can't do this." And then, at the end, he said, "You know, I said I would do it, so I'm doing it." After this litany—and I mean litany—of reasons why he shouldn't be doing it, he agreed to do it.

JA: *What factors compelled you to structure the film according to his eleven lessons? Obviously, you don't see the film as an autobiography or biography.*

EM: I think it's a number of things. In part, the film is this very odd primer. He talks about lessons at the very beginning of the movie. I should point out that we had one disagreement prior to my coming to Cannes, and that was about the lessons. The lessons were put in by me very late in the game. They were in the last versions of the movie. I put them in for a whole number of reasons, and people criticized them for a whole number of reasons. Does it reduce the movie in some way to a set of lessons? I think not. Do people look at the lessons at complete face value or do they reflect on them and how they relate to the other lessons? I hope yes.

What McNamara said is, "These are not my lessons in the sense that if I were to choose ten, eleven, or twelve lessons to pass on to posterity, I wouldn't choose these lessons. I would have my own list. Maybe there would be some of these lessons on my list as well, but I would have a different list. So I don't like these being called my lessons." So, for what it's worth, I changed my subtitle from "The Eleven Lessons of Robert S. McNamara" to "Eleven Lessons from the Life of Robert S. McNamara."

And I told him that if anyone asks—in fact, I'm doing it even though no one has asked—I would say, "Okay, these are strictly speaking not the lessons that Robert McNamara would have chosen. These are my lessons, but I would remind everyone they are still abstracted from things that McNamara said."

JA: *What else has he said about the film?*

EM: He, of course, wishes there was a lot more material in the film about the World Bank and the various roles he played there. [McNamara was president of the World Bank from 1968 to 1981.] He is aware that the World Bank has itself become controversial in its own right, but there are things that McNamara can point to in his tenure at the bank which do strongly inure to his credit. That's why there's that title at the end of the film. He didn't ask me to put that in, by the way; I put it in.

There are so many things that could have been put in the movie. A major thing for me—let alone him—was that he was instrumental in creating the Nuclear Test Ban Treaty and has actively worked to promote various forms of nuclear disarmament, including the ABM treaties. McNamara's argument against ABMs has always been very, very clear and it's a very simple argument. An anti-missile missile is what? A missile. And if you build a bigger anti-missile missile—that is, a missile—then what will the other side do? They will in turn build an even bigger missile, forcing us to build an even bigger anti-missile missile, which is also a missile. And so on and so forth, ad infinitum. Perhaps that isn't ad infinitum—it's really until we blow ourselves to kingdom come. So he's always been clear. And one of the truly wonderful things our new administration has done is scuttle the ABM treaty and to restart the arms race. And we shouldn't forget that the reason that we have the Pentagon Papers is because of Bob McNamara. McNamara asked for them to be collected, written, and we would not have that account if not for him.

JA: *How much did you and he talk of the current political situation?*

EM: We actually talked quite a bit about it. I didn't want to make a movie that was about it because I felt I had made a movie that was about the current situation nevertheless. It was unnecessary to cross all those 't's and dot all of those 'i's. I think its relevance to the current situation is pretty damn clear.

JA: *If you could elaborate a bit: the film seems to make distinct connection between the warmongering of the Johnson administration and similar behaviour in the Bush.*

EM: Well, yes. I often think that when the framers put together our particular brand of democracy, they had no idea about nuclear weapons. When they imagined the set of checks and balances between the legislative, executive, and judicial branches of government, no one imagined that one man in the executive branch of government could press a button and destroy the world. It wasn't part of their calculations, and how could it be?

One thing to me that's clear is that in the post–World War II period, it's not just that we can destroy the world, it's that this capacity to destroy the world has distorted everything. The executive branch of government is no longer one of three equal branches as the framers intended. It's something distorted way out of shape. And more to the point, it's not the entire executive branch that's changed, but the apex. I often think what a difference two or three years can make, but think of the differences that occurred when Kennedy was assassinated. For people who love conspiracy theories, they can point to this thing, that thing, and the other thing, but the truth of the matter—speaking as someone who is a great disbeliever in conspiracy theories—is that the death of one man changed everything. What happens when you have a president who wants to wage war? What the hell do you do?

It Could All Be Wrong: An Unfinished Interview with Errol Morris

PAUL CRONIN/2003

PC: *Tell me about the Interrotron. It seems surprising no one ever thought of the idea before.*

EM: Yes. Odd. I used it for the first time in 1992—on Fred Leuchter—and can find little evidence that anyone used it before then. Puzzling. Because it seems obvious. But as I like to point out, nothing is so obvious that it's obvious.

PC: *Okay. But what was your underlying motivation?*

EM: I've always been suspicious of *cinéma-vérité*, the fly on the wall school of documentary filmmaking where supposedly you're not interacting with things, you're just observing and recording them. The observer is hidden. I want to bring the observer stage-center.

Almost all interviews are filmed *vérité* style with a camera, an interviewer, and subject. You have a triangle where the camera takes the role of an observer, even voyeur. The camera is the third person observing two people talking. It's off to the side, and even though I'm looking into your eyes and you're looking into mine, this eye contact is something that the camera, sitting some feet from us both, doesn't capture. This means that the audience isn't really part of the conversation. They are merely observing it.

But our heads are wired up in a way that means eye contact is very important. It's really an essential part of our interactions with other people. Everyone recognizes the power of this connection when it happens, and

---

This interview, conducted between 2003 and 2006 in Errol Morris's office in Cambridge, Massachusetts, is previously unpublished. Morris has called this piece "the best interview that has been done with me." Reprinted by permission of Paul Cronin.

I'd always looked for ways to close up that triangle. When I made *Gates of Heaven*, I tried to simulate eye/camera contact with the people I was filming to the point where I would press my head against the side of the camera to narrow the parallax so it looked like they were looking into the camera, even though they were actually looking slightly to one side. Sometimes my hair would flop into shot. Sometimes my cameraman would grab my head and pull it out of shot. And sometimes that hurt. I avoided close-ups because the eye-lines would have given the game away. But I always knew this wasn't *real* first person filmmaking. Today I call it *faux* first person. So I had this crazy idea: what if the interviewer and the camera could become one and the same? What if I could *become* my camera?

And so, using a system of mirrors and video images, I created a way in which people can look into my eyes *and* directly into the camera at the same time. My invention is called the Interrotron—patent pending—the name of which comes from my wife, and is a combination of "interview" and "terror." I use a modified teleprompter that conveys video images instead of text. Teleprompters are used when someone needs to read text and look into the camera at the same time. The copy is placed on a half-silvered mirror in front of the lens. But a newscaster looking into the camera is not looking at anyone—he's simply looking into a dead lens—and it's a relationship only between a person and a machine. I took two of these contraptions and set them up in a studio. The idea was to wire the image from one prompter, camera A, which is filming my subject, and play it through the camera B prompter, and vice versa. The subject sits in front of one Interrotron and I sit in front of the other, which means we're both talking to live television images. We could be in separate rooms, or even on separate planets. The Interrotron gives me the ability to interview someone one-on-one, but watching the video image of me on the half-silvered mirror on front of the camera lens means that the interview subject can also make direct eye contact with the viewer. Of course interviewing this way means there is also a recording of me listening, or at least me looking like I'm listening. Seeing myself on screen like that for the first time I remember thinking, "How could anybody talk looking at this person?" But thankfully they do. With the Interrotron, I become one with the camera, and it's no longer a *cinéma-vérité* moment.

My production designer, Ted Bafaloukos, said to me, "The beauty of this thing is that it allows people to do what they do best: watch television." But the people being interviewed aren't watching regular TV. They're watching a TV set that really cares and wants to know more.

PC: *You're sure it's not just a gimmick?*

EM: It's something of a gimmick, but a gimmick with genuine metaphysical content. If you just sit someone down and ask them to talk to the camera for hours at a time, they won't do it. You need someone sitting in front of them who they can interact with, even though there's not anyone physically there. In fact, it's even better that someone is not right next to them. The Interrotron plays on the idea that you can say things on the phone that you would never ever in a million years say to someone sitting directly across from you. In effect, greater distance means greater intimacy.

PC: *And what about the Megatron?*

EM: Well, that's the *real* gimmick. I was very much interested in the possibility of shooting an interview with multiple cameras and all the possibilities of combining the images. Think of the Megatron as a supercharged Interrotron with twenty cameras all at different angles, though most aren't behind the mirror. As with the Interrotron, a really interesting editing style becomes possible. It means there is huge variety of closeups and medium shots. There really are so many potential stylistic possibilities. In theory there's no limit to the number of cameras that can be used. It gave me something like the compound eye of a bee.

PC: *How often have you used the Megatron?*

EM: I used it for a few of the *First Person* shows, but basically abandoned it in favor of the Interrotron. I never had a chance to experiment with the Megatron as much as I'd like to. One reason was that I don't like the look of digital video, and the cameras on the Megatron were all DV. And I don't like thirty-frame interlaced DV. Maybe I just never figured out the best way to use it, but I don't think I would ever shoot an interview again in DV. The interview for *The Fog of War* was shot on twenty-four-frame Hi-Definition, and I thought the HD cassette that we digitally projected at Cannes looked really good, better than a film print.

PC: *How have your interviewees reacted to the Interrotron over the years?*

EM: Fred Leuchter loved it, but Robert McNamara, who has done thousands of interviews over the years, took one look at the contraption and said, "What is this?" I told him it was my interviewing machine. He looked at me and said, "Whatever it is I don't like it." But he sat down and we started talking. He got used to it pretty quickly.

PC: *Has video changed the way you shoot interviews?*

EM: Absolutely. Back in the old days I called myself the Eleven-Minute Psychiatrist because I was shooting with eleven-minute magazines. At

the pragmatic level there's a big difference between shooting an interview in units of eleven minutes and being able to shoot for an hour and
forty minutes in one go and then be able to switch tapes in only a few
seconds. These days I often have two decks running, which means I don't
even have to switch tapes. My subjects can just talk and talk. We never
have to stop. Not having to interrupt an interview really makes a big difference, not least in McNamara's case because I always was afraid he was
going to get up and leave. I figured that the fewer opportunities I gave
him to do that, the better off I was.

PC: *Doesn't having so much material cause problems during editing?*
EM: More is more. Generally I shoot for as long as possible. It really depends on how much time the interviewee can give me. There doesn't
seem to be any benefit to shooting less. Why stop if someone's saying
something interesting? My interviews regularly run five or six hours. I remember shooting an interview with Rick Rosner for *First Person*, the episode *One in a Million Trillion*, which went on for something like eleven
or twelve hours. It was insane. I think we were both hallucinating by the
end of it. It would be great to get someone to talk non-stop for twenty-
four hours.

PC: *Your editor Karen Schmeer told me that often during interviews you'll
have some sitting next to you suggesting certain things, reminding you of certain things.*
EM: Yes, sometimes Karen and a researcher will be sitting with me. You
often hear this notion that editors shouldn't be on set because it can
cloud their ability to look at the material "objectively." But I don't agree.

PC: *Presumably the possibilities afforded by editing systems like Avid are
a factor?*
EM: Absolutely. With the Avid, just by pushing a single key, there's a
way to cycle through all twenty cameras, one after the other. If you had
twenty cameras with independent time-code and you had to go through
the material separately in order to find it and cut it in, it wouldn't really
be feasible. Having to do it that way wouldn't be of interest to me. Today, the fact that it would be financially possible to hook up twenty HD
cameras to the Megatron, combined with the remarkable potential of
the editing system I use, make it something worth exploring in more
detail.

PC: *Do you think you would ever go back to film?*
EM: I never left film. Given the opportunity I would go back to everything. I like all media. Why does it have to be A rather than B, or B rather

than C? Why not A, B *and* C? There's this idea that the future erases the past. In some instances it does, but what usually happens is that you end up with all these layers. It's not as if LPs don't exist any longer. Some people love and collect them, and people will collect CDs long after CDs go out of existence. My guess is that unless the companies stop making film altogether, and there is actually no way to shoot film, someone will always want to use it, experiment with it. People will always be intrigued by the various technologies from the past because there's a specific look or sound you get with them. Maybe that look or sound can be replicated digitally, but there's still something appealing about going back to the original.

PC: *Did you shoot the short film that opened the 2002 Oscar ceremony on the Interrotron?*
EM: Yes, over five days in Boston, San Francisco, New York, and the White House. I had more than twenty-four hours of footage which was reduced to four minutes and fifteen seconds. I'd really like to do something more in that vein, perhaps a whole movie. I know there's life in the thing beyond the Academy Awards. Some of the material has ended up on my website. Donald Trump talking about *Citizen Kane*, for example. Isn't it possible that in an alternative universe, Donald Trump actually starred in *Citizen Kane?*

PC: *Your work as a TV commercial director is something that seems to take up more time these days than your features do.*
EM: I started doing commercials shortly after *The Thin Blue Line*. Clearly someone thought that with my passion for justice and my interest in re-enactments I could effectively sell things to people. Often I see little difference between advertising and anything else. Branding isn't just part of commercials, it's part of how we see the world. It's all just an effort to "sell" someone on an idea, on a conception of reality. Commercials are films, albeit little films. My job is to create something compelling in the time available, whether it's two hours or thirty seconds. Think of commercials as American haiku.

PC: *Do you come up with the concept of a campaign yourself or do you have to follow ideas laid down by the advertising executives?*
EM: It all depends. I'm a director for hire. Advertising agencies sometimes ask me to come up with an idea and sometimes they have their own ideas. Sometimes I have real input in a campaign, other times I am given no input whatsoever, though generally I try to avoid jobs like that.

PC: *You have done political advertising.*
EM: Politics is too important to be left to politicians. The same could be said about political advertising. My producer Julie Ahlberg and I tried for months to provide advertising for the Democrats, for John Kerry, but in the end no one was really interested in doing much of anything. Or, if they were, no one could make decisions. The two of us were on a conference call with the Democrats and I muted the phone, and told her: "They're going to lose." No one could agree on anything, even to disagree. It was hopeless.

PC: *You clearly take a great deal of pride in your work, so presumably when you take on a campaign you always want to see it through to the end?*
EM: I prefer to edit material myself. Sometimes I get involved in ways that are unnecessary and even counterproductive, at least on a business level. But I actually think it's appalling that many commercial directors don't edit their own work. I would have a hard time working that way. A director who doesn't edit what he shoots isn't really a director.

PC: *Would you be able to make your features without the revenue generated by your work as a commercial director?*
EM: No. My films wouldn't be possible without the commercials. Often I've been able to shoot segments of my features on the back end of commercials. In *The Fog of War* there are scenes we filmed in Shanghai and Tokyo. I didn't take a crew over to those places specifically to get those shots. We were there shooting a commercial and at the end of the working day spent a time collecting material for the McNamara film. Commercials have given me a certain freedom that I would otherwise not have. I'm not constrained to make money from my movies because my primary income comes from my commercial work. I like the idea of what I do being an experimental form of filmmaking, that every time I do it I can redefine and re-examine what I do. I can rethink the underlying assumptions and premises, and try different things, all because I know I've got the commercials to fall back on.

PC: *Presumably working with such big budgets on commercials has been useful.*
EM: Sure. I usually have an awful lot of money at my disposal. I like the opportunity to experiment with all this equipment and cinematic toys. I've gained a lot of experience in this way. Plus the time commitment is much less. Compare producing an advertising campaign over three weeks to a feature project that can take two or more years.

PC: *Many of your commercials feature real people, not actors.*

EM: Yes and no. I use actors all the time in my commercials. When I started working on ads, people wanted me to do reenactments because of what they had seen in *The Thin Blue Line*. None of my commercials had interviews in them, that came after 9/11 when I was hired to shoot a campaign for United Airlines, a series of scripted ads to be shot at O'Hare airport. We were scouting various locations when Bush announced the invasion of Afghanistan. It meant that overnight we lost our permission to shoot at the airport. The whole job was going to be cancelled but because they had to pay us anyway, I told them I would take some employees of the airline into a studio and shoot something. So we did a series of real-people ads, and from that point on I've been asked to do more and more.

PC: *This leads us to your thoughts about the role of truth in documentaries versus feature film. Isn't the key difference that documentaries have to be true?*

EM: Are you kidding? Of course not. Who came up with such a preposterous idea? *Cinéma-vérité* clearly carries some kind of preposterous epistemological claim. The very name suggests some kind of truthful document. The idea is that you follow the stylistic rules and out pops truth. But style most certainly does not guarantee truth.

PC: *Your interviews appear to be quite investigative.*

EM: Yes. I never know what to expect or what I am going to hear. The same goes when the tables are turned and I am being interviewed. There is one thing I can predict, however. I always know an interview is going to be bad if the interviewer shows up with a list of questions and ticks them off one by one.

PC: *Is this interview going to be bad?*

EM: We'll have to wait and see.

PC: *It's not bad so far, though that stuff about United Airlines was pretty boring.*

EM: My apologies.

PC: *You would agree that interviews are essential to how you make films?*

EM: Yes. It's part of what makes my documentaries documentaries. It's that element of reality. The interviews are investigative and unscripted. My intention in the interview process is always to get a monologue on film that I use to create a story told in the first person. I edit this material into a kind of script and then create visuals to go with it. This seems, to me at least, to be very different from how most documentaries are constructed.

PC: *Many writers have commented about your interviewing technique.*
EM: My wife has said that I can be a real nag sometimes. Maybe that makes me a good interviewer. But there really aren't many rules to follow here. I just try not to be a threatening interviewer. I allow people to go all over the place, I don't rein them in. They're not being interviewed as such, I'm just allowing them to talk about themselves. And never go in with a fixed agenda because otherwise you learn nothing. It's always better to let the interview take whatever direction it takes, however surprising. In fact, the more surprising an interview the more interesting it usually turns out to be. Most of the time I don't know what questions I'm going to ask. I try not to bring in a preconceived plan. I'm not out to judge, I'm there to listen to what these people have to say. I truly believe my role in such situations is not to editorialize about my own feelings.

I was interviewing people long before I started working with cameras and my goal was always to say absolutely nothing. I would put my tape recorder on the table and hope that the person would just start talking. The game was to keep them talking as long as possible and not interrupt, no matter what. Because of this, a prerequisite of appearing in my films is an ability to talk at length. Extended monologues is what I like, not some kind of cross-examination. But I do try to encourage them to continue talking in such a way that my voice doesn't appear on the recording. I have one tape that I'm especially proud of that goes on for three hours where you don't hear me speak once. Basically, I'm a member of the Shut Up and Listen school of investigation. I might use only twenty or thirty seconds of an interview fragment that's ten minutes long, but the feeling you get is that people are talking not in response to some specific question that's hanging off-screen, but that they're talking at length. I like to think this is an essential part of the style of my movies.

Probably the best example of this is Emily Miller, the platinum blonde from *The Thin Blue Line*. Remember that Randall Adams was sentenced to death because of various eyewitness testimonies, including Miller's. She got on the stand and uttered that famous line—you've heard it in countless Perry Mason episodes—"That's the man! That's him!" So the jury hands down a guilty verdict and Adams is sentenced to death. During my interview with her, Miller completely forgot that at the capital murder trial she testified that she had picked Randall Adams out from a police lineup. I never asked her a specific question, but all of a sudden she started to explain why she had failed to pick Adams from the lineup. She went on about how he'd changed his physical appearance, his hair was different, about how he was looking at her in a funny way. I was really puzzled, so I said, "How do you know you failed to pick him out of a police lineup?" She said, "Because the policeman sitting next to me told me I had picked out the wrong person, and then pointed out the right person so I wouldn't make that mistake again." How can you not love that kind of thing? She had forgotten she had testified the exact opposite during the trial. It was essentially an admission of perjury. The point is that I would never have been smart enough to ask her about this. If I had been more adversarial with her—and the same goes with Fred Leuchter and Robert McNamara—I wouldn't have uncovered such interesting stuff. In fact, in McNamara's case he would have just walked out on me.

PC: *Is it true you don't even listen to what your interviewees are saying to you?*
EM: No. I listen, but I try to look like I am not listening. When you look like you are listening to another person there's a tendency to react to what you're hearing. You might twitch or look away, at which point the other person becomes aware of these reactions and in turn feels the need to ask you what you're thinking and interrupt themselves.

I devote myself to encouraging my interviewee not to stop. I'm aided and abetted in this enterprise by the fact that people really do want to tell you their story. If you let people talk without interruption, pretty quickly they'll show you who they really are. I figure people are going to say pretty much the same thing no matter what I ask them. Sure, I can prod them in certain directions, but many people have stories that will appear regardless of the questions thrown at them. In fact in *The Fog of War* McNamara even says, "Never answer the question that is asked of you. Answer the question that you wish had been asked of you." Just after McNamara said this, I asked him, "Are you doing that to me?" He just smiled.

A good interview needn't be a tug of war. I like confrontation as much as the next person, but it's not what I'm about as a filmmaker. I don't set out to impugn the character of whomever I'm talking to or to trap them in contradiction.

PC: *That sets you apart from many documentarians, at least of the journalistic style. Does your work connect with the history of documentary filmmaking, at least in your own mind?*

EM: Recently, for the first time, I watched several films by Robert Flaherty which I found extraordinarily beautiful. What surprised me is that his work—considered to be some of the first "documentaries" ever made—is highly stylized. As we all know, the igloo scene in *Nanook of the North* was achieved by using a cutaway igloo so the camera crew could get specific shots. This all goes to the whole idea of reenactments and staging and faking things. Even then Flaherty was telling us that there isn't a single way to apprehend reality, that it's not just a case of casting the net out and bringing the captured reality back into the boat. I looked at the DVD extras on *Nanook* and what's really surprising is the series of photos Flaherty took of Eskimos. What's interesting is that he divided them into two categories: looking into the camera and not looking into the camera, posed and unposed. The rule in narrative film is: Don't Look at the Camera, don't break that line. In documentaries we have people inhabiting a world of their own, and the same rule applies. In both cases, we're recording these performances. It's interesting to me that Flaherty was aware of these two categories. To my mind, all these things address the deep question about the relationship between our consciousness and the world, and our relationship between photography and the world and how it's mediated by our consciousness.

PC: *Are there documentary filmmakers who have influenced you?*
EM: Of course. Herzog, Wiseman. Hara's portrait of Kenzo Okuzaki in *The Emperor's Naked Army Marches On*. Flaherty for his own brand of whacked-out romanticism. Vertov's *Man with a Movie Camera* and *Kino-Pravda*. The reverse slaughterhouse scene is as good as it gets. And, of course, neorealism. Everything by Bresson. Look at Werner Herzog's films which straddle the line between drama and documentary, perhaps hopelessly blurring the distinction altogether. He's made "documentary" fictions and fictions that are hopelessly documentary in character. He's a neorealist expressionist. Bruno S is an actor in *Stroszek* and *Every Man for Himself* much like Nadine Nortier is an actor in *Mouchette*. *Aguirre* can be thought of as a documentary film of Herzog and Kinski's excellent adventure in the Amazon jungle.

PC: *You often claim that the differences between documentary and fiction are faint.*
EM: Of course. There are more similarities than dissimilarities. We expect, for example, documentaries to have stories in the same way we expect fiction films to have stories. Every piece of film contains elements of both fact and fiction. What I like to do is draw people's attention to the

fact that the line between fiction and nonfiction—between documentary and dramatic films—is somewhat more illusory than we'd like to think. For someone like Fred Wiseman, this line is probably in a very different place than it is for me. Some nonfiction films, mine for example, are highly controlled, while some fiction films, like *The Battle of Algiers*, have very strong elements of *cinéma-vérité*. Where does the real world end and fiction begin? Is an Astaire and Rogers film a documentary of them dancing or is something more than that? I've always been fascinated by the idea of the world a filmmaker creates and its relationship to the real world out there, this notion of making a documentary that doesn't contain a single "real" image. I like to think that a film like *Gates of Heaven* treads a path between reality and fantasy. And look at *A Brief History of Time*, where all the interviews were actually filmed on studio sets constructed to look precisely like actual rooms and offices.

When we talk about the differences between fiction and nonfiction filmmaking and photography, what we're really talking about is control and lack of control. With fiction we imagine everything being tightly controlled: the actors are told where to stand, told what to say, they are lit and framed in a very conscious way. With nonfiction, however, things just unfold with—so the theory goes—the filmmaker merely observing and not interfering in any way. In one sense my films are documentaries simply because the people in them are not reading from a script. But what makes the medium of film interesting is this interplay between the controlled and the uncontrolled, something I like to draw attention to, for example by being so precise about framing the shots.

But I really have no idea what the people I'm interviewing are going to say to me, and I take pride in the fact that I don't tell people what to say. I like to think I'm receptive to everything and anything. I might write out a list of questions but then make no use of them during the interview. It's just a way of preparing myself, doing my homework. Perhaps because of this people often say surprising things of their own volition. But once the interview is over, everything's up for grabs. By the time I get into the editing room I've created a series of uncontrolled moments on film, instances of pure spontaneity where the "real" world creeps in. I have spent literally years cutting a series of interviews into little pieces and reassembling them, even if the hope is that the end result still contains an overriding element of reality and spontaneity.

With *The Thin Blue Line* I wanted to do a nonfiction film as something like a piece of art rather than a piece of journalism, and in this sense the film tells its story in a very dreamlike way. The audience is meant to wonder what's true and what's not. I couldn't imagine telling that story as a narrative film, mainly because it would mean everything would be spelled out for the audience. Some true stories work well told by real people, others are best when fictionalized. With *In Cold Blood*, Capote was trying to call attention to the tension between reporting and art-making, between trying to portray a real story and at the same time try-ing to produce something carefully crafted and, above all, personal. I've always wanted to have my cake and eat it too, to make a well-crafted film that's aesthetically interesting and entertaining, and at the same time tackles various concerns of mine and might even produce some kind of social benefit.

PC: *Such an approach seems to irritate some people.*

EM: I'm often told that I am debasing the notion of documentary. But think about it: the so-called blurring of the line between fiction and non-fiction doesn't mean we're denying or manipulating the truth. What it does is make us think about truth and our relationship to the world out there.

PC: *You say that every image contains elements of both the controlled and the uncontrolled. Can we ever know where the line between fiction and non-fiction lies just by looking at an image?*

EM: No. I've been reading Sontag's book *On Regarding the Pain of Others* that was published a few years ago. She writes about photographs that are posed versus photographs—or so the argument goes—that record something that "just happened" in front of the lens of the camera. She says that when we talk about a fake painting, usually what we're talking about is a picture by Rembrandt or Vermeer which is actually painted by somebody else. It suggests intentional fraud, that somebody painted it with the expectation that audiences would be fooled into thinking it was an original by one of the old masters. Sontag says that when we talk about a "fake" photograph, we're talking about something completely different, about a photograph that has been posed, and she cites various well-known examples. My own view is that the posed/unposed distinc-tion may be a little harder to define than she imagines and may even be spurious.

There are many unanswered, deep metaphysical questions about how the world works. One is whether it's controlled or chaotic. Is the universe completely determined and ordered? Look at the so-called *auteur* theory of filmmaking, this idea that a film is completely under the control of one person. Some people complain about the idea by saying, "Sure, there's a director in charge, but there's also a production designer, a director of photography, a casting director, a bunch of actors, and a host of other people involved in a film." Of course they're right: everyone knows that the director as the all-knowable controlling force on a film is something that never happens in the real world. There's never a situation where absolutely everything is controlled because despite our best efforts, certain kinds of happenstance always sneak in.

So what's the opposite pole to this notion of attempting to control absolutely everything? It's our old friend *cinéma-vérité*, which tells us that nothing has been orchestrated or controlled or authored, that the director is merely observing and not influencing what's happening in front of the camera. Everything you see apparently happened completely independently of the filmmakers. Of course, as soon as you put down the camera in one position rather than another, you've made a decision about framing, content, and a myriad of other things. The idea of the spectator as the fly on the wall who observes but doesn't influence reality is something of an idealization.

For what it's worth, here's my argument. It seems to me that in every single instance of both filmmaking and still photography, there are instances of both the controlled and uncontrolled. How we look at an image and how we think about it is contingent, I believe, on how we think it was produced. Yet often we have no knowledge about how the image was produced, so we make assumptions. Let me give you a thought experiment. Look at a piece of *vérité* filmmaking, something that the Maysles brothers or Fred Wiseman might have shot. Someone turns on the soundtrack and you hear the voice of the director telling the people in the frame exactly what to do: "Walk down the street, stop, look up" and so on. Regardless of what you're hearing, what is there exclusively in the picture that tells you it's fiction or nonfiction? Take out the sound, or even include the sound because you could argue it was put in afterwards and that the picture is actually completely uncontrolled and has been made to look as if it were not uncontrolled. What is there in the picture that might conceivably tell you this is a genuine piece of *vérité* filmmaking? What is there in an image that tells you it's one or the other? The answer, I think, is nothing. My argument would be that you have to know more about how the images were constructed. Whenever I hear people talking about photographs being "true" or "false," I don't know what they're talking about. I don't think the term has any meaning. I sort of know what people are talking about when they say a sentence is true or false because the notion of something being true or false is one that can certainly be applied to language. I believe that it's only when language is added to a photo, when a caption is put underneath a photograph, that you can begin to meaningfully talk about what might be true or otherwise. But the photo itself is neither true nor false. Look at Robert Capa's 1936 photograph of the death of a Republican soldier, taken during the Spanish Civil War. It's called "Falling Soldier." But regardless of whether or not it was staged—and there has been much debate about that—it is still a real photograph of whatever it was photographing.

PC: *So you're suggesting that to think of a particular photograph as being a fake is to miss the whole point of the medium.*
EM: Yes. And it's also worth thinking about how images have been used to charge history and historical events with certain significance, how they have even been used to create history. Take the photograph of the raising of the flag on Mount Suribachi. Many people think it was faked or posed. It really doesn't matter. What's clear is that the image has taken on heightened significance quite independent of the reality that is being photographed. It has been used to envision history, not simply to depict a historical event.

Truth is elusive, and we avoid it. We're often wrong about things even when we are convinced that we are in complete possession of the truth. It's our capacity to believe in untruth that fascinates me. I suppose you might call this self-deception. Ultimately I suspect our conscious explanations do not take into account the hidden layers of motivation, intention, and belief that determine what we do. If I may quote from my own *New York Times* op-ed: "Unhappily, an unerring fact of human nature is that we habitually reject the evidence of our own senses. If we want to believe something, then we often find a way to do so, regardless of evidence to the contrary. Believing is seeing, and not the other way around."[1]

PC: *You talked about journalism earlier. Do you absolutely reject any kind of journalistic approach when it comes to your films? Are you attempting to do something other than merely convey information to the audience?*
EM: I think that most good journalism, in whatever medium, does more than merely convey information. I should also say that I'm not quite sure what people mean by "journalism." Are my films something more than journalism? I would think so, yes. But if someone were to say that what I do is a kind of journalism, I would have no problem with that either. In

---

1. "Not Every Picture Tells a Story," *New York Times*, 20 November 2004.

fact, I would be flattered. But what I do is more than convey information, and my style is not purely journalistic.

For example, in *The Thin Blue Line* I didn't identify the interview subjects by name. Some people didn't like this, but to my mind the important thing is that you understand who the people are in the context of the story being told to you. You know the cops are the cops, the defense attorney is the defense attorney, the wacko eyewitnesses are the wacko eyewitnesses, and so on. In *A Brief History of Time*, I also avoided naming people as the movie progressed, and feel that the short biographical descriptions at the end of the film cleared up any ambiguity.

When we talk about style—journalistic or otherwise—and documentaries, what we really are talking about, once again, is truth. Again, my line on this is: "Style does not guarantee truth," no more so that the font of a newspaper guarantees truth. The font of the *New York Times* might make us feel comfortable and believe we're reading something that's true, but this has absolutely nothing to do with truth. There are no "truth-telling" fonts. A documentary film is as likely to be "true" or "false" as a newspaper. A newspaper may contain sentences that are true or false, but what sense would it make to talk about an entire newspaper being true or false? Similarly, there is no "truth-telling" style of filmmaking, but lots of documentaries use *vérité* methods as some kind of guarantee of truth. It's this idea that if you put the right ingredients in, like a hand-held cameras, use only available light, and have an unobtrusive crew, that somehow—magically—this produces truth on film. I have nothing against *cinéma-vérité* as a style of filmmaking, but to think that because you adopt that style of Maysles and Wiseman what you're doing is somehow more truthful is just plain wrong. I find this claim quite repellent. Truth is not something that you go out and collect with a camera. It is something to be pursued. I've said this many times before, but it's worth repeating: truth can't be manufactured, only the appearance of truth. And there's actually another word for this: falsehood.

The idea that a director is a slave to reality when making a documentary is nonsense. Filmmakers always have the licence to do almost anything. My own particular style is completely intrusive: careful compositions, theatrical lighting, people always aware they're talking to camera. Essentially, my subjects are being asked to perform. But I certainly believe that my films are just as concerned with truth as any *vérité* film might be.

PC: *I'm interested in the fact that you shot all your interviewees in* The Thin Blue Line *sitting in the same chair that was exactly the same distance from the camera. Clearly you had a specific aesthetic in mind, even though you were making a nonfiction film.*

EM: The aesthetics of *The Thin Blue Line* were clearly very important to me. Filming was strung out over a long period of time and there were various different cameramen on the project, but I was careful to use the same 16mm Zeiss high-speed prime lens for every interview to establish some unity in the imagery. This all started off as an aesthetic choice and then became a compulsion. I wanted a uniform look for the film, a level playing field for all the interview subjects.

This idea ended up causing me an enormous amount of difficulty. David Harris was in jail at the time. It took close to two years before I could film him because I wanted the interview to have the same look as all the others. I could have met him earlier but chose not to, and he ended up being the last person I interviewed. I'm very glad I did manage it because without his interview I feel the film would have been a shadow of itself. David was on death row in Texas. The Texas Department of Corrections has all these rules about how death row inmates can be filmed. It has to be on a certain day of the week and through a wire screen and so on. But David would have looked different from every other interview I'd shot. It would have set him apart visually. I kept negotiating with the TDC for months to try to get permission to shoot him so I would be in the same room and without a wire screen, where I could light and record him in the same way I'd recorded everyone else in the film. Finally David was brought to Dallas, where they allowed me to be in the same room as him and light him as I wanted to. He had to wear handcuffs, but it's only quite a way into the film that you realize this when he raises his hands up. It becomes a very dramatic moment in the movie. So in the end David Harris was in that same chair, he was the same distance from the camera as everyone else in the film, he was lit properly. But getting that on film was a nightmare because of my stylistic requirements.

I've always thought of the interviews I do as my own version of the Museum of Natural History, where they have animals standing in stylized dioramas behind glass. It's like I'm attempting to create some kind of exotic environment and put it on display. I do hope that all of my films have an expressionist feel to them.

PC: Gates of Heaven *and* Vernon, Florida *seem to rail against everything that* cinema-vérité *stands for.*

EM: Most definitions of "art" are both pretentious and unacceptable. Why should mine be any better? This is the best I've been able to come up with: set up an arbitrary series of rules and then follow them slavishly.

When I made *Gates of Heaven* my contrarian streak really came to the fore. The film came out not so much of filmmaking but of the audio interviews I had done. The idea was to replicate the idea of uninterrupted talk on film. I looked at all the basic tenets of *vérité* and threw them out. I hated them anyway, so I consciously and totally disregarded them. I did everything precisely the opposite of the way it was supposed to be done. If the camera is supposed to be hand held, I put it on a tripod. If the equipment is supposed to be lightweight and portable, I looked for the heaviest equipment I could find. If possible, I attached a brick to it. If you're supposed to use only available light, bring in big lights. If you're there to record the world and not interfere with it, make sure you interfere in as many ways as you can. Be unobtrusive? Why? Be as obtrusive as possible. Stage scenes and put objects in the frame. In fact, carefully compose frames and put people in them. Avoid zooms. Use prime lenses so you can't zoom. And get everyone to make eye contact with the camera.

I had terrible trouble at the start of *Gates of Heaven*. I got into a big argument the first day of shooting with cameraman Ed Lachman, who I knew through Werner Herzog. He arrived the day they were digging up the dead pets at the failed pet cemetery at Los Altos and had his own ideas about how this material should be shot, namely he should be running around the site with a hand-held camera. Of course that was anathema to me. Ed told me he knew how to shoot these kinds of films and that I didn't know what I was doing. The truth of the matter, of course, is that there is no one way a film should be shot. There's no formula to be followed slavishly. I fired three cameramen from *Gates of Heaven* because they would compulsively zoom in and try to heighten the action. I had a similar kind of problem on *The Thin Blue Line*. Randall Adams was finding it difficult to talk on camera and I said something like, "I really believe that you are innocent. This is your chance to talk." The cameraman, who clearly found my whole approach abhorrent, took me aside and told me I was sick and debased. "If I'd wanted to work with a moral philosopher," I told him, "I would have hired Emmanuel Kant."

PC: *What about the reenactments in* The Thin Blue Line*?*
EM: Those came from that fact that I never liked the way reenactments looked in other films. I didn't want to have an omniscient narrator, someone telling you what apparently and definitively happened, because the main thrust of *The Thin Blue Line* is an investigation into exactly what happened that night in Dallas. Simply, the reenactments were never used to make you think you were looking at the real world. It was my hope

that they would take you into the ambiguities of the story by illustrating the various lies that people had told, or what they thought and claimed they had seen that night. I always wanted people to question the reenactments in the film, just as we should question the flawed accounts of the witnesses. They are all just different articulations of lies, existing to take you deeper into the mystery of what happened on that roadway and into the world of untruth. I scrupulously avoided showing the one single version of David Harris alone in the car shooting the police officer, which is the one that's closest to what actually happened. The film makes no attempt to tell you whether what you are seeing on the screen actually happened, and because of this some of the reenactments—which are illustrations of what people claimed happened—inevitably contradict each other.

This is all very different from what you see in most traditional television journalism where reenactments have some ironic significance. There's clearly a difference between using a reenactment to acknowledge that nobody knows what really happened, and one that purports to show you reality. There has been a dangerous tendency in television journalism to stage reenactments in such a way as to suggest that they aren't reenactments at all, rather the real thing. There are lots of tricks employed here, things like purposely degrading the image to look as though it's been filmed by a hidden camera. Amazingly, when *The Thin Blue Line* came out, someone accused me of trying to trick people into thinking that I had actually filmed the murder. As if I'd had a 35mm camera and a film crew out there that night, ready and waiting. It just goes to show that images—and also writing that purports to be "nonfiction"—often bear a very complicated relationship to reality. As I said in my *New York Times* piece, "Photography, because of its causal relationship to the world, seems to give us the truth or something close to the truth. I am sceptical about this for many reasons."

PC: *What about daydreams of things that haven't happened?*
EM: They're kind of reenactments of imagined events. One other thing about reenactments brings us back to the idea of what is controlled and uncontrolled. For *The Fog of War* I used footage of the U.S. Government's reenactment of the Gulf of Tonkin incident that was staged a couple of weeks after the actual incidents. History, in fact, is replete with stories of reenacted footage. When the Russians liberated Auschwitz in January 1945, there were no cameras present, so they went back and re-liberated it several days later for the cameras. I suppose you could say cynically that

the Defense Department filmed their reenactments of the Gulf of Tonkin incidents in order to make them more real and to give credence to the fact that they actually happened.

PC: *You often say that what people say and how they say it is more revealing than physical action.*
EM: There's an idea I've had for a long time, that each of us live in some private reality, and that our private worlds can be revealed through language. What really interests me is the act of self-presentation, how people see the world and their place in it, this tension between how people want to be seen and how, in fact, we perceive them. I love listening to people describe themselves, how they paint a picture of themselves through language. In fact, language and how people use it to express their inner world might be my central concern. I've always been interested in speech revealing something unintended or even unconscious. As a filmmaker I am able to create something that is incredibly contrived in so many ways, and yet manages to preserve an element of the real, the spontaneous, the uncontrolled, namely language. The only true "documentary" element in my films is speech. I could never invent the language, the kinds of things that people say in my films. It's probably what I'm most proud of, that moment where people say the unimaginable. Cal Harberts in *Gates of Heaven* about the pet explosion, Phil Harberts and the R2A2 formula, the Martins and the sand that grows.

My favorite line comes from Emily Miller in *The Thin Blue Line* when she says, "Everywhere I go there are murders, even around my house." She's confused, she's confabulating, she's a fantasist living in some crazy world of her own devising. Surely there aren't people being bludgeoned to death in her kitchen or immolated in the living room. To me, this line sums up so much about her and people in general, that we all live in a personal fantasy world a good measure divorced from the real world, that there can be a radical disjunction between how we see ourselves and who we are, between what we believe is true and what is really true.

This is why paper edits of my films have never worked for me. There's something so absolutely different about actually listening to an interview and seeing it transcribed on paper. What makes some of my favorite moments so interesting is something that transcends the actual spoken words. It's an odd combination of emotion, gesture, and the words themselves. The key to editing—whether it's a full-length film or a short commercial—is to be aware of cadence, the subtleties in the voices, the timing, how people speak as much as what they are saying. I've been musician, a cellist, for forty years, and for me there's certainly something musical about editing an interview. When it works, when the editing is just right, there is something musical about the human voice.

PC: *Where did you get the idea to make a film about a pet cemetery? And who paid for it?*

EM: First things first: I never saw *Gates of Heaven* as being about a pet cemetery, though I couldn't really put my finger on what it is actually about. The film was inspired by an article that appeared in the *San Francisco Chronicle*, the article you see spinning on the screen in the film: "450 Dead Pets Go to Napa." I'd been spending a lot of time with mass murderers and at the time was working on a script about Ed Gein, a murderer and grave robber, called *Digging up the Past*.

Once it was finished, it was unclear if *Gates of Heaven* would be seen by anybody at all. The whole business was so different back then. There weren't that many film festivals, whereas now you can't swing a cat without knocking over a couple of them. People just didn't know how or where to distribute a film like that. There wasn't any precedent. It was accepted into the 1978 New York Film Festival but there was a newspaper strike that year, so hardly anyone reviewed it. At the Berlin Film Festival it played without subtitles and I really couldn't sit through the film again, so I wandered around outside and came back just before the ending. The theatre was empty. Everyone had walked out. Many people caught up with the film years later because Roger Ebert put it on his list of the top ten films of all time.

PC: *If it's not about pet cemeteries, then what is it about?*

EM: I've listened to so many audience responses to *Gates of Heaven*. Everyone seems to have their own reading of it, which is great. You have all these people in the film talking about an unsuccessful pet cemetery and the removal of all the pets to a successful cemetery. But it's not clear what the film is really actually about. There are so many people expressing themselves about things are really important to them—and that have nothing to do with pets or cemeteries—that the film becomes about them. There are some oddly powerful moments in the film. When Danny is playing the guitar on that hilltop, I feel he's up there with his dreams and hopes intact, surveying his world. But there's also the reality of where he is. It's not an amphitheatre filling with thousands of adoring screaming fans that he's looking out at, it's a universe of dead pets.

It's said that people have pets because they can't have effective relationships with other people. I believe it's the other way around: people have relationships with other people because they can't have effective relationships with their pets. Maybe that's my version of the human condition: a mixture of desperation, misplaced romanticism, isolation, and a sense of being totally and irrevocably lost. *Gates of Heaven* is an incredibly misanthropic film, and yet in the *New York Observer* Ron Rosenbaum called it a "Lucretian meditation on the nature of love." I'm not sure I know what he means, and I'm not sure what the nature of love is, at least in the context of dead pets and living people. I suppose Samuel Beckett came close to a working definition when he described love as a form of "lethal glue."

Someone once asked me how I might characterize my films. Well, I think of a pie chart with three equal parts: sick, sad, and funny. People seem to respond to *Gates of Heaven*—maybe more than my other films— in different ways at different times, from finding it sick or sad or funny or sick and funny or funny and sick, and on and on. But I think it can be all of those things at the same time. I used to think I was stupid because if I'd only made a film with a certain level of gravitas, more people would have taken it more seriously. Not to compare myself to Nabokov, but in his books—particularly *Lolita* and *Pale Fire*—he managed to combine the profound and the profoundly silly. The notion that the two are incompatible is simply wrong.

PC: *The accusation sometimes thrown at the nonfiction filmmaker is that he making fun of the people he is documenting. For some people the characters in* Gates of Heaven *are being made to look ridiculous.*
EM: I used to defend myself by denying I was making fun of them, but that seems a little disingenuous. People *are* ridiculous. Is a documentary filmmaker responsible for creating some sort of advertising campaign for humanity? Should documentaries be offering a paean to the human condition, to the supposed wonder that is man? I think despair is a more appropriate response. Let's put in this way: I don't see myself as any more or less ridiculous than the people in my films.

My mother once told me that the lowest form of humor is the kind that makes fun of other people. But what other kind of humor is there? Are you supposed to make fun of rocks? Some people seem to think that because a film is funny, everything that's going on in *Gates of Heaven* is vitiated by that humor. Not so. Humor seems to be just one part of the story. Having said that, I don't think there's a real distinction between laughing at and laughing with. There's just laughing at. I suppose my final thought is, "So what?" I think the film is about loneliness, disappointment, and desperation, and the fact that it's funny as well doesn't detract from those elements.

I identify with almost everyone. Well, maybe not the lady with the singing dog. But take the two brothers who worked at the successful pet cemetery in Napa: Phil, the older brother with the trophies, and Dan, the younger brother with the guitar. They're both like flies on flypaper, as trapped in the pet cemetery as the pets that are interred there. Dan with his melancholy new-age romanticism and Phil with his insane sales formulas and insurance trophies. I like them both.

For me, the end of the film is a kind of fetishistic nightmare. Phil with his insurance trophies, Danny with his Pioneer SX-1010 speakers, Cal talking about the Garden of Honor, and then Mr. Howard talks about disposing of an inanimate object with some kind of reverence and care as a living thing. I'm hoping for the day when not only people and pets are buried, but furniture as well.

PC: *You said you were spending a lot of time with murderers?*

EM: While I was at Berkeley, I read a book by Herbert Fingarette called *The Meaning of Criminal Insanity* and thought about writing my thesis on criminal responsibility and the insanity plea. I started going to the trials of three mass murderers, including Edmund Kemper, who I had first visited along with Werner Herzog. This was in Santa Cruz. And then in 1974, I went back to Plainfield, Wisconsin, to interview Ed Gein, the model for the Norman Bates character in *Psycho*. I was down there for almost a year and spent an inordinate amount of time in the courthouse reading through trial documents to see what kind of crimes has been committed there, apart from Gein's. What amazed me was the number of murderers who'd come from Plainfield and the surrounding area, so I started interviewing them too. I've got literally hundreds of hours of tapes sitting in a box somewhere, and transcripts too. I transcribed it all with the intention of one day writing a book. At the time I remember my mother asking me why I didn't spend time with people my own age. I said, "But mom, the murderers *are* my own age."

PC: *Is this when you started interviewing people?*

EM: Yes. First with a tape recorder and only much later with a camera. With the tape recorder I would play a game: see how long you can get someone to talk before you have to say something. It's become my shtick.

PC: Vernon, Florida, *your second film, wasn't quite the film you first had in mind.*

EM: No. Someone called it "philosophy in the swamp," which is a description I like. At the time I was looking for a film project and read an article in the *New York Times* about Joe Healy, an insurance investigator. He mentioned many of his most notorious cases and then almost in passing made reference to a town in the Florida panhandle where there was an extraordinary history of insurance fraud. There had been something like twenty or thirty people who had lost various limbs in suspicious accidents. In the insurance trade the town was called "Nub City." This guy explained that these people were actually chopping or shooting off their own arms and legs. One guy even fell asleep with his foot over a railroad track and was rudely awakened by the evening express. To me it sounded like a perfect metaphor for America, a country full of people who want to enrich themselves but who literally become a fraction of themselves in the process. I told Healy that I wanted to go down there. He said it was the most dangerous place he'd ever been, that I would be—and this is singularly appropriate in this instance—risking life and limb if I started asking questions. At first he wouldn't even tell me the name of the town, though eventually he relented, and named Vernon, Florida. It's a town that I can honestly say is in the middle of nowhere, equidistant from Tallahassee and Pensacola. I told him I was going down there, and he said, "Well, whatever you do, don't stay long and don't go out at night."

It's hard to know what I was thinking, or if in fact I was thinking at all. At first I had no plans to make a film. I wasn't a filmmaker at that point. My first trip down there was before I'd even made *Gates of Heaven*. I'd been working on *Stroszek* with Werner in Cherokee, North Carolina. I left and headed south, through Georgia and Alabama to Vernon. It was my first trip down there. I stopped at Chipley, the county seat of Washington County, Florida—Vernon is smack in the middle of Washington County, Florida—to take a look at documents at the courthouse and noticed there really weren't any murders in the county. I asked the sheriff about it. He said, "Down here we don't have murders. We just have disappearances."

So I ended up living in Vernon for a while, initially to assemble material about the nubbies, which is what the insurance investigators called the claimants with self-inflicted injuries. I wanted to find out how many there were, the nature of the insurance claims, things like that. I even went to interview a double nubbie and got beaten up by his son-in-law who was a Marine. I remember that night very well because the nubbie was wearing shorts and a T-shirt. His nubs were really apparent. There was no doubt about what I was looking at. It's an illustration of how incredibly stupid I am. What was I thinking? That I was going to start interviewing people who've successful defrauded insurance companies? The parlance in the private investigation trade is "door-stepping," where you just show up at someone's door and start asking questions. If I'd continued in that vein I would have disappeared. It became self-evident that I couldn't make that movie, at least not as a documentary. I finally decided to make a film in the town that had nothing whatsoever to do with Nub City, though I'd still like to make a feature about the nub club. It's a fantastic story.

To me, Vernon is a magical place, and it has a unique look to it. It's a swamp, but a certain kind of under-vegetated desolate swamp. I've never seen anything quite like it elsewhere in the world. I remember taking a lot of photos at the time. It's a kind of parallel universe which just happens to be our own universe. There was the feeling that I had entered a different dimension in which there was some kind of metaphysical component that came out no matter who I was talking to. Everything and everyone had this philosophical bent to it. No one ever seems to remark on it but when Coy Brock, the preacher, is talking about God he says, "Let's call God 'That just happened.'" I really do wonder: what's the difference between God and caprice? It's God as a form of complete godlessness, of happenstance. I find it compelling. God as anti-God.

PC: *Is* Vernon, Florida *a kind of ethnographic film?*

EM: Are you kidding? I'm not an anthropologist. The film is not a survey of their society or culture. It's a dreamscape. It goes back to what I was saying about truth. What we know about photography is that it exists in causal relationship to the world. A relationship always exists between an image and that which it is an image of. In other words, every image has a certain reality about it. But I would never make the claim that *Vernon* is in any way a thorough sociological examination of the town.

PC: *Once you started work on the film, what were your plans? Did you have a firm idea as to what you wanted?*

EM: No, I really didn't know what movie I was making. Once it became unclear whether anybody was willing to talk with me and that I wasn't going to be able to make a film about Nub City, it wasn't clear to me what I was doing down that at all. We began to assemble these very odd characters, one by one. The production wasn't easy. For technical reasons a lot of the material I shot was unusable. We had a small crew and lived together in a house. I used to joke that people who knocked on the door would want one of two things: to kill you or convert you. Either way, highly undesirable. I remember one afternoon Ned Burgess, my camera-man, was outside the town hall with the camera on a tripod, when one of the double nubbies tried to run him down with a truck. It became some-thing of a joke. People would ask, "Why are you shooting here?" I would answer, somewhat disingenuously, "Oh well, Vernon's such a strange and magical place." Then they would ask me, "Does it have anything to do with Nub City?" and I would insist that it didn't, that the movie wasn't about the nubbies at all. And oddly enough that came to be true. I think there's one single nubbie in the film, but that's it. He's sitting on the bench in front of the gas station, and he lost his limb through natural causes, not insurance fraud.

PC: *And the film's structure was conceived during editing?*

EM: Pretty much, yes. I edited it with Brad Fuller. We were desperate be-cause we'd done things in such a different way that we weren't sure that there was even a movie there. The same was true of *Gates of Heaven*. A friend of mine from Berkeley who has worked on all of my films, Charlie Silver, has a basic principle of editing, one that's unfortunately often for-gotten: editing is taking out the bad stuff and leaving in the good stuff. We took a long time trying to figure out how to do that.

PC: *There is no music in* Vernon, Florida.

EM: And there's no music to speak of in *Gates of Heaven* either, save for Danny playing the electric guitar or Zella Graham singing to her dog. I started thinking about music in my films with *The Thin Blue Line*. At that point it was because of Philip Glass. He provided an essential component of that film. Once I started putting his music up against the interview I was shooting, it was clear he had to do the score. But I never thought of music in my first two films. I felt they didn't need music.

PC: *There was a gap of quite a few years between* Vernon, Florida *and* The Thin Blue Line. *What were you doing?*

EM: Feeling sorry for myself. When *Vernon* came out, lots of people told me I wouldn't have any trouble getting money to make my next film. I had horrendous trouble and was effectively out of the business for years. My brother Noel died, and it nearly destroyed my mother. She lost my father when I was only two. Of a massive heart attack. And then, my brother. My father was forty-three when he died, my brother was forty. I had always looked at my brother as the smart one in the family. He was a computer scientist and a genius. I always held him in awe. Years later, my mother told me that Noel considered *me* to be the smart one. Go figure.

PC: *Did you have the feeling that you'd never make another film again?*
EM: Yes.

PC: *What was the starting point of* The Thin Blue Line?
EM: I'd been out of work as a filmmaker for a long time but working as a private investigator, among other things. Finally I was given money to make another film. Actually I got money to work on a story that had nothing whatsoever to do with *The Thin Blue Line*. I was so desperate that I submitted a proposal that I thought would interest executives at public broadcasting, even though it didn't interest me, a project about "future dangerousness" centered around Dr. James Grigson, a Dallas psychiatrist notorious for his anti-defendant testimony in death-penalty cases. They call him Dr. Death, the Killer Shrink, the Hanging Psychiatrist, things like that. I spent quite a bit of time with him and became quite fond of him even though I find his views completely repellent. He had lost all his private clients and said to me, "You know, after I got that name Dr. Death, they just stopped coming."

Texas has a very odd death-penalty statute. In order to execute someone there you have to make a prediction about their future behavior. It's not enough to say they've done something very naughty in the past. You also have to show they're going to do something very naughty in the future. The trials were bifurcated. There would be a guilty phase and then a penalty phase. To help juries make these kinds of decisions, prosecutors would hire Grigson who, on the basis of a ten or fifteen minute examination, was apparently able to make such predictions. He always said the same thing: "This person is a dangerous psychopath who is going to kill again and again, so you had better fry them." In Texas executions are preventive murder. Kill them before they kill you. Or something like that.

I'm profoundly skeptical about our abilities to predict the future in general and human behavior in particular, except when it comes to what Dr. Death will say in the penalty phase of a capital murder trial. This can be predicted with 100 percent accuracy. Grigson suggested I visit various prisons in Texas and interview people he had helped sentence to die in the electric chair about the crimes they had committed and about whether they might do similar things in the future. I must have spoken with fifteen or sixteen people, picked entirely randomly, including one man who turned out to be innocent: Randall Adams, who had been convicted of killing a Dallas police officer.

Adams interested me, but not because I thought he was innocent. He had a singsong way of talking, as if he was convinced that no one was really listening to anything he had to say, that he was going through some kind of formal recitation that he felt compelled to go through, even though he knew it would fall on deaf ears. Of course in Grigson's eyes such lack of remorse on Adams's part confirmed he would kill again. Using the testimony of David Harris, the kid who actually pulled the trigger, Adams had been convicted for capital murder and sentenced to death. The story that emerged in *The Thin Blue Line* evolved around me as I started looking into it, and as soon as I started uncovering weird stuff I was kind of trapped into investigating further and further.

Grigson actually examined both Adams and Harris, and got it doubly wrong. It's very hard to be 200 percent wrong in one situation, but Grigson managed to achieve this unlikely outcome. Not only did he say that David Harris hadn't killed anyone, adding that he wouldn't kill in the future, he also said that Randall Adams had killed and would continue to kill. Adams has been out of jail for many years now, without so much as a misdemeanor. David Harris, on the other hand, was freed by the state of Texas after Grigson testified that he was a nice boy who would mend his ways and wouldn't get into any more trouble. Of course, that diagnosis didn't prevent him from going on to kill another person.

PC: *But didn't he have a problem with violence?*
EM: And with authority figures. He enlisted in the military and tried to kill his commanding officer, ending up in Leavenworth. He was released and stole a car, drove to California, picked up a hitchhiker, and robbed a store. He tried to kill a police officer when surrounded, his gun jammed, and he was taken into custody where he tried to blame the hitchhiker. It's not much different from the story he successfully told in Dallas. When I first met him, he had just been paroled from San Quentin to his family in East Vidor, Texas. That's the home of the KKK in case you didn't know. It's a really frightening place.

Incidentally, I was wearing glasses at the time but stopped wearing them in Texas because I became convinced that the glasses secretly said J-E-W and that I would do better without them. I had a bizarre conversation with a police officer in Vidor who asked me if I lived in New York. I said yes, to which he said, "There are a lot of deli restaurants in New York, aren't there?" I said to myself, "Is this going where I think it's going?" I said, "Yes, there are a lot of deli restaurants in New York." And then he looked at me and he said, "I bet you really like deli food, don't you?"

PC: *So when you started investigating Randall Adams's case you assumed he was just one more guilty man claiming he was innocent?*

EM: I never set out to find an innocent man, but I did become more and more interested by this particular case. I went to the Texas Court of Criminal Appeals in Austin because every single capital murder trial is automatically appealed there. I sat there and read the trial transcripts for days on end. In the transcript of his trial Adams maintained that David Harris—who had given him a lift on the night of the murder—had killed the police officer, so I set out to find Harris and get his side of the story. I found him through a parole officer. Remember, this is almost ten years later, and he'd just been paroled from San Quentin after five and half years. I made arrangements with his parole officer to have David contact me in order to arrange a meeting but he wouldn't give me David's phone number. I figured I'd never hear from him. Ten minutes later David called me back and we arranged to meet at this lonely bar in the swamp near Vidor, Texas.

At this first meeting I got the feeling he was the real killer almost immediately. I didn't want to ask him any questions about the case for fear I'd spook him, which meant he might not want to be filmed. Also because I find there's an element of spontaneity lost if things aren't filmed the first time around. I should say I find that interviews work best if I spend very little time with the person ahead of time. But he started volunteering all of this information about the case and asked me about Randall Adams. He wasn't even sure that Adams was still alive—that had been one of his first questions. I told him he was. At one point I started to get nervous because I was thinking he was the real killer. I don't know if you've ever had this experience. You think someone is thinking that you're thinking something, and you don't want him to think that you're thinking something, so you tell him you're not thinking that, and in the process of telling him you're not thinking that, you tell him the exact opposite. I said to David, "I'm really glad I got a chance to meet you because I can see now that you couldn't possibly have been responsible for the murder of the Dallas police officer." And he gave me this very disturbing look. At least it was disturbing to me. And as I left, he told me three times to be very careful driving home. When someone says that to you once, they're asking you to be very careful driving home. When they say it to you twice, maybe they're asking you to be very, very careful driving home. When they say it to you three times, it's a threat. I left the bar, and I was convinced he was following me. I was driving these back roads back to the motel in Huntsville, Texas where I staying.

A while later David didn't show up for an interview because he was busy killing somebody in Texas. That night, he broke into an apartment.

A guy and his girlfriend were asleep. He abducted the girl naked and screaming and locked the boyfriend in the bathroom. The guy broke down the door, grabbed a gun, and there was a shootout in the parking lot. The girl got away, but David shot and killed the man at point blank range. It's one of my favorite excuses for missing an appointment: "I'm sorry, I was busy killing somebody." I was at his trial in Beaumont, Texas. It's come full circle now. He was executed by lethal injection in June 2004 for that murder. It was a couple of weeks after Grigson died of lung cancer.

David Harris—and the whole case—had a profound effect on my life. It's a chapter that's more or less closed now. There's a kind of guilt that sets in. Having gotten Adams out of prison, should I have tried to prevent Harris from being executed? Could I have done anything? I hate the death penalty. State-authored death seems to be a pretty bad example of death in general. But I didn't do anything.

PC: *Did your time working as a private detective help you when making the film?*

EM: I still feel myself to be something of a detective. Actually, sometimes when I was working as a detective I would pose as a filmmaker, which really was quite depressing. But part of what made me a good private investigator was the ability to get people to talk.

I've always believed there has to be some investigative element to a nonfiction film. There are thousand of movies that tell stories about detectives investigating crimes, but I don't know of any other movies where a crime is actually investigated with a camera. For example, the interviews with the three eyewitnesses—Emily Miller, R. L. Miller, and Michael Randell—was submitted as evidence in federal and state court. The film doesn't just chronicle a murder investigation after the fact, it *is* a murder investigation. The footage I shot is actually evidence that was used in a court of law. People say that *The Thin Blue Line* is the only film to get a man out of jail. Sure, the movie brought the case to national attention, and that made it impossible for the authorities to sweep it under the rug. But it's the investigation I did—which goes far beyond anything in the film—that really led to Randall Adams's conviction being overturned. Adams was convicted on the basis of some crucial evidence, for example the eyewitnesses who happened to be driving by at that moment. I spent a long time tracking them down and interviewed four of them on camera. Each of them had, at this capital murder trial, committed perjury without even knowing it.

For a while I wanted to turn the film into the strongest possible argument for Adams's innocence. I actually filmed an interview with myself in the same style as all the others which I tried to edit myself into the film, but it turned the whole thing into a very ordinary-looking piece of investigative journalism that was far more prosaic and less believable. Unfortunately, when I took myself out of the film, I also had to drop a lot of the material that only I could explain. If I look back objectively at what I was trying to do it's clear that though there was no evidence that Randall Adams didn't do it or that David Harris did, there was plenty of evidence that Adams didn't get a fair trial.

I might add that if I'd taken a more adversarial approach to interviewing, some people might have found the film more interesting and fun to watch, but Randall Adams would probably still be in prison.

PC: *Could you say something about the legal dispute between you and Randall Adams after he was released from prison?*

EM: The whole thing was bizarre and hurtful. And was all about money. When he got out of prison, he was angry that he'd signed a release giving me rights to his life story. He felt as though I had stolen something from him. I was determined to prove his innocence and would have spent another three or four years trying to get him out of prison, but as a filmmaker I also had a proprietary interest in finishing and releasing a film.

I don't speak with Randall Adams anymore for obvious reasons. My wife summed it up very succinctly: "Just because he's a victim, doesn't mean he isn't an asshole." But of course I'm still very proud of what *The Thin Blue Line* was able to do, which was get him out of jail, no matter what he might say, whether he appreciates it or not. For not-so-obvious reasons I was sporadically in touch with David Harris until his execution. He was bright and often personable. He was described by many people, including Adams, as "the kid." And it's true, he was a fresh-faced kid at the time of the killing. There was something sweet and even sympathetic about him. It just doesn't square with what he did. I found him endlessly fascinating even though when I met him as a free man he scared me. Do you remember the sequence in the film when he tells the story about his brother drowning? It's a moving story, and I wonder what kind of psychodrama he was acting out again and again later in life.

PC: *Did Harris ever really confess the murder to you?*

EM: When I interviewed him one last time on audiotape, I asked him whether he had killed the policeman that night in Dallas. He smiled and nodded his head. You can't hear it on the tape, but it's something quite unforgettable for me. It was a moment of enormous sadness and vindication at the same time. My belief in Adams's innocence was right but there was sadness that it had come to all this, that it had happened at all, that there had been this loss of life. It all felt so utterly meaningless. I've never been terribly interested in psychiatric nomenclature because such terms seem to explain very little. I wouldn't call David Harris a sociopath or a psychopath, but I do know he killed for reasons I don't completely understand.

PC: *Why do you think the Dallas authorities were intent on prosecuting Adams for the murder rather than Harris, to whom all the evidence pointed?*
EM: One answer to that question is that Harris was sixteen years old at the time and couldn't be given the death penalty, whereas Randall was twenty-six and could be sentenced to death and executed. Harris looked like a sweet kid while Adams, with his long hair and moustache, looked more like a cop-killer. My own theory as to why Harris wasn't prosecuted is that they simply didn't have a case against him. It became a choice between a weak case and no case. If Harris was telling the truth about what happened that night, then he was sitting next to Adams in the passenger seat and would have been an eyewitness to the crime. If Adams was telling the truth, then Harris was alone in that car and there were no witnesses, save for Harris, himself.

PC: *What's the meaning of the title of the film?*
EM: I took it from the summation the prosecuting attorney made to the jury at the end of the trial when he spoke about "the thin blue line" of police that separates the public from anarchy.

PC: *The film raises questions not just about the American legal system but also about how bad luck and chance play a part in all our lives.*
EM: Adams came within a week of dying of a lethal injection. It was only an appellate court decision on a technicality that saved him. He came from a good Ohio family and was a workingman, and one day his car broke down and he happened to be picked up by David Harris. *The Thin Blue Line* is about destiny and luck in general. It's about how our perch in this world is a very insecure one. Adams's story is the ultimate paranoid dream where one small incident sets off an inexorable and ultimately tragic chain of events that nearly destroys everyone involved. In this sense, it's quintessential *film noir* of the forties and fifties, like Edgar Ulmer's *Detour* or *The Reckless Moment*, or a real-life *Twilight Zone* episode, the Kafkaesque nightmare of being a stranger in some faraway place

where everything you say is taken to be a lie, where things happen for no reason. It was cold that morning in Dallas. Adams, who had come to Texas from Florida, had no warm clothing and was shivering. He started walking down the road with a plastic milk jug, stopped at a gas station and was told by the attendant that it was against the law to put gas in a plastic container. He started walking back toward his car when David Harris pulled up and offered his help. Just plain bad luck.

PC: *After proving such a success as a documentary filmmaker, why did you feel the need to make* The Dark Wind, *a narrative feature?*
EM: The simple answer is that I did it for the same reason that everybody does anything and everything in Hollywood: vanity and greed. I really had no idea what I was getting into and the whole experience was miserable.

PC: *Were you comfortable working with the actors on* The Dark Wind?
EM: I never had any trouble working with actors. Actors are people too. Conversely, people are also actors. Coaxing a performance out of someone in an extemporaneous interview isn't so different from coaxing a performance out of an actor with scripted lines. You, as the director, are creating a situation were people feel comfortable and want to perform for you.

PC: *Do you know what your next fiction film might be?*
EM: I've got lots of ideas, including a feature about Nub City and the story of Einstein's brain. For years I've been working for years on a story about King Boots, a dog from Michigan put on trial for murder. I have six thousand pages of trial transcripts. It's such amazing material. The dog allegedly killed the owner's mother, an eighty-seven-year-old-woman. This was no pit bull, it an Old English sheepdog called Boots who had won more prizes than any other dog in American history. Under Michigan law, Boots was impounded and the state wanted to destroy it. It was charged with murder, even though we know dogs can't frame an intention to commit murder. The owners hired defense lawyers to get Boots acquitted. The coroner originally said the mother died from "multiple bites," but a second autopsy concluded it was a heart attack. Boots was visited in jail by a vet who found a wound on the dog's nose that had been made by a kitchen fork. It was suggested that the woman—who had a good relationship with Boots—had tripped over the sleeping dog and accidentally stabbed it. The dog bit her and she died. It's a very rich story about the American family and the justice system. Boots wasn't

acquitted, although the evidence certainly suggested he should have been. He died shortly after the trial, I like to think of a broken heart.

PC: *Sounds like stories that could equally be made as nonfictions.*

EM: There are some stories that need to be told in fiction form and others that need to be told using real people. I can imagine *The Thin Blue Line* as a scripted drama, but it would be far less interesting. There is an inherent drama is looking at each of the interviews in the movie and wondering whether the speaker is lying or telling the truth. I shot several interviews with the people involved in the King Boots story, but some of the most important characters didn't agree to be filmed on camera. I believe that the story would work best as a fiction, though my viewpoint might be hopelessly infected by the reality of not being able to get some of the important interviews I wanted.

PC: *Which do you find more challenging: fiction or nonfiction?*

EM: Documentaries are probably harder to make than narrative features. Most people really don't understand just how hard it is to make these films. *Fast, Cheap and Out of Control* and *The Fog of War* are full to the brim with images and sounds. It's not easy taking all this material and finding a narrative. Documentary combines script writing, directing, and editing. And it also involves performance. What's more, you can reinvent the form with each film. *Fast, Cheap* took me three years to edit. The entire structure of *The Fog of War* was developed during editing. Originally it had a relatively simple linear structure to it but it wasn't a film, it was just a chronology. It was only when we started to take the movie radically out of order and impose an idea of what it could actually be about that it really started to become a real film. Discovering your film in the dailies is not something that generally happens in narrative filmmaking. It's very hard being at sea not knowing if you have anything, not knowing how to shape it.

PC: *Where do you find your ideas?*

EM: It's not as if I have some hidden source, a dumpster filled with material, hidden out back. Many of the stories that have interested me over the years have come from the most ordinary places. I try to keep my eyes open. I got the idea for *Mr. Death* from the front page of the *New York Times*. Most of the stories for my movies came from newspapers and magazines. I like to take the inconsequential—those stories that other people might ignore—and find something consequential in them.

PC: A Brief History of Time *is a film that seemed to surprise many people. It's certainly nothing like a cinematic physics lesson.*

EM: No, nothing like that. Whatever cinema is, it's certainly not a good place to teach theoretical physics. Someone could make a film that goes on for a hundred hours that still wouldn't do justice to the many ideas in Steven Hawking's book. What I wanted to do was look at the kind of people who have devoted their lives to doing science, so the film is full of this fantastic cast of eccentrics. I interviewed an evangelical Christian who lived with the Hawking family and would forever try to convert Hawking—who is a confirmed atheist—to evangelical Christianity.

I felt there was a kind of metaphorical connection between Hawking's book and his life. As a child, Hawking believed in a universe without end: a savage, unchanging universe without boundaries. Then at the age of twenty-one he gets a death sentence when he's told he has two and half years to live. So then what does he go on to prove? That the universe doesn't go on forever, that it has a beginning and possibly an end, and so in some way has human attributes. When Hawking talks about black holes, it's hard not to be struck by the connection between his life in science—his interest in stars that collapse in on themselves—and the premature burial inside his own body. It's a Poe-like horror story of a man being buried alive, someone who is utterly dependent on other people for his survival but who has beaten the odds and has the temerity to ask these vast questions.

While making the film I used to joke that it was an extended essay on the naturalistic fallacy, the idea that the world around us has humanlike attributes, that it's born, it lives, and then dies. Of course, the ultimate irony is that that naturalistic fallacy may be no fallacy whatsoever. John Wheeler—the man who gave black holes their name and who taught me at Princeton years ago—says that if the universe collapses much like a black hole, if it all comes to an end, how is that different from the life of each one of us?

PC: *Was the film your idea from the start?*

EM: I had approached Steven Spielberg with the King Boots project. His company was working on the Hawking film and they asked me to get involved. I did know of Hawking but hadn't read the book and wasn't even sure I wanted to make the film until I actually met Hawking in his office. He's an incredible person on so many levels. On meeting him for the first time I was struck that here's a person who is totally incapacitated yet who is totally in control. One feels quickly dominated by the man despite all of his physical infirmities.

I was fascinated by his voice and made a decision very early on not to interview him on film. When you spend time with Hawking, you very quickly learn to accept these amazing pauses. Upon entering his office the first thing you see are computer screens that obscure his chair. There's a screen that's part of his chair and a desktop computer sitting there. You ask a question and then all you hear is this clicking that goes on and on and on, and you don't really know what's happening. Even though I was told all about this previously, you still don't really know what's happening. Or at least you're unprepared for it. Does Stephen like the question? Is he answering it? Is he annoyed by it? Is he ignoring me altogether? And there really is little warning when he's about to speak. But after spending some time with him I wouldn't sit in front of him, rather beside him where you can read the computer screen as he's writing. As a result there's a strange kind of intimacy about all of it, and rather than being a painful experience, it becomes very natural. I grew to really like the voice. Stephen was concerned that his voice in the movie should sound exactly the way it sounds in real life. For him, the voice synthesiser is his real voice. There have been various upgrades on the voice synthesiser but he refuses to use them because he doesn't want to sound like anyone else.

PC: *Hawking's book is hardly obvious cinematic material.*

EM: No. It combines some of the more difficult abstract ideas about theoretical physics with a man who essentially doesn't move and can't speak in any traditional sense. As I like to describe him, Hawking is the first non-talking talking head in media. But at the same time, the story is a pretty big story. In fact, it's the biggest story out there: the creation of the universe, the birth and death of the cosmos. And of course, one of the reasons I was so interested in making the film was that so many people told me it was an impossible project.

It became apparent at a very early stage of production that there was a popular misconception about Hawking's book, probably because people have an idea about its contents without having read it. It's generally seen as science pedagogy—"Let's learn a little general relativity and cosmology"—but I saw it as a romance novel. It's not purely about science. To me the book is also about Hawking's personal struggle with the universe, about how he sees the world. I was fascinated by this relationship between his life and his science. It's similar to what drew me to the characters in *Fast, Cheap*, where my primary interest wasn't in the objective details of what these four men actually do but in how they describe their work, how they envision what they do. In *Brief History*, Stephen's frailty becomes a kind of symbol of human frailty in general, particularly when you consider the scope of his investigation. We're all not in that different a position than he is when you survey the cosmos as a whole. So the film is not explicitly about scientific ideas and it's not explicitly a biography on a factual level. Rather it's "biography as dreamscape."

PC: *How did you tackle Hawking's approach to religion?*

EM: I know that when asked if he believes in God, Stephen has said that he doesn't believe in a personal God. Notwithstanding, the book and film are both filled with references to God. Stephen's relationship with God and/or the Creator is certainly a central theme in his work. I think that's one reason why the book has such wide appeal, the fact that he does address these very large philosophical concerns. Having said this, however, I have never felt that Stephen's God is a man with a long, grey beard or a God who intervenes in human affairs.

The book mixes a kind of fantastic optimism with total despair. I think that's one of the reasons I find the material so persuasive. At the end of the book and film Stephen talks on the one hand about the possibility of knowing everything there is to know about the universe, about the world around us, about the mind of God. For me this is a fantastically optimistic idea. And on the other hand, he speaks almost like a prophet of doom with his belief that the universe is going to come to an end fifteen billion years from now. He also once told me probably the most pessimistic thing I've ever heard. He was asked about the possibility of extraterrestrial life. Stephen's explanation for why we haven't heard signals from outer space is that in the last million years our DNA really hasn't changed at all. We're still those same creatures running around in the jungle, but our destructive capacities have increased millions and millions–fold in only the last one hundred years. Why don't we hear those intelligent signals? Because if a civilization ever reaches a point where it is able to send such messages, it would have already destroyed itself.

I admire Stephen Hawking tremendously. I find myself capable of cynicism about almost anything, but I am quite incapable of being cynical about Stephen. He's an incredible human being and scientist, and it really was an honor to make the film.

PC: *You mentioned earlier that all the interviews in the film were filmed in a studio.*

EM: Usually you bring the crew to the people but in this case we brought the people to the crew. We shot all the interviews in studios, mostly at Elstree in London. I wanted to be able to control the sound and lighting, and give the movie a constructed look. As I said earlier, there isn't really a single "real" image in the whole film. Even the chair Hawking is using was built especially for the film, and for some of the shots we had a Hawking stand-in. I felt that since he is the central character of the movie it was important to replicate his office exactly, which means that the Marilyn Monroe posters on the walls and the books on the shelves are all identical to his actual office at Cambridge University. I wanted to create a visual unity around Hawking, and I think the fact that we shot the interviews in a studio gives them all a timeless feeling. With Hawking's mother, for example, you see a window behind her, but it's not a window looking out over anything real. There is an endless sunset behind her, a world suspended for a moment outside of time.

PC: *You shy away from fancy visual displays to show the ideas Hawking is talking about. Was that a conscious decision?*
EM: Even though there was a certain amount of pressure to fill the film with high-tech graphics, I avoided this because the book is full of examples from everyday life. I really wanted to give the graphics a human face. Who's to say what a black hole really looks like anyway?

When it came to filming Hawking himself, I wanted to build up a kind of library of images to work from while editing. We ended up with hundreds of shots of him and the chair from every conceivable angle. I should say that although Hawking was involved in the movie from start to finish—he wrote the narration, looked at rough cuts, offered comments—he never approved of the chicken. We had this ongoing discussion about the chicken all through the editing process. I felt I had an unassailable argument, namely that this was going to be my only opportunity to put a shot of a chicken in space in one of my films and I should avail myself of that opportunity. In its own way it takes us into the central theme of the movie, about what started it all off, what was there at the very beginning, and if there was a beginning, what was there before that. It's a chicken-and-egg thing. And I believe Stephen has grown to like the chicken.

The soundtrack to the film is certainly as crucial as the images. For me, the clicking of the mouse on his wheelchair is one of the most important elements because it's the only real connection he has with the outside world. It's the first and last thing we hear in the film. The narration was drawn from a mass of different material—from the book, his lectures, and scientific papers—that I edited together and recorded.

PC: *Some people were probably put off by the film because its subject matter is not an easy one. Do you understand everything that your interviewees say in the film?*

EM: Of course not. I like to think I'm somewhere in the middle, between people who know nothing about this, and people who know a great deal.

PC: *There was some criticism that the film doesn't tackle the more personal aspects of Hawking's life. Does he like the film?*

EM: Yes, to my relief he does. The decision not to deal with such things was made for me in the simple sense that a number of people I would have liked to interview for the film declined to talk to me, including Hawking's wife. It was also very clear to me that he didn't want me to go into the details of his private life. I felt responsible to him in a whole number of ways. I certainly wanted to make a film that in the end would represent his scientific ideas and that he would approve of. In terms of the story I was telling, the details of his marriage didn't seem integral. I certainly don't feel their absence in the movie.

PC: *How did you find the four characters whose stories make up* Fast, Cheap and Out of Control?

EM: My wife read about Rodney Brooks, the insect robot guy, and for years told me to get in touch with him. He worked down the street at MIT, and when I started work on the movie, I contacted him. I'd read something about mole rats, the only mammal that lives like a social insect, and went to meet some mole rat scientists but they just didn't seem suitable. And then I met Ray Mendez, mole rat enthusiast, and he was just perfect. A really fascinating character whose main job at the time was as an insect wrangler for the movies. He did the moths in *Silence of the Lambs*. Then I found out there was a topiary garden close by to where I live, in Portsmouth, Rhode Island. I met George Mendonça and realized his story fit perfectly into this mixture of animal stories. Dave Hoover, the lion tamer, I actually knew from years before, and some of the footage in the film I shot even before I made *The Thin Blue Line*. So you've got a guy who cuts animals out of privet, one who studies insectlike mammals, another who works with wild beasts in the circus, and one who builds robotic insects he thinks will eventually replace all carbon based life on the planet.

PC: *Didn't you first plan to include Fred Leuchter in the film?*

EM: The first interview I shot with Fred, which was done in 1992, was six or seven hours long. For *Mr. Death* I shot another twelve hours of footage. I did toy with the idea of putting the original Leuchter interview into *Fast, Cheap.* At that point I hadn't done anything with it, but pretty soon I realized that Fred's story raised unique questions, independent of those in *Fast, Cheap.* And my wife has this line: "Whatever Hitler is, he isn't a spice." By adding Hitler to the soup, it immediately becomes Hitler-flavored. It dominates everything, so I decided to leave him out.

PC: *How did you go about cutting the four stories into a single narrative?*

EM: With *Fast, Cheap* I was fascinated by the possibility of making a movie where there was no clear story line at first, where it emerges slowly and unexpectedly out of the relationships between these characters and the ideas they express. It's clear quite quickly to the audience that the film has four principal characters and that their stories will eventually fuse together in some way as the film progresses.

PC: *So you shot the interviews and then pieced the film together once you had all the elements?*

EM: That's about it. While I was making the film, I had that Yeats poem in my head again, "Lapis Lazuli": "All things fall and are built again / And those that build them again are gay." He's suggesting there's dignity in doing something even if it's destined to be destroyed. What I like is that you can't look at this assemblage of characters and say, quite definitively, "This is what it's all about." The themes of the movie, whatever they may be, are pretty complex and elusive. It's the ultimate low-concept movie, one that utterly resists the possibility of a one-line summary.

People often ask me to explain what I was trying to do with *Fast, Cheap,* but that's probably not my job. Without an explanation the movie doesn't fall apart, it's still the same movie. With a film like this it's inevitable that there are such divergent interpretations because there's so much in there. There's so much room for discussion about the various ideas. In *Gates of Heaven* there's a whole set of surprising and unexpected connections thrown up between these characters to the point where the film isn't really about pet cemeteries at all, and it's the same with *Fast, Cheap.* At first glance these four characters don't seem to have much to do with each other, but soon certain themes start to emerge and take over the movie: the control of nature, our ideas about mortality and obsession, about how humans use animals as a way to project images of ourselves on the world. I'm tired of talking about the film as a piece of weird and eccentric Americana because for me, it's a deeply romantic movie that has real emotional substance to it.

Part of the story is this idea that all of us would like to create something that outlasts us, a microcosm of the world we can control. Maybe this is our fondest hope, to create a world where death plays no part. What I find powerful about these four stories is that with each of these people, death has managed to sneak in anyway. George Mendonça, the gardener, spends fifteen years creating a bear out of a privet hedge. He's an artist who makes these larger-than-life creations that are so absurd and beautiful and of absolutely no use. He knows they're not going to last. His life's work could be destroyed overnight by a hurricane or bugs. It's all so ephemeral. There's probably nobody to take George's place after he's gone and yet he persists. I think there's a nobility in it all. Actually, I see him as the quintessential artist because his cause, however futile in the long run, is so noble.

In this way the film is a kind of elegy. It deals with the impermanence of all our lives and of how what we do is, ultimately, kind of useless.

PC: *Another connection between the four men is something you've already pointed out: animals.*

EM: All four stories in the film are control-of-nature tales that emerge from these men being able, in some small way, to construct a world for their own purposes. In a way it reflects the Frankenstein story, the need to create life and at the same time control it, that by manufacturing a facsimile of life we can better understand the world and ourselves, with the unfortunate codicil that something bad is going to happen.

Another possible theme in *Fast, Cheap* is that each of us constructs fantasies about ourselves and our place in the world so we feel safer about things. It's a basic survival mechanism and probably has something to do with self-deception, with this idea that in order to survive some people have to live somewhere other than "the real world." So one question the film asks is, simply, where do we belong in all of this?

Perhaps the most basic thing that links the stories is the idea of mental landscapes. Just as with *Mr. Death* and *Brief History*, the stories of these four men are excursions into an internal rather than external realm. How much of the world is our dream of the world and how much is real? That's why I introduce each character with their childhood dream of what they want to be.

PC: *We've been talking a lot about intellectual ideas. How important are the visuals for your films?*

EM: Whenever I hear a good story, images immediately come to mind, and it becomes difficult to resist the temptation to film them. I often use visual techniques to telegraph certain ideas I think are worth considering. A good example is the slow-motion shot of the milkshake toss in *The Thin Blue Line*. It's a strong image, but surrounding it is this very important question of what actually happened on that roadway in Dallas. We have the police diagram of the road that evening on which is marked the spot where the milkshake landed. The milkshake collects your thoughts on where the murdered policeman's partner was when the shootings took place. Was she in the car or, as procedure dictates, was she standing outside? What did she see that night? The milkshake-toss shot was used to underline the fact that, in all likelihood, she stayed in the car and threw the drink as she was getting out of the car as the murderer sped off. She didn't get the licence plate number, she didn't get the make of the car. She got nothing.

There is something of a motif in McNamara's story, and in turn in *The Fog of War*, which comes out of the fact that he always seems to be dropping stuff from the skies, whether it be ordnance, napalm, or skulls. His time during World War II working with Curtis LeMay used this motif in the sequence of numbers being dropped over maps of Japan. Another story that emerges in the film is that at one point McNamara was president of the Ford motor company, where he pushed for safety, arguing for collapsible steering wheel and seat belts, things like that. This was at a time when safety wasn't really thought of as being too important. In the film he tells this remarkable story about how they dropped skulls down the stairwell of one of the dormitories of Cornell in order to determine the effect that automobile crashes had on the human body. When I heard this story, I immediately felt this was something I actually had to show, and I illustrated it using a kind of stylised imagery. The images are my attempt to illustrate and dramatize what's going on inside McNamara's head.

PC: *Does this idea of "mental landscapes" tie into your use of archive footage?*
EM: Sure. My films don't document news stories or external events, they're more excursions into people's personal dreamscapes. When someone's talking on camera describing the world around them, to a certain extent they're describing themselves. It's as if the arrow points inward, not outward. The first voice we hear in *Vernon, Florida* is that of Albert Bitterling, my Cartesian philosopher-in-the-swamp. It's one of my all-

time favorite lines on film: "Reality. You mean this is the real world? I never thought of that." The point is that when we think of nonfiction stories we often think of people doing things out there in the world. But I'm not so interested in describing what people do but in how they see the world in a very subjective way, hence the title of my TV series, *First Person*. It's something I feel precludes any kind of journalistic approach. Film clips are, of course, an effective and cinematic way of taking us into the fantasy world of these characters. After all, our brains are littered with these strange collages, these incredible conglomerations of virtual and real images picked up over time from real life, movies, television, newspapers. *The Fog of War*, for example, is just that: a fog, an assortment of facts, letters, presidential recordings, archive footage.

Look at the clips from *Boston Blackie* in *The Thin Blue Line* when Emily Miller is talking about how she always wanted to be a detective or the wife of a detective, and how much those television crime shows influence her. Or the clips of Robin Hood saving the day when Andrew Capoccia in *First Person* is talking about how he helps regular people save money when they're up against the big corporations. Maybe the best example is all the sequences from the Clyde Beatty films in *Fast, Cheap* that Dave Hoover loves so much, these cheesy adventure movies he watched as a kid and that made him want to be Clyde Beatty. I think all of us probably live in some kind of dreamscape. Maybe one thing we all struggle with is moving from that fantasy world into the real world. This is the idea at the heart of *The Thin Blue Line* and *Mr. Death*, and maybe everything I've ever done.

The McNamara film was constructed on my belief that I could do history as a stream of consciousness from a single individual instead of a structured chronological narrative moving from one event to the next. History books are full of footnotes which lead readers to primary source material. With *The Fog of War* I wanted to start with this primary material, construct a film around these intensely subjective references, and then see how they fit into the overall historical picture. Those numbers falling over Tokyo, for example, are taken from McNamara's actual handwritten notes we found in the National Archives.

PC: *Compared to* Mr. Death, Fast, Cheap *is much more descriptive.*

EM: I think the real difference between a film like *Mr. Death* and *Fast, Cheap* is that we're concerned with how these four characters see the world, instead of whether what they say is right or wrong. When George Mendonça is talking about hand shears versus electric shears, it's really not important whether one is better than the other. What we do care about is his personal belief that hand shears are better and that he's spent so many years using them in his work. It would do us little good to bring in experts and have them talk about the various virtues of one kind of shears over another. But that's not the case with *Mr. Death* because when Fred says that poison gas was not used at Auschwitz, he's making a claim we absolutely have to respond to.

PC: Fast, Cheap *is probably your most structurally complex film. How long did it take to make?*

EM: Editing is such a terribly obsessive process. It's like what George the gardener says in the film: "Cut and wait." *Fast, Cheap* took about four years to edit, including a chunk of time after shooting to let the material gestate. I really needed time to think about what I was going to do with the footage. It wasn't easy editing the movie because there were no models or principles to fall back on as examples. It was the same with *Gates of Heaven* when I brought in several co-called "professional editors" to give advice. They all said, "It can't be done, there's no way to put this together."

For a time I really did wonder if the footage was editable at all. It's not like it was made up of regular talking heads that could be stitched together thanks to some kind of pre-imposed narrative, plus the odd piece of visual detritus. At times I felt the same about *Fast, Cheap*, not least because my mother and stepfather died during editing and I really lost faith in my craft. I took some time off, and when I did finally come back to it, the movie somehow came together relatively quickly. Maybe it was because I was fascinated with the way mortality interferes with our plans, whether we like it or not. But at first I had a terrible time in the editing room because I was trying to interweave the overlapping but still quite discrete stories of these four men into one, and I found it very difficult. My general approach was to create some kind of preamble to the whole story, almost to fool audiences into a false sense of security and then play out the four characters one after the after. We started cutting each character up and shuffling the order, interweaving the dialogue and images, until about two-thirds of the way through the film the story is in free fall. Everything is all mixed up, and the audience doesn't really know where they're going.

Technically it was a complex film. The cameraman Robert Richardson had wanted to make a film as a kind of collage. I wanted to create a whole palette of textures and colors, and so we used a variety of film stock:

fine grain 35mm, grainy 35mm, 16mm, Super 16, High 8, Super 8, video transfer to film, infrared, black and white, color reversal, color negative. Anything goes. For some shots, like the one at the end with George Mendonça, we actually spent a whole day inventing the look we wanted. We shot at a hundred and twenty frames a second, five times the speed of sound, which means we need five times as much light. We brought in fog machines, water towers, camera cranes, and lights. We're talking about something that is a really substantial deal with a crew of forty people. After that scene a friend told me, "If you're a fly on the wall, it's a five-hundred-ton fly."

We talked earlier about the Avid. It would have been very difficult to cut *Fast, Cheap*—or something like *The Fog of War*—on a flatbed because we were using so many different formats. We would have had to blow up everything to 35mm, which for financial reasons alone just isn't feasible. Editing *The Thin Blue Line* wasn't easy for the same reason. The reenactments were all shot on 35mm and the interviews on Super 16, and as I had so very little money, I chose to do reduction prints to 16mm of all the 35mm material. So we edited everything in 16mm, but the 16mm reduction prints of the 35mm footage looked awful. While editing we could hardly see anything, and when we printed the finished film and actually saw the 35mm as 35mm, it was shocking how good it looked.

PC: *It seems that the structure of almost all of your films, commercials and TV programs is found in the editing room. You shoot and shoot, then piece the story together afterward.*

EM: I've struggled for months, sometimes years, finding the structure of a film. It's got me into trouble sometimes, as the final result can be very different from the place where I started out. The process of discovery is something I always look forward to in the editing room. And yes, it's exactly the same thing with many of the commercials I've done, especially because so many of them have not been scripted in any real detail.

PC: *You cited Hannah Arendt's book* Eichmann in Jerusalem *more than once when talking about* Mr. Death. *But Fred Leuchter doesn't seem to conform to her description of the paper-pushing bureaucrat.*

EM: No. Fred is no dispassionate bureaucrat. He's genuinely passionate about what he's doing. An entrepreneur. A self-made man. Arendt's phrase "the banality of evil" has been endlessly bandied about, interpreted and reinterpreted. But she, herself, describes the banality of evil as a kind of thoughtlessness. To me that speaks to the absence, not the presence, of thought. I believe this applies to Fred, a man who seems to be suffering from a massive lack of self-awareness. You can see this in the film, not least when I ask him if he ever thinks he might be wrong. He just says, "I'm long since past that. I made a decision that I wasn't wrong." Curious. It's like he made a decision to stop thinking. I'll give him credit for that. Most people stop thinking without ever having to make such a decision.

How do we read something like this? Throughout the movie he portrays himself as a humanitarian, a scientist, a concerned citizen, someone who wants "painless executions"—my second favorite oxymoron—and a champion of the First Amendment. He's the good guy who wants to take the sting out of capital punishment, the Florence Nightingale of death row, the champion of the underdog.

Fred rushes in to defend Ernst Zündel—a Holocaust denier—because Fred's a self-proclaimed civil libertarian and lover of free speech. For Fred it would be remiss for him not to offer his services. But is this just a ploy on his part to sell his services to various people, or does he really believe it? The answer is probably both: he's a salesman who does such a good job that he's started to convince himself. Though he sees himself as a hero, most of us see him, at best, as a deeply misguided and creepy guy.

PC: *What's your favorite oxymoron?*
EM: It changes from day to day. Right now it's a "nice person." And we're always hearing about this thing called "regime change." What we really need is species change.

PC: *Did Leuchter see the film before you screened it publicly?*
EM: Yes. I wanted to show the film to Fred before it premiered at the Sundance Film Festival. I have to admit I was a little apprehensive about what he would think, but nothing Fred saw in the movie caused him to change his views in any way. He went away believing the same things that he believed going in. Eventually, I realized it wasn't my problem—it was his.

Mr. Death is a little morality play. It's a study in hubris and vanity that tells the story of one man's downfall. Fred shows us that if you want to believe something, you can believe it no matter what evidence there is to the contrary. Human credulity is unfettered and unlimited. It's kind of frightening that people are able to believe absolutely anything. This is what I love about Fred's story, this radical disjunction between his image of himself, and what he's actually doing. His is the opposite of the examined life. You couldn't possibly invent a character like Fred.

So the film is an examination of his state of mind, of how Fred fell into error, and because of this I don't think his response to the film is that important. He does actually like the film. But given that it's about someone who is so clueless, is it so surprising he would see the film differently from how I see it? I suppose the question is just how clueless can Fred really be? Do we all live with the same kind of self-invented fables? There's no mystery about whether his claims are right or wrong. Of course they're wrong, all wrong. The mystery is about why he's making them and about whether he really believes them.

The Holocaust has been used in so many movies to push an idea about the triumph of the human spirit. Are they kidding? Whatever the Holocaust is about, it is not about the triumph of the human spirit. By trying to enter the world and mindset of the Holocaust deniers, *Mr. Death* captures the very nature of false belief. Of not just what made Fred Leuchter possible, but what made the Nazis possible. If the uncontroversial and unsurprising thesis of *Schindler's List* is "Anyone can be a hero," then my film has what I believe to be a far more disturbing thesis: "Anyone can think he's a hero."

PC: *Would it be fair to say that your interest in Leuchter mirrors your earlier interest in murderers?*

EM: Sure. It comes back to the same question: "Am I capable of doing something like this?" I couldn't say that Fred's crimes are on a par with those of Ed Gein, but it's this kind of aberrant behavior that interests me. I think we can learn a lot by studying it. And here's one more irony: Leuchter never killed anyone. None of his execution machines have ever been used. McNamara, on the other hand, has been linked with the death of millions.

PC: *It would have been easy to represent Leuchter as a lunatic psychopath foaming at the mouth.*

EM: Yes, and I think *Mr. Death* is more disturbing and interesting precisely because I chose not to do this. It's much easier to condemn Fred Leuchter than to try and understand him. Personally, I find the idea of Fred as a misguided and bumbling idiot more frightening than the view of him as some kind of Iago-like figure who sits in the wings rubbing his hands with an evil grin on his face, conniving, calculating, and plotting. The world would be an easier place to live if there was an easy way of identifying the malefactors in our society. What seems to disturb people about Fred is that they don't come out hating him. They see him as a vain and confused human being. They wonder, is he really monstrous? Or is he really this kind of accidental Nazi, this loveable idiot? Might I be capable of this kind of grand folly too? I suppose at the end of the film the audience is left with two questions: do I know who Fred really is? And do I know who I really am? I think it's a good film because it throws so many questions back at the audience.

You know, I'm not terribly enthusiastic about films that just tell you "War is bad." I need more than that. I believe that history without detail is worthless. History is built with detail, and when it becomes bowdlerized so that it becomes about everything, it in turn becomes about nothing.

PC: *How do you respond to the suggestion that you weren't hard enough on Leuchter, or that you don't handle the historical facts of the Holocaust as profoundly as you should have done?*

EM: I was criticized by some people for not plumbing the depths of Leuchter's past, for not trying to find some event that would identify the evil within him and make everything else clear. But you know, I can't even say for sure that Fred is anti-Semitic. There's no smoking gun, like the young Leuchter found desecrating Jewish graves. To me the fact that he probably wasn't propelled into this thing because of anti-Semitism is what makes his story all the more horrifying. So often what we see as evil perpetrated by someone is always construed by themselves as some form of doing good.

As for the Holocaust question, this simply isn't a movie about the Holocaust. It's a far more interesting story about not only the denial of the Holocaust but also of reality. It's about Fred Leuchter trying to avoid the world, about his attempts to come to terms with who he is. Need I add that the film doesn't make light of the Holocaust? My mother's family came from the area around Krakow and I lost members of my family in the Holocaust. Hopefully what the film does is open this historical subject to examination. Personally, I don't learn anything from tedious documentaries about how horrible the Holocaust was. I know it was bad, I've known it all my life. There is already overwhelming evidence about what happened at the death camps and I certainly don't need to prove the world is round. I'm comfortable with the fact that the film makes it absolutely clear that Fred's ideas are pernicious and false.

PC: *The story moves away from a "first-person" approach when you bring in experts like Robert-Jan Van Pelt and James Roth.*

EM: Most documentaries purport to give you an objective point of view. My films are explorations of subjective elements, how someone sees himself. I made this film to explore why Fred did what he did, and his views are presented in the most objective way I could get away with. *Fast, Cheap* is four characters saying an awful lot of stuff about what they do with no one commenting on whether they're right or wrong. Originally *Mr. Death* was going to be only Fred talking, but it became clear that this was untenable.

What happened was that I screened an early cut of the film, one that featured interviews only with Fred, at Harvard University. What amazed me was that there were students who thought he was right and who seriously started to wonder if the Holocaust ever happened. I thought it was so obvious and clear that what I was presenting in the film was wrong, but they still asked me why I believed what Leuchter was saying. Some students even called me a Jewish Nazi. Obviously this was all very disconcerting to me—and remains so—and I realized I had to go back and rethink the movie. Pretty soon I decided I'd have to open the story out beyond just Fred. I had to put in other voices, though even today I still feel I shouldn't have. The problem was that I don't want to be seen as being irresponsible, or, actually, also be irresponsible. Though I didn't want to get trapped into some long recitation of why Fred is wrong, it would have been irresponsible not to make clear that *The Leuchter Report* was worthless. Bringing in scholars like Van Pelt and Roth into the movie was a simple necessity. I wanted to avoid people coming up to me saying, "You made a movie about a Holocaust denier but you don't say whether he's right or wrong." I can come back and say, "Well, it's obvious he's wrong. Just listen to him." But once again, there's nothing so obvious that it's obvious.

I love irony, but to have only Fred talking—and to assume that the audience would understand that my point was to have this man indict himself—just didn't play. If I didn't add all these other interviews, the film would have been morally compromised, though doing so compromised the film artistically, because it spoiled that splendid insanity of Leuchter babbling away.

PC: *I gather you never liked the title* Mr. Death.
EM: It's terrible, really. My wife wanted to call the film *What Fred Said*. I liked *Honeymoon in Auschwitz*, but I was scared of calling it that, even though Fred did actually spend his honeymoon there.

PC: *Can we talk about composer Phillip Glass, with whom you've worked on several of your films?*
EM: I remember complaining to him while we were working on *The Thin Blue Line*, "You know, this music just isn't repetitive enough." He

gave me this very strange look and said, "That's a new one." It was certainly due to Philip's music that *The Thin Blue Line* started coming together as a movie. I edited the film with scratch music assembled from a variety of Glass records and it worked really well. I was worried about what I was ultimately going to replace this music with. Who would I find to write Philip Glass–type music? Pretty soon the obvious answer surfaced. He does existential dread very well. There's a certain gravitas to his work.

I've always been careful about using music in my films. The main issue for me is that the music is playing underneath a monologue so it can't drown out the words, but at the same time it has to enhance what's being said. I never really know what music I want to use in a film until I actually have the images up there on the screen, because music combines with images in ways that can't always be anticipated.

PC: *Are you able to see any connecting threads through the* First Person *interviews?*

EM: They don't really cohere, if one were to be scrupulously honest, because they were produced over such a long period of time. To me the characters of *First Person* are simply a group of obsessives. Each episode is a portrait of someone truly committed to what they do, even if some of them would fit perfectly on a tabloid-style TV show. But it's not oddity for the sake of oddity. If there isn't some emotional depth to the story, I'm not interested. There's always something deeper and more interesting going on. Take Saul Kent, who decapitated his mother and froze her head for future resuscitation. Where his story gets really interesting is when he talks about devoting his life to becoming immortal, and only then deciding what he really wants to do. I love this kind of stuff. I've always had more ideas than time, and half-hour TV episodes are the perfect outlet for me.

Of course, the other connection between the films can be found in the title. They all capture what these people are saying, and nothing more. It's one person, and only that person. I'm not interested in whether they are right or wrong, credible or not credible. It's not about balance, about providing the audience with all sides of the story. That's not the point. In fact, I'm doing the exact opposite.

PC: *What are your thoughts about film schools?*

EM: I'm quoting Godard here, I think, but the real university of film is the movie theater. If you want to learn about film, go to see movies. Lots and lots of movies. As a graduate student at Berkeley, I got my real education at the Pacific Film Archive, where I must have seen two or three movies a day.

PC: *Werner Herzog has said that he doesn't understand irony at all, while you've said that irony is a kind of religion for you.*

EM: Herzog would tell me one of his Nazi *Übermensch* stories: how he single-handedly battled four hundred man-eating pygmies in the Amazon jungle or walked across Mongolia hopping on one foot. In turn I would counter with a Jew-boy story: how I cried myself to sleep every night because I lived at home with my mother, had no friends, and wet the bed. I'm pleased to say that these stories never failed to irritate him.

PC: *Okay, but can you give me some examples of irony in your films?*

EM: Sure. Although explaining an irony is probably like explaining a joke. McNamara is a control freak, yet he explains to us that the world is, essentially, out of control. That's ironic, but my favorite example is in *Mr. Death.* For me there are three ironies in the final scene of the movie. It's a layer-cake kind of deal. Fred is sitting in his own electric chair and comes out with a truly absurd line. He's talking about prison guards: "They came to realize that their children shouldn't sit in the electric chair." Why? Because one of these kids later went on to commit capital murder, was sentenced to death, and executed in the same chair that he sat in as a child. You sit in the chair—the legend goes—you die in the chair. That's irony number one. Fred then goes on to tell us that he sat in that same chair, and went on not to die in the chair but to design and repair electric chairs. That's irony number three: I outwitted death. Those are the two intended ironies, but he comes up with a third, unintended irony with the final line in the movie. Fred is wistful, contemplative, and says, "Maybe I created a new legend and some good has come of this after all." Good?! What's interesting about the scene is our knowledge that Fred, without knowing it, has been destroyed by his own execution device. In some metaphorical sense it's as if he did sit in that damn thing and was executed. And that's irony number three. Isn't he, when all is said and done, an example of the walking dead?

To go back to the reenactments in *The Thin Blue Line,* there are strong elements of irony in all of them because they are visual representations of things that people claimed they saw and never what actually happened. They are dramatic reenactments of unreality. There is also a very ironic line at the end of the film that no one ever seems to notice, much to my disappointment, though when I see the film it still strikes me as being absurdly ironic. It's David Harris's epiphany at the end of the movie—this moment that seems to combine self-knowledge and self-deception at the same time—when he's talking about the death of his younger brother, about his life of crime and violence: "I came to realize I was only hurting myself," he says. Well, I look at this and there's a part of me that wants to stand up and raise my hand and say, "Not exactly, David. There were other people involved as well."

PC: *Do your films tell us as much about you as they do about the people you are taking to?*

EM: What is the hallmark of a really good documentary? Isn't it a film that somehow captures the complexity of the relationship of the film-maker to his subjects? I like to think that a good documentary somehow preserves the relationship between the person making the movie and his subjects. It's not necessary to hear my questions or see me on screen, but I like to think I'm still very much part of the interviews and of the film as a whole. One of the things I find so fascinating about documentary film-making, and why I'd like to continue making documentaries no matter what else I might do, is that they seem to be a form of almost pure movie-making, offering almost unlimited possibilities for self-expression.

PC: *As we talked about earlier, the notion of truth as being objective appears more than once in your interviews. I'm curious to know how the ideas you must have tackled as a student of philosophy of science have affected your work as a filmmaker.*

EM: I think they have affected pretty much every aspect of my life. I got an awful lot out studying philosophy. At Princeton, at a time when Hilary Putnam and Saul Kripke were writing about realism and reference, I ended up with Thomas Kuhn as my advisor. One of my great night-mares. Kuhn was basking in the glory of his "shifting paradigms." There were students who lapped up every word. I'm sorry, but I found his book *The Structure of Scientific Revolutions* deeply confused. Hey, if meanings are incommensurable, then how is history of science possible? To make a long story short, he physically assaulted me and shortly after that threw me out of Princeton. I ended up at Berkeley. The philosophy department was really bad. If I thought Princeton was bad, this was unimaginably worse. Paul Grice, their *éminence grise* from Oxford, as far as I could tell, spent most of his time picking his nose, hitting on women, and chain-smoking Player cigarettes. I guess that made him an expert on intentions. I couldn't take it. They were driving me crazy, and so I started going to a lot of movies at the Pacific Film Archive. At least it was dark in there.

PC: *But have those various philosophical concerns of yours become part of your movies?*

EM: I guess so. For example, Karl Popper is one of my heroes. Going back to *Mr. Death*, it's interesting to consider what the Popperian account of Holocaust denial would be. From Popper's point of view I don't think we have anything to fear from Holocaust denial. In fact it might even be a good thing. Isn't the starting point of Popper's idea: propose a theory, one that is potentially falsifiable? Then you see whether you can falsify it. In this particular incidence, our theory is eminently falsifiable. It's "conjecture and refutation" *par excellence*. The Holocaust deniers, just by being out there, have encouraged people to do so much important Holocaust research. They have been invaluable—or a better way of putting it—they have been valuable in establishing the existence of the Holocaust. That, too, is ironic.

That's why it is so important to examine and to refute *The Leuchter Report*. Look at the Spielberg technique of recording thousands and thousands of eyewitness testimonies, of just going on and on uncritically, as if somehow the answers will emerge from the accretion of one eyewitness account after another. It's a Quantity over Quality approach. Compare this to the historian Robert-Jan van Pelt who helped formulate a new way of looking at the Holocaust, of exploring and understanding history. In the seventies there was a famous trial in Vienna of the architects of Auschwitz crematoria. They were acquitted. Why? Because no one knew how to read the files. No one knew how to read the drawings and blueprints in the archives. Van Pelt—who was trained as an architect—came in and started to study this material and discovered how the original plans for the crematoria had been modified to include homicidal gas chambers. If what he discovered had been known at the time of the Vienna trial, these people would have hung. The one thing we know about architecture is that it's premeditated.

There are always difficulties in discovering that truth. Whether we like it or not, scientific theories are only an approximation of how the world works. I like to call the brain a "virtual reality generator," a lump of protoplasm that processes the things we see and hear and feel. In this sense, truth is nothing but an unending quest, something that's constantly eluding us. Searching for the truth is our attempt to get beyond our brains, our selfish protoplasm. It's never just handed over to us on a plate. One of my favorite lines in *A Brief History of Time* is when Hawking's mother calls him a "searcher." It's not as if he has possession of absolute knowledge or truth, but he is involved in trying to uncover the truth about what the world might really be like. For someone to insist that a particular line of inquiry is closed, that everything about a certain idea is resolved, is to me quite unhealthy. There's never a cow so sacred it can't be examined. Maybe it turns out to be neither sacred nor a cow.

But I certainly do believe in scientific progress and that we are approaching greater truth. Quite to what end I can't say, but we are learning more about the world every year. There's this ridiculous postmodernist idea that there is no such thing as "the truth." Truth doesn't exist. I see myself as the ultimate anti-postmodernist. Even with all the obstacles to truth-seeking that exist—self-deception, self-interest, things like that— there are very few things we can't at least try to look beyond in order to clarify the truth of a situation. To me, truth is never subjective. It's not up for grabs, it's not subject to a vote, even if it might sometimes be difficult to determine absolutely.

People think that ambiguity is somehow wonderful in its own right, an excuse for failing to ask questions. I find this view reprehensible. If the world is a mystery, then there is nothing more noble than trying to solve that mystery or at least exploring it in an attempt to find out more about the world and about ourselves. The bottom line: there is a real world out there where real and knowable things actually happen, and this is what my films are about. If you look at what took place in Dallas in November 1976, it is clear that someone was most definitely sitting in the driver's seat of that car and shot Robert Wood. That person, it seems quite safe to say, was David Harris.

There is a very big difference between saying there's no such thing as truth—that truth is subjective, that we all see the world in different way, that just thinking something makes it true, that there's no way in adjudicating between all those different "truths"—and saying that truth exists but we all have a vested interest in not seeing it. There is such a thing as truth. It's not that we find truth with a big "T." We investigate, and sometimes we find things out and sometimes not. There's no way to know in advance. It's just that we have to proceed as though there are answers to questions. The alternative is unacceptable.

The Thin Blue Line was compared by some people to *Rashômon*, a film I hadn't seen in many years. I went back and looked at Kurosawa's film, wondering if I'd missed something. I always thought it was about the subjectivity of truth, but as I understand it *Rashômon* is a very different film. It's about that fact that we all see the world differently and all have our own reasons for burying the truth. The greatness of *Rashômon* is that at the end you have the feeling that out of all of these divergent stories, you still know what really happened. Through these various self-centered subjective accounts, we gradually glean the information that allows us to determine the underlying truth.

As should be clear by now, self-deception interests me a great deal. It's part of the human condition and is a theme that runs through much of my work. We're basically a bunch of weird monkeys doing weird monkey things that are only dimly apparent to us. It's the "Fog of Everything." I'm acutely aware that I'm no different from the people in my films, that I don't have any special access to the truth, that I'm as self-deceived as anyone I've ever interviewed. It's the old Garden of Eden story. As God was kicking Adam and Eve out of the Garden of Eden, He began to feel guilty and decided to come up with a way to make the whole experience a little easier for them, so He gave mankind self-deception. "Things will still be really, truly horrible out there for them," says God, "but they'll never notice."

PC: *And of course there is a strong element of self-deception in Robert McNamara's story.*

EM: Like Fred Leuchter, McNamara is tortured by his past. But while Fred is tortured in a clueless way and feels completely misunderstood, McNamara is not entirely oblivious to the reasons why people dislike him and are angry at him, although I'm sure that to a certain extent he also feels somewhat misunderstood.

A good example of how self-deception might play a part in McNamara's story is what happened in the Gulf of Tonkin in 1964, which for me is something of a microcosm of his whole story. You have these two incidents in the Gulf, one on 2 August and 4 August, followed by the Senate ratification of the Gulf of Tonkin Resolution that Johnson and subsequent administrations used as justification for escalating the war. In *The Fog of War*, McNamara tells us something that many people know, that the 2 August incident did happen but that the 4 August incident did not happen. What he doesn't tell us in the movie is that the 2 August incident was provoked by us. Johnson and McNamara stood before the American public and repeatedly talked about the "unprovoked attacks" in the Gulf of Tonkin.

I've talked in detail about this with McNamara, and his justification for what happened is, "Well, they weren't really provoked. We were blowing up radar installations, but those were just pinpricks." From this arise the questions of exactly what a pinprick is and what a provocation might be if it isn't the result of having your radar installations blown up? For example if the North Vietnamese blew up a radar installation in South Carolina would that be considered a provocation or a pinprick? What about if they blew up a radar installation in New Jersey? The other question that emerges is: does McNamara really believe it's a pinprick? Is he being sincere about this or he just giving excuses for what happened? Maybe he does believe it and maybe in this equation of great power politics and international affairs there's a kind of language that I personally don't adequately understand, which equates in some way to people like McNamara really believing that the military's actions weren't really provocative.

On the other hand, it could all be about lying. Daniel Ellsberg, of *Pentagon Papers* fame, once told me that you could say anything about McNamara. Call him a war criminal, a monster, whatever. No problem. The one thing he won't tolerate? You can't call him a liar.

PC: *How did you get McNamara to agree to being interviewed at such length?*
EM: I had wanted to interview him for years but once I asked him it actually took very little convincing. We were all set up shooting *First Person* and had the studio booked so I thought, "What the hell, I'll just call him and see if he's willing to come up to Cambridge." He'd just written a book and had been traveling around the country on a book tour. I think—I don't know this for sure—that he saw me as part of his book tour. He called me two days before we were due to shoot the interview. I guess someone must have told him that he shouldn't talk to me. He said, "I've been speaking to people about you and they say it's a very bad idea for me to talk to you. Actually, it makes no sense at all. There's no reason why I should do it. You're the wrong person." He went on and on giving me all these reasons why he shouldn't talk with me, and then said, "But I said I'd do it, so I'll come up and do it." A friend of mine pointed out to me that this is also the story of the Vietnam war.

At first he was going to talk for a very limited amount of time—such conditions are very characteristic of McNamara—but we convinced him to extend it from one day to two. We ended up with six hours, and most of the film actually comes from that first set of interviews. They were just amazing interviews. Before he agreed to come back for more I had to put together a forty-minute cut of the film, which he liked. I truly feel that McNamara was quite courageous in sitting for these interviews. I've often wondered what motivated a man of his age to agree to make this film. He exposed himself to someone he didn't know, while knowing there's a public out there who really don't like him. There have been violent demonstrations against him. People have even tried to kill him. He's been accosted by Vietnam veterans. But even with this litany of reasons why he shouldn't work with me, he agreed to come to Cambridge.

The first interview was done pre-9/11, in May of 2001. He came on a Tuesday, the Sunday after the *New York Times* had published an article on Bob Kerrey, his Congressional Medal of Honor and his possible war crimes in Southeast Asia. It had also been the subject of a recent report on *60 Minutes*. McNamara came into the studio and we started talking about that article because it was on both of our minds. He vigorously defended Bob Kerrey, saying, "How can you hold him responsible for those things that his superiors did?" Then I mentioned to him I had read an article by Richard Rhodes about Curtis LeMay that was in the *New Yorker* years ago in which LeMay had been quoted as saying that if the United States hadn't won the war, he would have been tried as a war criminal. He was referring to World War II, the firebombing of Japan and the use of the two atomic weapons.

Early in the interview I asked McNamara about this, and within the first twenty minutes of our conversation he said that he too considered himself a possible war criminal. He wasn't talking about the sixties in Vietnam but rather in the forties in Japan. I remember thinking at the time that was quite extraordinary. It's the kind of thing you maybe expect to hear after twenty hours of interviews, not twenty minutes. What's even more interesting is that I knew nothing about McNamara's involvement with the firebombing of Tokyo and his service under LeMay in the Mariannas, and as far as I know nothing substantial has been written about it. It's not in any of the books about McNamara or any of the autobiographical material McNamara has written. Yet all of a sudden he starts talking to me on camera about the firebombing of Tokyo, and mentions that he had written memos for General Norstad—the chief of staff of the 20th Air Force—about the height of bombing, or more specifically about the relationship of the altitude of the B-29s to the accuracy of the bombing. One of his lessons is: maximize efficiency. McNamara pointed out that it's not an arithmetic relationship. Above 20,000 feet, the B-29s lacked any real accuracy. His suggestion: bring the bombers much lower, at the time an almost heretical suggestion. The B-29s had been designed to fly higher and further than previous bombers in an effort to minimize the terrible losses that the B-17s had suffered over Europe. Anyway, after this first interview my research assistant went down to the National Archives and found a folder of material filled with McNamara's memos from 1945. I don't think anybody had looked at it since 1945.

PC: *Many people feel you were far too easy on McNamara when interviewing him.*

EM: Yes, but when critics write that I'm McNamara's "lapdog" or that I allowed him "to call the shots," it's obvious they've failed to take into the account the very nature of the movie they've seen. Critics have written that some of the things McNamara says are self-serving; that he focuses on certain details and omits others, that he's rewriting history in his own interest. Well yes, they're right on all counts. If I'm too easy on McNamara by not including other voices that explicitly criticize him, then I admit it: I'm guilty. I did it deliberately. I wanted to do away with the traditional formulas of historical storytelling on film with the endless yin and yang of experts conceptualizing and explaining.

The Fog of War is part history, part self-analysis, part mystery, part self-justification. By my interviewing McNamara and no one else, he reveals to us many of the contradictions that have fascinated me about him for years. Something emerges that is otherwise lost. The way he responds to certain questions, his refusal to answer certain questions, his silences: this is what the film is really about. I like the idea that actually there are two people in the film, two McNamaras talking to each. One is forty-five years old, the other is eighty-five.

Of course there will be people who look at the film and judge it on the basis of what they think it should be about or what it should look like. Some of these criticisms are formulated on the notion that there should be at least one other voice in the film—perhaps a narrator—telling you what to think about McNamara, explaining whether or not he's to be believed, pointing out which things he's saying are true and which are not, exclaiming when he's being sincere or otherwise. Part of what I was doing in the film was eschewing all of those ancillary voices under the belief that by examining this one voice—alone on the screen talking about his life—the audience is able to enter into his mental landscape. It's pretty clear to me that what voice-over narration does is not give us information about what we're looking at, but rather information about the speaker, and in turn the filmmaker. Language is the ultimate tool of concealment. Sometimes I think it was invented to facilitate lying, so that we can lie more effectively, not only to other people but to ourselves too. But McNamara isn't trying to justify the Vietnam War. That's not his mission. He may say things to try to convince us that what he did wasn't evil or irrational or ill-considered, but he himself has admitted all kinds of error.

PC: *In his book* Explaining Hitler, *Ron Rosenbaum alludes to the idea of "evil incarnate." Do you think such a thing exists? Is McNamara "evil"?*

EM: I believe in evil acts, not evil persons. I've never really believed in evil persons, and I'm not sure I even understand the concept of good and evil people for the simple reason that people are just too complex to be summed up that way. Much to my surprise I came to really like and respect McNamara. He's someone wrestling with his demons, a man involved in a real attempt to understand his place in history even if, like most of us, he's willing to go only so far. I believe the world is a better place for having someone like Robert McNamara around. He's a man who evokes very strong feelings in some people. There are people who hate him and will continue to hate him no matter what. They consider *The Fog of War* as one big excuse, an attempt to make himself look better or even to whitewash himself. But when he suggests that he and LeMay were probably war criminals, he's telling a very different story. To me, this kind of self-analysis is hardly an attempt to whitewash the past, but rather a sincere attempt to think about history. Has he gone far enough? Who has?

How many other public figures from the Vietnam era have shared their agony with the public in the way McNamara has? I really respect the fact that in this crazy spirit of enquiry he traveled to Vietnam to talk with his former counterparts, an experience detailed in his book *Argument Without End. In Retrospect*—and to a certain extent his participation in the film—shows that this is a man who is trying, perhaps struggling, to understand and analyze his past motivations and action. I feel he should be applauded for asking himself, "How did this happen?" I never felt that what McNamara did with *In Retrospect* was born out of self-interest or malice, rather a desire to do good, and therein lies the essential tragedy of his story.

To my mind McNamara is in many ways a very ethical man. This is not someone who denies everything and takes responsibility for nothing. Or let me put it this way: he's certainly not oblivious to the ethical dimension of life. I find it very moving to see him wrestle with the question, "Am I a good man or a bad man?"

PC: *Why do you think McNamara was fired? Was he playing an adversarial role within the Johnson administration? In* In Retrospect, *McNamara writes about talking to Katherine Graham of the* Washington Post *and wondering if he actually had been fired or if he quit of his own volition. Even he doesn't even seem to know if he was playing an adversarial role.*

EM: It's quite possible he didn't know precisely what kind of role he was playing within the administration just before he was fired. The usual question arises: how much are we really in control of our own behavior? This is not to excuse him, by the way. I think people are wrong when they imagine that with his books and this film, McNamara is involved in some simple attempt at an apology. It's really much more complex than that. I think he's involved in a complex attempt to understand who he is and what he did. Maybe part of it has to do with denial too. In fact, I'd be surprised if it didn't. But it's never as simple as that.

PC: *So you think the book is more of an explanation than an apology or an excuse?*

EM: When you listen to these kinds of things, if you're kindly disposed to McNamara, then you'll seen him as being full of explanations. If not, what he's coming out with are just excuses. A friend of mind said to me that the definition of an excuse is "an explanation for something that turned out badly." I think this is correct. Part of it is that something really bad happened: the deaths of millions of Vietnamese and 58,000 Americans. We can all agree that this was a bad thing. It certainly horribly affected me as a young man and still affects me to a certain extent. What explanation could McNamara offer of this that wouldn't sound like an excuse, at least to some people? I suppose something like "I'm a maniac who always had to be the best in my class, and my attempts to excel were so unfettered that I would stop at nothing in trying to advance myself" would suffice for some. But if that's true, why the hell is he telling Kennedy to get out of Vietnam when the president is extremely reluctant to do so?

There's a recording of a Security Council meeting on 2 October 1963, a few weeks before Kennedy's death. We hear McNamara, who has recently returned from Vietnam, telling the president we need to get out of Vietnam, arguing for the removal of a thousand American advisors by Christmas and of the remaining fifteen thousand by 1965. Kennedy isn't entirely convinced by this. In fact, McNamara told me there was terrible disagreement at the meeting, something confirmed when I made a transcript of the meeting. McNamara even urged the president to publicly announce withdrawal of American advisors from Vietnam to prevent "backsliding," people going back on this policy. That night Pierre

Salinger, the president's press secretary, announces this and there are news reports about it that show American servicemen boarding planes in Vietnam about to fly home. A few weeks later Kennedy is killed and we then hear, on the Johnson tapes, the president chastising McNamara during a phone conversation and making explicit reference to the Security Council meeting. He says, "I always thought it was foolish for you to make any statements about withdrawing. I thought it was bad psychologically. But you and the president thought otherwise, and I just sat silent."

Perhaps the recording I heard of this conversation is unique. Maybe there are hundreds of others that I haven't heard that contradict it, which means my understanding of what happened back then is completely skewed. But this recording does exist and I find McNamara's line about needing to find a way of getting out of Vietnam very powerful. He is seeking a non-military way out of the crisis. The question is: was he willing to find a non-military way out at the risk of losing the war? I just don't buy the various simplistic conclusions about McNamara. It's much more complex than that. In fact, to the extent that I understand everything in this movie, I feel I've done a poor job of telling the story.

When people say, "McNamara didn't go as far as I'd like in the film, he didn't really apologize," I ask myself, "What exactly is it that these people want to hear? What are they looking for?" Do I want to hear McNamara apologize for the war? Not really. Maybe I just don't believe in redemption, but I think there would be something obscene about saying sorry for the death of 58,000 Americans and more than three million Vietnamese. How do you redeem the Vietnam War? Isn't the point that it's unredeemable? What could bring back everyone who died? I have my own theory of apologies, that we love them because they empower us. You say, "I'm sorry, will you forgive me?" and then the ball is in their court. I think that what McNamara has done is far more interesting than apologizing. Simply, what he tried to do is analyze how the country—and he—ended up in Vietnam. Don't forget this is the man who ordered the creation of the Pentagon Papers. It's that same instinct to go back over the past, to go back and try to understand it. He's a man who's looking for redemption and who is trying to revise the past in his own mind. But he's also very interested in exploring why certain things happened in his life, things that affected many of us, and how we can learn from history.

PC: *Was there a certain view of McNamara—and by extension of what we might call "human nature"—that you were trying to put across in* The Fog of War? *The historical incidents he talks about in the film to a certain extent take a backseat to timeless questions of self-knowledge, of how we see the world.*

EM: I often think that if my movies are any good it's because they are full of u•1resolved questions you can keep thinking about.

PC: *What was your own stand on the Vietnam War at the time?*

EM: As I told McNamara at the start, I demonstrated against the war when I was at the University of Wisconsin and as a graduate student at Princeton. All of those demonstrations were after he had left office, but they were very much against the Vietnam War. It's been interesting making *The Fog of War* because the responses to the film have been so generational. Those people who came of age during the Vietnam War know about McNamara and have strong opinions about him, but younger people know little or nothing about him.

PC: *In your office there is an entire bookshelf of background material on McNamara. Clearly you felt the need to prepare for your interviews with him.*

EM: I like buying books. But notwithstanding, I did make a real effort to prepare for the interviews by reading a lot and talking with historians. Even though I've never believed in having a formal list of questions to ask someone, I believe in preparing for interviews. I was, of course, aware of McNamara's brilliance. I wanted to show him respect on a very basic level. Before we met I read and thought about his books very carefully. He told me that most of the people who interviewed him had never read his books.

McNamara himself is very persnickety. He told me that when he was writing his books he tried not to put in anything that couldn't be corroborated by independent evidence. For example, he remembers telling Kennedy to pull the American military advisors out of Vietnam, but couldn't remember exactly when. So he went to the Kennedy Library and found the tape recording of his conversation with the president. Part of that conversation can be heard in *The Fog of War.*

PC: *What about the newly released tapes from the Johnson Library? What new light do they throw on McNamara's role in the war?*

EM: I call it the Halberstam Thesis because it appears in *The Best and the Brightest,* his book about the Kennedy-Johnson whiz kids who dragged us into a loathsome, disastrous war in Southeast Asia. The thesis is that McNamara was a number cruncher, man devoid of ethical sensibility, who through his obsessions with statistics, blundered into the Vietnam

War. That he was the bellicose secretary of defense egging on a vacillat-
ing LBJ. That he was the hawk who belatedly became a dove, and a dove
very late in the game, too late for him to ever engage our sympathies. The
David Levine cartoon from the *New Yorker* probably sums it up, the image
of McNamara crying alligator tears when the damage had already been
done. Halberstam's version of the story is that the war was a bad war conceived of by bad people. It's perhaps inarguable that the war was wrong,
but was it really conceived by evil or shallow people? The Halberstam
book just made me more curious about McNamara.

The newly released presidential tapes from Johnson's administration
tell a different story, to me at least. The tapes tell us that the Halberstam
Thesis is wrong. McNamara was probably a dove all along. Not that this
lets him off the hook. Rather, it opens up a different story. Not a better
story, just a different one. If he opposed the war, then why did he go along
with it? How did he allow himself to be pushed into such a position?

The Fog of War tries to outline these questions. When you hear McNamara saying to Kennedy that they need to find a way to get out of Vietnam, and that pulling out advisors is a way to do it, to me that's not a
hawk speaking. I suppose if you are completely convinced that McNamara is a hawk is a hawk is a hawk then you can find some way to provide an alternative explanation of these remarks. But there they are, to be
reckoned with one way or the other.

Johnson then becomes president by accident and in the early months
of his administration we hear McNamara repeatedly telling the president to limit involvement, to curb the various troop levels and bombing
sorties advocated by the joint chiefs of staff. We repeatedly see McNamara trying to mitigate and ameliorate, diminish the level of conflict
rather than expand it. But then we hear Johnson telling McNamara he
basically wants to escalate the war, saying things like, "How the hell does
McNamara think he's going to win a war by pulling advisors out?" Perhaps this is my own simplification, but I have a very hard time reconcil-
ing that with the picture of McNamara as being the chief architect and in-
stigator of the war in Vietnam. To me it doesn't tell a story of McNamara
pushing Johnson into war, but rather the other way around. Vietnam has
been seen as "McNamara's War," but maybe it was actually Johnson's war.
So the questions change: who was McNamara in all of this?

PC: *How did the structure of the film come about, the "Eleven Lessons"?*
EM: I struggled to find a workable structure for the film until just before
Cannes, when I put in the lessons which were extracted from things he

says in the film. McNamara's main complaint to me was that they weren't his lessons and that if he had picked eleven lessons they would be different. What's odd to me is that people talk about the lessons without pointing out at there might be intended ironies with each and every one. Take "Maximize efficiency." Well, that seems like a good lesson, but what if that ends up killing 100,000 people in single day? Or "Get the data." But what if the data's all wrong? One thing I really like is the set of ironies that are set up at the start of the film and that hopefully pay off at the end. The final lesson is "You can't change human nature." It's saying that this is the way we are—confused, bellicose, crazy—which is basically saying that you can't put an end to war. Or that the other ten lessons are meaningless. One of McNamara's most powerful lines in the films is when he says, "Rationality isn't enough." Sure, man is rational, but rationality may not be sufficient to save us from our own inherent need to destroy each other. And this from a man known for being hyperrational, the efficiency expert, the data cruncher. I even have Harry Reasoner, in a McNamara profile from CBS, describing him as an IBM computer with legs. There's something ironic about basing your entire life on rationality, and then deciding that rationality can't save us from ourselves. And if rationality can't save us, what can?

PC: *So what is the difference between your lessons and McNamara's?*

EM: He's an optimist and I'm not. McNamara believes that by examining our conduct, and through his examination of his own conduct, we can make the world a better place, that we can avoid repeating the mistakes of the past. What's my take on this? Max Brod, Kafka's close friend, asked him, "Franz, surely there is some hope?" "Yes," said Kafka, "but not for us." Look at Faulkner's Nobel Prize acceptance speech in 1946. The speech is remembered for the phrase "Man shall not merely endure, he shall prevail." But it contains a far more interesting and pessimistic line: "Our tragedy today is a general and universal physical fear so long sustained by now that we can even bear it. There are no longer problems of the spirit. There is only the question: When will I be blown up?" Indeed. Beastliness is the norm and not the exception. I've always wanted to make a movie that would make people wish they'd have never been born. But alas, reality beats me to it.

PC: *Why did you bring in McNamara's first memory, that of Armistice Day in 1918?*

EM: It's related to the lines he quotes from Eliot's "Four Quartets' about going back to where you began: "We shall not cease from exploring / And at the end of our exploration / We will return to where we started / And know the place for the first time." Namely, you can learn from experience. You can review the circumstances of your life and derive lessons, and that perhaps others can profit from these lessons as well. There is something to be gained, something to be learned. Life has some benefit. I have a slightly different gloss on all of this. What was Armistice Day? It was a celebration of a great self-deception, of a delusion, of a great irony. We might well call it Woodrow Wilson's self-deception about the Great War as the war to end all wars, about 1914–18 having taught mankind that it shouldn't engage in something like that again. Ha! "Those who cannot remember the past are condemned to repeat it." Santayana's quote. But I wonder whether we can learn from what we did five minutes ago. We keep on making the same mistakes, and it's unreasonable to expect we can do better regardless of whether we remember anything or not. I prefer, "Those who cannot remember the past are condemned to repeat it without a sense of ironic futility." Or even: "Those who cannot condemn the past repeat it in order to remember it." And don't forget, in the light of the recently released presidential recordings, the far more interesting quote from Santayana: "All history is wrong and has to be rewritten." As more archives are opened up for us to study, the full picture becomes clearer. In a sense, history is about the struggle between what actually happened and what we imagine happened.

PC: *You have written about "preventive war."*

EM: If the notion of a war to end all wars is oxymoronic, the notion of "preventive war" is, as well. "This is a preventative war, an antiwar war," we're told. But all wars produce more wars. Every war in history has produced unresolved tensions that in the end produce future conflict. It's like McNamara's view of antiballistic missiles: it's still a missile. If you build an antimissile to protect yourself from missiles, then they build a bigger missile to destroy your antimissile missile, and in turn you have to respond by building a bigger antimissile missile. And so on. So there's McNamara saying he's come back to where he started. It has this kind of circularity, an element of tragedy to it that I like. It's horrific, but I find it artistically satisfying.

PC: *Did you go out of your way to link McNamara's story with the current political situation?*

EM: Not directly, but it was certainly in the back of my mind. As our interviews progressed, the events of forty or fifty years ago that McNamara was describing became more and more relevant to what had happened only five or six days ago. The Gulf of Tonkin story seems to be a WMD story of forty years ago. History was catching up with the movie, not the other way around. Perhaps the most obvious example is when he explains that during Vietnam, none of the United States' allies gave any direct support. America went into it alone, regardless. It's a line we actually put in very late in the day, just before we finished the film. He asks, "What makes us omniscient? If we can't persuade nations with comparable values of the merit of our cause, we'd better reexamine our reasoning." The issues of *The Fog of War* are inevitably related to things happening in the world today simply because they're about the most basic and universal problems: self-deception and conflict. When considering how relevant the eleven lessons are to the current situation, the question of whether we're doomed to repeat our mistakes of the past over and over again comes up.

PC: *Are you saying that Vietnam equals Iraq?*

EM: Although my feelings about Iraq are not so different from my feelings about Vietnam, I don't think that Vietnam equals Iraq. History is like the weather, and all historical situations are different. But though history never exactly repeats itself, there is one thing that remains the same in history: human idiocy. Our capacity for self-deception, ignoring history, for historical amnesia, for ignoring evidence if it's unpalatable to us, even if it means accepting untruth, all this remains constant. It's only part of my job with this film to contribute to the debate about what's happening today in the world. As McNamara said to the audience when we spoke in Berkeley a few months ago, "You make the connections."

PC: *In an interview, McNamara described you as having a high IQ, being an extraordinarily interesting conversationalist who is very well-read, and someone who works hard to try and understand his subjects. Is this the trick to your success as a filmmaker?*

EM: Having a high IQ? I guess I forgot to tell McNamara that I was tested with an IQ of 87 when I was in grade school.

PC: *That's retarded.*

EM: Exactly. My guidance counselor told me: "You know, you appear to be a lot smarter than you really are." I guess I like to make that extra effort. I remember reading an article in the *National Inquirer* on "How to Look Smart When You're Really Very Stupid." I've tried to follow several of their recommendations: drink a lot of coffee, carry around a book with you wherever you go, and smile and nod as often as possible. These suggestions have been invaluable.

PC: *You seem to have a strong contrarian streak.*

EM: Contrarian? Also, skeptical. I believe that we should always entertain the possibility that everything we know is wrong. Ultimately it may be that our conscious explanations don't take into account the hidden layers of motivation, intention, and belief that determine what we do. We observe at best one percent of ourselves, maybe zero percent. I've always wanted to recast the Cartesian *cogito*. How about, "I think therefore I think I am."

One of my favorite quotations comes from the last living member of Zoar, a failed utopian community in south central Ohio. The Zoars really fascinate me. Unlike the Shakers they really had very little going for them. The architecture was execrable, the food was bad, and not too surprisingly their community became extinct. But in an archive in Ohio I found a record of the last words of the last inhabitant of Zoar. In her nineties and on her deathbed, she said, "Think of it. All those religions. They can't all be right. But they could all be wrong."

There's one last thing I'd like to say about this notion of self-deception. Not too long ago I was giving a lecture at Brandeis University and showed various clips from my films, including the one from *Vernon, Florida* about the sand that grows. Mr. and Mrs. Martin appear with their bottle of sand. They had collected the sand at White Sands Proving Ground in New Mexico and had brought it back with them to Florida, and they talk about how they put very little sand in the jar and how the sand almost filled up the jar. They are both absolutely convinced that the sand is growing. I said, "One thing we know about the sand is that it isn't growing. But clearly they think it is. How could that possibly be the case? Can our desire to have the world accord with our fantasies be so great that it influences how we actually see the world?" And I went on and on about this, until someone raised their hand and said, "You know that the sand at White Sands Proving Ground is not beach sand. It's gypsum, which is very sensitive to changes in humidity. It absorbs water. So perhaps when they brought the sand back from the low humidity of New Mexico to the high humidity of Florida, the sand actually did expand." And I thought that's great! Just when I think I have an absolutely perfect example of self-deception, it turns out that the only one who's deceiving himself is me.

Film and Friendship: Werner and Errol

ALICE ARSHALOOYS KELIKIAN/2007

ALICE ARSHALOOYS KELIKIAN: *Welcome to today's program with Werner Herzog and Errol Morris. There is no format for today. And when I asked Werner if we could tape the event, he said, "Only if there's a rampage."*

ERROL MORRIS: Rampage?

ALICE: *Rampage. So, no rules, no format. I thought I'd ask a question, and there are two microphones on either aisle for those of you who'd like to ask a question if they stop speaking, by any chance.*

ERROL: Rampage really depends on a hostile and aggressive audience.

WERNER HERZOG: I, in all respects, am always on attack.

ALICE: *Then I guess we can take the gloves off. Werner and Errol have known each other for almost thirty-five years. They were very close friends, and they remain close friends. Errol, with* Gates of Heaven *and* The Thin Blue Line, *you reacted against the conventions of cinéma vérité in documentary filmmaking. You said that documentary style does not dictate truth.*

On the other hand, Werner, in the 1970s and 1980s you claimed that you could find greater truths in fiction than can be found in the documentary. So, what you effectively did—I'm thinking of Aguirre: The Wrath of God *(1972) and* Fitzcarraldo *(1982)—is create a world and then document your characters within that world. Errol borrowed from noir to make documentary films, and you looked to independent documentaries in some of your fiction films. Is this a parallel, or is this completely wrong?*

Discussion with Werner Herzog and Errol Morris following a screening of *Encounters at the End of the World* at Brandeis University, 23 October 2007. Introduced by Alice Arshalooys Kelikian. Reprinted by permission of Alice Arshalooys Kelikian.

ERROL: I would say completely wrong.

WERNER: I do not feel comfortable with it either, saying that I looked for "documentaries" in fiction films. No, it was always something that came more from—and I say it with great caution—experimental films. Those influenced *Fata Morgana* (1971), which I consider a fiction film. Errol is quite convinced it's a documentary, and just as a documentary should be—pure fantasy, pure mirages.

ERROL: The distinction that has been set up seems to me spurious. This distinction between films with actors, films with real people, documentary films, drama, so on and so forth. The distinction is spurious in this sense: I think that all films—and I'm not even saying anything remotely controversial—have elements of both.

Werner's films, which really influenced me as a young man and continue to influence me now as an elderly, rapidly aging man, clearly had elements of both. Think of Bresson, who would use non-actors in his dramas, or Rossellini. Werner is clearly part of that neo-realist movement for me, because—and sorry for all of this exegetical material—but Klaus Kinski, properly speaking, is not an actor. He is a crazy person. A real, genuine crazy person put in a drama.

WERNER: That's totally correct. (Laughter) Yes, I see myself a little bit like having learned from Bresson. Even though I saw my first Bresson film a year ago, I had a hunch. My wife signed up for NetFlix, we got some Bresson movies, and they're most stunning. I thought, "That's what I should have seen thirty years ago, forty years ago." I didn't. But still, it's totally legitimate to say that yes, Bresson influenced my work concerning actors.

ERROL: Also, I think that both of us—and correct me if I'm wrong—have reacted strongly against this feeling that film has to be a certain kind of thing. I feel that more and more acutely as time goes on that most movies are cookie cutter movies put together on some grotesque, satanic assembly line for public consumption. The fact that there are movies that don't toe the line, that represent a divergence from mainstream cinema, is a good thing, not a bad thing. I thank God for the fact that I can do things differently, that I can reinvent what movies are every time I make a movie. It makes it worth doing. I couldn't go on otherwise.

WERNER: Errol, I always walk out of one of your films with the sense that I've seen a *movie*. That's very much the feeling of *Vernon, Florida* or even the film with McNamara—what's the title?—*The Fog of War*. Even there I have the feeling I've seen a feature, a narrative feature film with an inventive narrative structure and with a sort of ambiance created that you only normally create in an inventive, fictionalized film.

The new film that I saw, *Standard Operating Procedure*—you [the audience] haven't seen it yet, but you will eventually see it—feels completely as if you had invented characters, and yet they are not. We know the photos, we know the events, and we know the dramas behind them. And yet I walk out and I have seen a feature film, a fiction film.

ERROL: The intention is to create something that makes you think and puts you in some kind of odd place. I think that he shares this; ("he" being Werner, to my left). It's the perverse element in filmmaking. Last night, Werner was talking about ecstatic truth. And in truth—and this time I use the word in a way that I can understand more easily—in truth, I have no idea what he was talking about.

But what I do understand in his films is a kind of ecstatic absurdity. There are things to be captured on film that just make you question the nature of reality, and of the universe in which we supposedly live. We think we understand the world around us. Then we look at this material and we think twice. I have always, always liked that element of ecstatic absurdity.

When a friend of mine, Ron Rosenbaum, was writing a book on Shakespeare, we talked talking about the *meaning of meaninglessness*. Is there such a thing? I would respectfully submit: yes. You can be treated to the meaning of meaninglessness in abundance in this man's work.

WERNER: Thank you. It feels good to hear that. (Laughter) But, of course, I'm suspicious about the sources. Where does this come from, this textualizing of Shakespeare and poetry? I think we have discarded a part of *cinéma vérité*. We have hit at it enough—*cinéma vérité*, the answer of the sixties—that I hope that we have buried it for good.

But now what is emerging, and what we should really lower our heads and charge against—is this post-modernist, post-structuralist sort of aesthetic in film studies. You find it as an all-pervading abomination speaking about literature. I think there's a new enemy out there that we should really start to tackle more violently and more viciously. I mean with sucker punches wherever we can do it.

ERROL: I think it's the same old enemy, really. It's ourselves. I'm very fond of telling people when they say that they would like regime change in Washington, for example, that what we really need is species change.

The species itself is so impossibly, deeply degraded that one could well do with something else for a change.

But I don't think the problem is with *vérité*, per se. There have always been claims about truth telling in cinema. In fact, this man makes his own variety of those kinds of claims. I should point out that *Grizzly Man* (2005), a film that I really, really, really like and which resuscitated your career in many ways, is based on *vérité* footage.

WERNER: I would contest that. When you look at it, yes, it's found footage, but I think that [film subject Timothy] Treadwell always wanted to be the movie star in his own movie. You even see how he stages himself, how he directs himself, how he repeats one take after the other. Sometimes we know he's done at least fifteen takes: What survives in this footage is take two, take three, and take number fourteen, so we know he has shot at least fourteen takes and has erased twelve or eleven of them. This is kind of remarkable because it's highly, highly, highly organized.

He was also a movie fan. He was a great fan of science fiction, for example; a great fan of *Starsky and Hutch*; a great fan of the series *Cheers*, where he competed for the role of the bartender and didn't get the part. He somehow created his part in the movie.

So I would be cautious about *vérité*. *Vérité* comes in at certain moments when he is in *Starsky and Hutch* mode, wearing now his bandana, the sexy camouflage bandana, and he jumps away on the little path and disappears. He'll disappear for twelve seconds—which is a long time in the film and footage—and then reappear. But what is in between? All of a sudden you see reed grass, long stems, and wind bending the grass.

ERROL: That's an amazing sequence.

WERNER: Yes. Everybody overlooked this and I had the feeling that this was *vérité*, a *vérité* element. Yes, there is *cinéma-vérité* in it. I declared my brand here and you have your way of approaching it. We'll never grasp it anyway. Speaking of truth, we have to touch it with a pair of pliers anyway because we'll never even get anywhere close.

ERROL: And we probably wouldn't even know it if we saw it.

WERNER: But maybe by trying and attempting it, maybe through the illumination of trying to postulate an ecstasy of truth, there's an odd access to it. Still, I'm trying it.

ERROL: Yes.

WERNER: And every time it gives more—

ERROL: Werner, I take back the remark about *vérité* in this sense. You know I've been in the process of making a movie about Abu Ghraib and the photographs at Abu Ghraib. What is so very odd—and this is true of Treadwell, I believe—is that yes, he is presenting himself to the camera quite consciously. He is performing for the camera. But at the same time that performance is part of what is being captured. It's part of the *vérité* moment. There's this whole idea that something that's posed is not real, but that can be part of the reality you're looking at. What's so interesting about the Abu Ghraib photographs is that many of those scenes were orchestrated for the camera. They were actually posed photographs. And the fact of them being posed doesn't make them less real. In fact, it makes them more horrific and more deeply disturbing.

WERNER: Some of it not even posed. One of the women in the film, when you ask about her thumb—because in the photos she always has a thumbs-up—says, "Whenever I enter a picture frame, I don't know really what to do with my thumb and so I do this here." It's accepting a pose the moment you are going into frame. I like that moment.

ERROL: What makes *Grizzly Man* very modern and a kind of strange hall of mirrors is that Treadwell is, like you, a filmmaker trying to capture his version of reality as a set of images. Maybe that's the human enterprise.

WERNER: Some of the Abu Ghraib photos are purely staged. Some of them are not. When they take the photos, let's say from second floor, you see the soldiers and prisoners somewhat down in the corridor. In many of these occasions I'm fairly convinced that nobody down there was aware that there was somebody taking photos. But, of course, some of them are the real accumulation of, let's say, naked bodies in the infamous human pyramid. In my opinion, a great exercise in a very vile, inhuman stage art. It's like a modern form of drama, of theatre, the theatre of bodies to tie them up into a human pyramid and taking the last remaining dignity from them. It's not a random tossing of bodies on top of each other. The kind of staging of it makes it so horrifying.

ERROL: Yes. Treadwell seems to be interested in creating a theatre with bear actors. (Laughter) I think that we all take the images of our lives and try to make sense of them. We try to order them in a way that's congenial or acceptable, even flattering. Treadwell was involved in this enterprise in a rather bizarre setting. He eliminated almost all people, except for his girlfriend who really doesn't appear much, and populated his theatre with bears. He was, I suppose, in search of becoming the greatest bear director of all time. But it backfired. Or maybe it didn't. Maybe it was fulfilled.

WERNER: Quite often I'm asked to describe him or categorize him. I've tried it a few times and it gets more and more complicated. Yes, that's certainly one of his goals: to become a bear and be the great bear actor. He actually is on all fours and huffs at a bear. He somehow leaves the boundaries of his attempts to become the bartender in *Cheers*. He leaves that way behind, and aspires to something much deeper.

ERROL: I guess it's one of those undeniable facts of the human condition is that we really can't be bears, no matter how much we might try. I did a film about Temple Grandin who is autistic, or supposedly autistic. She designs humane slaughterhouses. Oliver Sacks profiled her in his famous piece *An Anthropologist on Mars.*

She makes the claim that she really can imagine herself as a cow. She goes to great pains to tell us, "It's not me in a cow suit; I *am* a cow." Of course, there's a voice inside of my head that rebels. I think, "You know, I'd like to be more accommodating. I'd like to go with the flow here. But I really don't think you are a cow. I think you are a human being who thinks she's a cow."

WERNER: But she appears to be credible when she describes how she constructs a runway into the death chamber.

ERROL: Yes, her stairway to heaven.

WERNER: There would be curves, and the cow would be curious. *What's behind there?* And the way she moves. She appears like a heavy set, clumsy woman, and all of a sudden she literally moves like a cow, being curious to follow this curved path. *What's behind there?* And that's where you get killed then. The cow is not really frightened; it's more curious than frightened.

I like very much how she moves. I think sometimes about footage I've seen by Jean Rouch, the wonderful French filmmaker who died two years ago or so. He made films in Africa, and some are about hunters and the way the hunter moves in facing a lion or in facing an antelope. *The hunter moves like the antelope.* This is really, really good stuff. And in a way—

ERROL: Other hunters or other people think he moves like an antelope. I wonder if antelopes think he moves like an antelope.

WERNER: Apparently yes, because he gets very close and kills them with an arrow. Normally you can't get close to an antelope; they are quite shy.

Moving like an antelope makes the success of the hunter. I truly like this kind of stuff.

ERROL: I've always been fascinated by how people see themselves, and their capacity to see themselves as virtually anything. It's like our capacity for credulity, our capability of believe utter nonsense, to imagine things that are utterly ridiculous and clearly untrue. Our abilities are unfettered in that direction.

WERNER: Yes, but we seem to lose it from age four onwards.

ERROL: Self-deception? It's enhanced with age.

WERNER: No—like my little son walking up to me and declaring with total conviction that he is a tiger. It's very convincing how he does it and that little one—I had no doubts that he was totally into that, and I accepted it. But it's harder to accept it from a ten-year-old, and it's harder to accept it from a grown-up. It's easier to accept it from unusual characters into whom you eventually run. . . . Like Kinski. He comes to mind.

ERROL: Yes, I think that we've all . . . well I, at least, feel trapped inside of myself, like I'm in some kind of prison. So there is what I would call an *insane curiosity* to look beyond that, to imagine how other people see the world, or how they imagine themselves in the world. I don't even think ultimately it's about film. I think film is a great way to present those ideas, but I think there's some deep curiosity, innate curiosity, that stands behind that.

When Werner and I first met each other, our first trip together was to see this serial killer in this prison in Northern California.

WERNER: Vacaville, yeah.

ERROL: It was Dr. Saxer—Werner's producer, Walter Saxer—Dr. Morris, and Dr. Herzog allowed in because—

WERNER: We were scared shitless. Kemper, Edmund Emil Kemper, was a very huge man. Still fairly young, I think twenty-six by then, but something like six foot five or six foot four.

ERROL: I think bigger.

WERNER: Maybe bigger, yes. And he had since—

ERROL: Very large.

WERNER: Capital punishment was suspended at the time he was condemned. He chose seven or eight consecutive life terms, but he wanted to die in the gas chamber. The only way to get to the gas chamber when it was reinstated at that time was to kill someone inside the prison. . . . So the attorney was really scared. He was relieved that he had some solid men as his guards or his company. Reading all the transcripts of Kemper, what was interesting was that the man, in my opinion, was that he made a lot of sense. In a way, why he killed and how it all originated makes a lot of sense.

After having killed seven or eight or so co-eds, hitchhikers, he killed his mother and put the severed head on the mantle shelf and threw darts at it. There happened to be some leftover turkey in the fridge from Thanksgiving, so he called the lady next door, the neighbor, and asked—am I correct?—yeah, asked her if she would like to pick up the turkey leftovers. She walked in and he killed her as well and put her in a closet. Then he fled in his mother's car and criss-crossed the West until he ran out of money and ran out of gas. In Pueblo, Colorado, he kept calling police. You know better what happened there. I think they thought he was kind of gaga and didn't believe him—

ERROL: He desperately tried to turn himself into the police by making repeated phone calls from this one phone booth—of course, now he would have had a cell phone—and the police kept hanging up on him. They just—

WERNER: He was down to his last quarter to make his last call when two detectives picked him up at this phone booth. I remember their names because they sound very German: Schmidt and Grubb. Schmidt and Grubb took him to the police station, and what was smart of them was that they randomly turned on a tape recording and Kemper spoke for six hours pretty much nonstop. This transcript is really wonderful.

ERROL: Quite amazing, yes.

WERNER: Very, very amazing. Kemper was, in a way, a very sensitive person. When you looked at his hands, they were like the hands of a violin player, in a way. I remember his hands looked like an elephant with a Mozart soul.

ERROL: I was just about to say that his description was of an elephant with the soul of Mozart. I'm not sure that most of the prison authorities would have used that description, but at the time I found it very, very interesting. I thought about it for a long time. It made it situational, as if God in his infinite perversity had somehow mismatched his various characteristics in order to produce some kind of nightmare, some kind of tragedy.

Yeah, what comes from Werner in these early years and what I myself was thinking is so mixed up in my mind, I have to tell you. I was a very disaffected graduated student at the University of California-Berkeley when I first met Werner. I think it was just shortly after you finished *Aguirre*, and these films were being shown in the United States for the first time. It was quite an amazing experience to see Werner's work. There was really nothing quite like it in America at that time, and probably not since that time. I became really fascinated.

Even now that we're talking about it on stage, I'm thinking about our attempts to understand, *What are they thinking? What is going on in another person's mind? How do they see the world?* Kemper was a perfect example. I would drive every day from Berkeley to Santa Cruz to attend the Kemper trial. I became a regular fixture. And I would say the trial transformed my thinking about many, many, many things. These trials were chopped in two: There would be a guilt/innocence phase and a penalty phase.

Kemper had killed a dozen people. He had killed his grandparents. He had been put away in a juvenile facility, released under California law when he reached a certain age, and then went on to kill ten more people. And Kemper had described how these murders occurred. He would be killing a woman that he had picked up in the car with a knife and had been talking to her saying, "I hope this isn't really unpleasant. I hope you're not uncomfortable. I hope this is not too frightening."

But there was this wacko psychiatrist, Dr. Joel Fort, who took the stand and said, "You know, this man is not neurotic. Not only is he not psychotic, he's not even neurotic because he can't empathize with the victim. He has a sociopathy or a psychopathy. He can be completely dispassionate while he is killing another person." I started to wonder—and I still wonder about this stuff—I started to wonder how in God's name does this psychiatrist know what Ed is thinking? Maybe Ed has this fantasy of being in control. Maybe in this writing after the fact he imagined himself as being dispassionate. Perhaps he was completely out of control, deeply psychotic. There's a discrepancy between the accounts that we provide ourselves and the world. In a way, that's very much in your films as well, and it's something that deeply inspired me.

WERNER: There is something about Kemper—and of course, Ed Gein as well. We had a falling out over Ed Gein some time later.

ERROL: Cannibals can turn friends into enemies. Go figure.

WERNER: We had a very, very intense rapport over it. Errol had a problem with me when we tried to find out in Plainfield, Wisconsin, where Ed Gein—probably the most notorious—

ERROL: Do you know about Ed Gein? Does this name . . . ? We're dealing with a younger generation here, so—

WERNER: Yeah, it was actually in the fifties that—

ERROL: The movie *Psycho* (1960) was based on Ed Gein. The writer of the novel *Psycho*, Robert Bloch, lived in a small Wisconsin town; Weyauwega, Wisconsin, about twenty miles from Plainfield. Ed Gein was the most notorious killer. It's the ultimate house of horrors. He was a human taxidermist, cannibal, serial killer, grave robber, necrophile.

WERNER: But the grave robberies were actually the point where we wanted to know more. Errol wanted to know more because apparently Ed Gein had not only murdered people, he also excavated freshly buried corpses at the cemetery. I think he dug up graves in a pretty perfect circle, and in the very center of this circle was the grave of his mother. Errol kept wondering: Did he excavate his mother and use her flesh and skin for some sculptures in things at his home?

ERROL: An innocuous question. (Laughter)

WERNER: There was only one way to find out. I proposed, "Let's go to Plainfield, grab a shovel, and dig at night." And I showed up in Plainfield, Wisconsin. I was doing some filming up in Alaska, and I came in a car all the way from Alaska down to Plainfield—

ERROL: At the time I was living with Ed Gein's next door neighbors, who I had befriended.

WERNER: You didn't show up. I was there, but you didn't show up. And we had a date. It was something like, "September 10. I'm going to be there, and you will be there." And you didn't show up.

ERROL: He's unfortunately correct.

WERNER: I would have dug, even though Errol wasn't there. I was kind of scared because people open fire easily in this town.

ERROL: I was living there. I had left and become friends with this very strange doctor, Dr. George Arndt. He had written one academic paper in his entire career called *A Community's Reaction to Horrifying Events*;

essentially, it was a compendium of Ed Gein jokes. And I had befriended Dr. Arndt and together we had gone to Plainfield Cemetery and—it actually reminds me of that scene in your movie [*Encounters at the End of the World*]. We had put our ears to the ground looking for hollow areas in the earth.

WERNER: I had forgotten about that completely. So things come back forty-five years later.

ERROL: Dr. Arndt, who was really quite mad—I should tell you at least one of the jokes, no? I crave audience response. Why did Ed Gein keep his chairs covered over night? To keep them from getting goose pimples.

So there I was with George Arndt in the cemetery. Arndt had this theory. It was George Arndt's theory that Ed was so devious that he wouldn't have gone down directly into his mother's grave. I had discovered that many of the graves that he had robbed had made a circle around his mother's grave, and he only robbed the graves of women who were middle aged and overweight, like his mom. Dr. Arndt took this information and his hypothesis was that Ed went down into one of the side graves then tunneled. So there would be this radial tunnel towards the center, towards his mother's grave, but that he would never have gone directly down into the grave. Psychiatrists have amazing theories. And I wondered, *Was she down there?* I could never get an answer. I could never get a straight answer from anyone. Is Mrs. Gein still buried in Plainfield Cemetery? I told the story—this was the big mistake here—I told the story to Werner.

WERNER: And I showed up in Plainfield.

ERROL: There was this horrible realization: *He's actually going to do it.* I have to say, I did get scared. You know, I really always was—I probably still am—trying to please my mother. I had been already thrown out of these various graduate schools; I was a ne'er-do-well and nearly down for the count. I saw myself arrested with the Germans. I saw this full moon, I saw the Plainfield Police, I saw my being led away with the Germans in handcuffs, the complete family disgrace. But this is an opportunity: I apologize for not showing up.

WERNER: I have to apologize for something. My car broke down, and there was no mechanic out there. But there was a wreckage yard, and I fell in love with the guy who fixed my car. I said that we were going to do a film there in Plainfield, and that really upset Errol a lot. He thought I was a thief without loot. This was his country, his territory, his Plainfield and I shot in Plainfield. I shot a film *Stroszek* (1977), which I think is forgotten and forgiven by now, and we can maintain friendship over this now.

ERROL: My line in those days was that for you, Werner, to steal a character or a story isn't real theft. But to steal a landscape, that is a very, very serious crime.

WERNER: I understand that. I take it to heart. But there actually is a film out there and we can't take it off the map.

ERROL: It's a very good film. I don't know how many people have seen this film, but—

WERNER: It has a beautiful end with dancing chicken, and I really like it.

ERROL: Yes.

WERNER: Movies are sometimes created by odd fascinations that return in very different forms. Often what is so fascinating about your films is how they originate. Very often the whole background story, how it originated, is worth as much as the whole film.

ERROL: Or much more than the films. One of the distressing things for me is that I couldn't write for years. All of a sudden I find myself writing, for reasons that elude me. I think I'll just turn over in bed the wrong way one morning and then it will all come to some abrupt, horrible end.

It's very odd when you're obsessional and crazy. Werner has this great blessing, something that I truly envy, of being prolific rather than being that kind of penguin that sits endlessly on an egg. He actually allows his eggs to hatch. I think I'm—well, it's not even that I think—*I know* I'm of a different persuasion altogether. I covet the egg. I study the egg. I turn it upside down and sit on it again and then turn it right side up again.

WERNER: Errol, it doesn't really matter how long you sit on an egg. Your films, they've always been satisfying. When you look at my films, you can easily say, "Oh, this should be cut much shorter here; it should be improved in sound; it should be improved here and there." Yes, we can say that easily. In your films, we can't. You can't.

In the films that Errol makes, very often there is a whole chain of mountains but we see only one peak. You might return to *Vernon, Florida*, because that was only a casual first subject that was sticking out there which you made into a film. There are also stories behind this *Nub City*. . . . But *Vernon, Florida*, in my opinion, is only one visible peak of a whole mountain range.

ERROL: At a time when I can't even quite say that my career was moribund because it was nonexistent—something has to exist before it can actually die—Werner very kindly translated the film *Vernon, Florida* into German.

WERNER: I did the German version, yeah, which was very hard. How do you translate the one who is hunting the turkeys here and the turkey gobbles, and even double gobbles? You can't really translate it appropriately into German, so you have to translate into some sort of stylized Bavarian. Then you'll get it right.

But what a great joy to work on that film because I know it bit by bit, by bit, by bit. It has become part of my joys in life—just to think about this is always a great joy. Sometimes you lose sight of the fact that there were four or five other summits sticking out of the ice in Florida; sometimes you think that you may eventually return to it. If not, it's okay. You have to accept that you can't do everything you set out to do. You can't do it all. There are just too many things, and the world is too confusing and too many-fold to grasp. But grasping it somewhere and hatching an egg is alright. It doesn't matter that you hatch on it for a year and a half or two. So what?

But I find it very remarkable that you have come back to music, and playing the cello. You may go back to writing.

ERROL: Yes.

WERNER: You might go back to God knows what.

ERROL: Yes.

WERNER: There's a question out there.

AUDIENCE MEMBER: *When you go into making a documentary, do you have a set narrative in mind, or is the process more organic? Werner, as a director of narrative films, on* Grizzly Man, *for instance, did you find yourself fighting that urge to get a performance out of the character, or did you just sit back and observe?*

ERROL: There isn't that fine distinction to be made between one and the other. There are elements of both. Always.

WERNER: *Grizzly Man* may not be the very best example because Treadwell was already dead. So it makes sense that I had to step somehow into
his mind. *What was he trying to achieve?* Among others he wanted to be a
movie star. I give him the opportunity to be the star in this movie. I give
him even the best, great movie music, by Richard Thompson. I did not
come in with a narrative. I only knew that some people out there knew
him fairly well, or could be witnesses: I knew there was a very, very fine
pilot out there, Fulton; and I knew there was a very fine coroner out there,
Fallico. I had met them before shooting fairly briefly. I actually stumbled
into the film from one minute to the next. I just heard about it and took it
away from a producer. I asked him, "Who is directing the film?" And he
said, "I'm kind of directing the film." And he said, "Kind of." Somehow
I knew he was not very sure.

I spoke to him directly and I said, "No. I will direct the movie." I shook
his hand, and I was in business. So there was no time conceptualizing,
no time. I had to start almost immediately because the salmon run was
going to be over soon, and the density of the bear population would
dwindle. They would go into hibernation after that. So I jumped into it.

I only viewed a couple of people out there. I wanted to meet his parents. I wanted to meet the coroner, who was very remarkable in the film.
He was a very, very nice and very philosophical man whose family emi-
grated from Italy. His father was a professor of philosophy at University,
and he was a very, very deep glowing man, very kind. I started filming
with him. I knew pretty much what I wanted from him and we talked
about it briefly.

But he steps in front of the camera and starts talking like the coroner
in court. After less than a minute I said, "Frank, we are here. We are making a movie. You are not the expert witness in court. This is something
different. This is not in court. This is a movie and you better be yourself now. I want to have an echo from you. I want to see the man and his
emotions. What did you experience when you had the garbage bags with
the few remains of Timothy Treadwell and his girlfriend? What was going on? You see that on a daily basis, but this was unusual." He looked
at me and he nodded, and now I turned on the camera. In a way, he
was directed, but he was directed only to loosen up and to show something deep inside of him, and it didn't take much persuasion. He understood, and he goes pretty wild in the film. So I have no hesitation to stage
things.

Or, for example, in the house of Treadwell's parents, there were teddy bears and little kid's porcelain ducks here or there. But I accumulated them. I raked them together from all over the house and so I staged the set. But the staging of the set makes you understand the parents, and the kind of climate in which Treadwell grew up, so I know no problem with that. I emphasized an essence, and I do that all the time. You'd do the same, I guess.

ERROL: I was a private detective for years after I started as a filmmaker, and I'd like to think that there's this detective element in everything I do. My movies start from interviews. *The Thin Blue Line* started from bizarre, odd interviews. Everything that I've really done—

WERNER: I want to add one thing: Errol has something that I don't have and I've never seen anyone who has it like him. You do not direct the ones you interview. Errol has a way of looking at them with such an intensity of curiosity and acknowledgement. Even before you had this device—how do you call it?

ERROL: The Interrotron.

WERNER: But having your face next to the camera, and the way he would look at people. . . . Whatever it is, it makes people talk, and they say things to you that they would never say to any one of you here in the audience. They wouldn't say it to me either, but Errol makes it by dint of his face.

ERROL: I think it becomes a "documentary," whatever that is, by its element of unpredictability. Now Werner goes to Antarctica. He has a limited amount of time and a limited amount of materials; he has no way of doing any kind of prep. And so, the movie is emergent, if you like, from just what happens there. There's a strong element of spontaneity, of the uncontrolled, of the unrehearsed, the unplanned, in every single film he's made.

WERNER: Yes. That's where real life enters.

ERROL: I feel that element of spontaneity because so much of what I do is controlled. My element of spontaneity is not knowing what someone is going to say to me in front of the camera; of having really no idea, of being surprised. I know that there's this moment in all of the interviews that I've loved where *something happens*. I had this three-minute rule that if you just shut up and let someone talk, within three minutes they will show you how crazy they really are. And it has happened time, and time, and time again.

WERNER: And you do have a great sense of the afterthought. The statement is finished, is over, but Errol is still sitting and expecting. Then all of a sudden there comes an afterthought and that's the best of all.

ERROL: Yes, often.

WERNER: I have learned that, in a way, from you. Wait for the afterthought. Be patient. Don't say, "Cut." Just let them do it. In the Antarctic film you have the man who all of a sudden, not knowing what to do—he showed his hands with very odd shaped fingers and he stands and stands. And I don't respond to him. He wanted to know should he continue to work and stands and then somehow—

ERROL: Now, why is that moment powerful? It's powerful because you know, looking at it, that it's unplanned. It comes from this moment of being deeply uncertain what to do, what to say, what will happen next.

WERNER: And he's at his best.

ERROL: Yes. It's a moment that is superlative.

WERNER: The unplanned, the unexpected, the afterthought. You are the master of that.

ERROL: If everything were planned, it would be dreadful. If everything were unplanned, it would be equally dreadful. Cinema exists because there are elements of both in everything. There are elements of both in documentary; there are elements of both in feature filmmaking. I think it's what makes photography and filmmaking of interest. Despite all of our efforts to control something, the world is much, much more powerful and deranged even than we are.

WERNER: Exactly. Film schools are not into the unexpected. Despite all of what film schools tried to teach you, and despite all the sort of rules that the industry has established, find your space into which all of a sudden the unexpected occurs.

AUDIENCE MEMBER: *Why did you not play the audio of Treadwell's tape in* Grizzly Man? *You explained why you didn't in the narration, but I didn't believe you.*

ERROL: Perhaps we should explain, because I realize people might not know what we're talking about here.

WERNER: Yes. When Timothy Treadwell died, he was attacked and eaten by a bear. What quite apparently happened was that his girlfriend, Amy

Huguenard, heard a commotion outside the tent. She switched on the camera, but it was then apparently dropped it to the ground. She never removed the lens cap because it got so violent out there. So there's only the audio portion of the tape, which was already at fifty-four minutes or so, with six minutes still to go. Then it stops because the tape runs out.

What is clearly discernable is that there is heavy rainfall. You hear the pounding of rain on the tent and you hear the camera somehow crashing down. It's certainly Amy Huguenard who switched it on because you hear Timothy Treadwell screaming in the distance.

At the beginning of the salmon run, when grizzlies catch salmon, normally they eat the whole salmon. A couple of days into it, they start to go for the tidbits, and they put their paw very delicately. They hold the head of the salmon and they skin them alive because the nutrients and the fats in the skin are particularly good.

I have seen photos at the coroner's office of the remains of Amy Huguenard. Amy Huguenard's head is remaining, and it was cautiously skinned. My feeling is, in retrospect, that the bear was killing Treadwell and then killing Amy Huguenard; not right with one swipe of the paw, but apparently skinning them alive. What you hear is so horrifying, beyond all. . . . I was kind of curious myself, but it's so horrifying that it was quite clear this is not going to be in the movie.

AUDIENCE MEMBER: *More horrifying than your telling us? I didn't believe that you really thought it was too horrifying to use in the film.*

WERNER: Why do we have to have this tape? It's very easily sensationalistic and it transgresses a borderline. I was reluctant to do it anyway, in principle. Why don't we see all the amateur video recordings of people who jumped from the World Trade Center when it was burning? Over two hundred people, I think, jumped from the windows, from 106th floor, 104th floor, and crashed. In a few instances I've heard about video where the person crashes into the pavement only a few feet away from the camera that films it. These things have never been shown in public and they will not be shown. It didn't need much thinking. It was just clear this is not going to be in my film, and I said to them, "If you insist to have that in the film, I'll step down and you'll have to do it. My name will be off. It's as simple as that."

ERROL: Isn't it the line from Keats that, "A heard melody is grotesque, but those unheard are even more grotesque"? If I were ever to write my book on ethics, I would say that ethics is a combination of two principles: *I'm sorry* and *I'm sorry I got caught*. As a filmmaker you have, shall we say, a primal scene. What could be more primal than being eaten by carni-vores? Hell, now that's a way to go.

If you play the scene for the audience, you could be accused of be-ing sensationalistic, of pandering, of showing—God forbid—bad taste. *Whatever you do, I don't want to hear that man being eaten by carnivores!* So you go through this sort of absurd hall of mirrors, this calculation. It's a version of damned if you do and damned if you don't. You play it? People criticize you for having no sense of decorum, no sense of human de-cency. You don't? They accuse you of being manipulative, holding back.

I think there is something really deeply manipulative about that scene that seems to me insane, and seems to be the essence of Werner—why I like him and I'm frightened of him. He makes us in the audience feel guilty; he makes us feel indecent. I was sitting there thinking to my-self, "Oh boy, I want to hear the guy eaten by the carnivore!" And then Werner comes in and says, "You should be ashamed of yourself. How dare you want to hear the man eaten by the carnivore?" And I think, "Oh, I should be ashamed of myself. I feel really bad about myself."

Then another thought came through my head and I thought, "No, no, no. I'm not ashamed of myself. I really want to hear the man eaten by the carnivore!" But somehow he had pulled it off. He had made me feel guilty for something that everybody in the audience, I believe, re-sponded to in some similar way. Of course, that is a critical move in art. *Withholding.* Not giving the audience all that they want. Why? It's always better that way.

WERNER: Yes, you are right, but I'm not as complicated as you tried to make myself.

ERROL: Not true.

WERNER: My approach is the one of a Bavarian peasant. In a way, when we did not dig in the cemetery in Plainfield, I somehow felt at ease with it. I tried to persuade myself that sometimes it is better not to know, to come out with a question and never get the answer.

ERROL: I call it anti-curiosity: How much will it cost me to know less?

WERNER: Don't try to be too distortive. I see it very simply: it is better that we do not know. And by "we," I speak of the audience because I have to exclude myself. I was the one who heard it. But "we," as the audience, have a question and don't get an answer. Sometimes having suspicions about the filmmaker himself—*Is he honest? Does he try to manipulate us? Does he make too much out of it?*—and all these secondary questions . . . let them linger. That's okay. Let them linger and you are kind of disturbed not so much what's on the tape, but by me, the filmmaker. There's a secondary aspect, and I can take it easily. Yes, go after me. In this case you can, because we are sitting only a few feet away. Fine, yes, go for the jugular.

AUDIENCE MEMBER: *Rampage.*

WERNER: Yes. Normally as an audience it's very unpleasant that you can't corner the guy who did it. Very often I'd like to do that.

ERROL: It's the purpose of art: extending the frontiers of guilt. Before seeing this film I never, never thought that I would feel guilty about wanting to hear a man eaten by a carnivore. But somehow this film introduced that to my thinking for the first time, and I still feel guilty. Because I still want to hear it. (Laughter)

AUDIENCE MEMBER: *Could you share the story of what led up to* Werner Herzog Eats His Shoe *and* Gates of Heaven?

WERNER: Oh, there are different versions out of it, I do believe. Errol, you have a version, right?

ERROL: It's the *Rashômon* (1950) of the shoe eating.

WERNER: Yes, the *Rashômon* eating of the shoe. I can remember we were sitting together. I was the only one who really took Errol seriously in an environment where some people thought that no, he would never make a film. Errol, at that time, had given up cello playing and was not so much into his studies anymore and didn't release a book . . .

ERROL: I'd been thrown out of school.

WERNER: Anyway, we talked about his project—and that was *Gates of Heaven*—and I found it instantly intriguing. But somehow there was this complaint in your voice: *How will I find money?* Money is so stupid. And I said to Errol, "This is a film that you can start with one reel of 16mm film, an eleven-minute reel, and it will carry you on somehow. Some people will see that this is something you can do and you will finish. This is the one you will finish." Just to challenge him and push him a little bit, I said, "I'm wearing these"—they were Clark desert boots—"I'm going to eat my shoes the day I see this film, and you better make it."

ERROL: My version is slightly different. My version is that Werner had a compulsive obsessive need to eat his shoe. (Laughter)

WERNER: I've heard quite often that I allegedly said to Errol, "You are never going to make any movie. You are a bozo. You will never make a movie, and I can even bet on it."

ERROL: The bozo part: True. Never making a movie: Untrue.

WERNER: Yeah, but it's an interesting aspect about bozo or not bozo. How do you make the bozo/non-bozo distinction? It's something that's mathematical and it's something deeply Bavarian as well.

ERROL: I do not believe that my film career really hinged on the shoe eating.

WERNER: Absolutely not. Or on any specific person, including me. It hinged on nothing but what you had in you.

ERROL: But his example of making these movies was incredibly important to me. I had seen someone else actually making movies, and it showed me that it was, in fact, possible. For that I am very, very deeply grateful.

WERNER: So I am also convinced that the shoe eating was just a little arabesque that happens once in a while in the life of a man.

ERROL: The shoe was also prepared by the best chef in America, so that also should be taken into consideration.

WERNER: It's actually a very manly thing. I cannot imagine that a female would feel like cooking and eating a shoe. It's a very male sort of thing going on in this case. I do believe there's a strong distinction there, how I distinguish myself from females. Yes, I would eat a shoe and they wouldn't.

ERROL: Makes sense.

ALICE: *Thank you so much for coming to Brandeis. (Applause)*

ERROL: Thank you, Alice, for having us.

WERNER: Thank you, Alice; you brought me here. And, Errol, you pushed her and me and everyone.

ERROL: Oh yes.

WERNER: So it's very, very, very kind to have me here. Thank you.

Hallway to Hell

JOSHUA ROTHKOPF/2008

"I THINK IT IS a horror movie," Errol Morris says about his latest documentary, *Standard Operating Procedure*, a viewing experience bound to faze even his most devoted fans. "Or at least, that's what I've been calling it: a 'nonfiction horror movie.' What was recorded in the fall of 2003 is a nightmare—a horrific nightmare."

Morris is referring not only to the infamous photographs taken at Abu Ghraib, the central subject of his new film, but also more generally to the conditions there, which still make him irate (in an entertainingly Elliott Gould–ish way). "Violations, endless violations!" Morris, sixty, exclaims over the hum of air-conditioning in a midtown hotel. "Even the very location of Abu Ghraib—forget about the symbolism of picking the most notorious prison under Saddam—is a breach of law. It's being mortared constantly. Prisoners are supposed to be taken to the rear of the conflict. So there you are, on Tier 1A, with your copy of the Geneva Convention, and what do you say? [*In a fussy voice*] 'Ahem, excuse me? This prison shouldn't even be here.'"

Clearly, Morris is just getting started. And while many others feel only lingering shame at this point, the director is making no apologies for digging in so late. "Of course, it would be nice if Abu Ghraib would just go away," he says. "That ain't gonna happen." And yet, much like the Oscar-winning *The Fog of War* (his 2003 profile of controversial Vietnam War architect Robert McNamara), *Standard Operating Procedure* bears the director's signature obliqueness. There are long, eye-to-lens interviews with the very soldiers caught grinning and giving the thumbs-up in front of prisoner abuses: Sabrina Harman, concerned with her own culpability

From *Time Out New York*, Issue 656: April 24–30, 2008. Reprinted by permission.

while taking snaps of naked human pyramids, and leash-tugger Lynndie England.

"I don't think the press was really interested in their stories," Morris offers. "Rather, it was all sound bites: 'Lynndie, look this way; Lynndie, are you sorry?' I would distinguish that from a real dialogue. I mean, imagine our shock when Lynndie came into the studio and was articulate. What I had read in the press was that she was perhaps retarded, unable to speak, kind of a lout. Subhuman. Clearly, these people were scapegoats and I have pulled them back from the edge of anonymity into something that is far more disturbing, namely being actual people."

In doing so—and for deploying his usual reenactments, in this case re-staging Abu Ghraib's torture sessions—Morris is facing the greatest heat of his career, certainly since his landmark *The Thin Blue Line* got a convicted prisoner off death row. "I may be aestheticizing Abu Ghraib," Morris says, addressing the question that will no doubt hound him, "but I'm also asking us to think about Abu Ghraib. Photos are these textless little pieces of the world, stripped of all context, stripped of before and after, right and left, top and bottom. They're a small scrap, a surface of something. And it's my attempt to tell a story visually, to bring that photograph back to life, that's being attacked. My reenactments are certainly not an effort to deceive people into thinking I was there. If I had been, I wouldn't be shooting at a thousand frames a second in Cinema-scope." ("Clearly Errol would have liked to have gone to Abu Ghraib itself," says production designer Steve Hardie, "and even considered that in early planning. I told him, 'Have a good time! Send me a postcard.'" The prison ended up being painstakingly built by Hardie on Hollywood's old Warner lot.)

The reenactments have led Morris to a dark corner—even to a private hearing with the MPAA over his (ultimately won) R rating. "In the middle of this conversation, an intelligent woman from the ratings board said, 'You know, horror films have changed since the beginning of the war. They're not just about killing people; they're about humiliating them.' And it seems to me that this was the entire foreign policy of the United States! (*Laughs*)" Morris feels justified in his dramatic tactics; ultimately, he contends, drama was the secret goal of Abu Ghraib. "That hallway was actually a stage," he says. "It was a proscenium, some bizarre theater created to intimidate the prisoners watching and also, presumably, the MPs who were orchestrating it. That insanity is my whole story."

Regarding the Pain of Others

LIVIA BLOOM/2008

WHY ARE AMERICAN soldiers smiling in the torture photographs from Abu Ghraib? They're bragging and proud; they're conducting business as usual; perhaps they're even satirizing conventional travel snapshots. Lynndie England, Charles Graner, Sabrina Harman, and the other members of the 372nd Military Police Company who were responsible for maintaining order at the Baghdad prison must be aberrant "bad apples." No one else would pose for pictures with naked, hooded Iraqi detainees while wearing those sickening, humiliating Disneyland grins.

But what is the correct facial expression for carrying out corrupt, inhumane torture orders, anyway? Should the soldiers have looked somber? Resigned? Defiant? Cold, competent, professional? Frustrated, because their desperate attempts to coerce information from inmates (who were often being held without charges) produced no results?

"They knew it was fucked up!" director Errol Morris said when we spoke at length about his engrossing new film, *Standard Operating Procedure*, which places the photographs from Abu Ghraib at the heart of an epistemological inquiry on the nature of photography. Despite a military-sanctioned "amnesty period" during which countless photographs and videos were destroyed, Morris gathered more than three thousand images from Abu Ghraib; these included the infamous pictures published by the *New Yorker* in 2004, as well as many never previously been made public.

Taking a different approach from Alex Gibney in *Taxi to the Dark Side* (2007) and Rory Kennedy in *Ghosts of Abu Ghraib* (2007), Morris uses the pictures to scrutinize photography's limitations as evidence, and the importance of looking outside the frame in order to see the full story. In-

From *CinemaScope* Magazine, Issue 34 (Spring 2008). Reprinted with permission by Livia Bloom.

spired in part by Susan Sontag's seminal texts "Regarding the Pain of Others" and "On Photography," Morris has examined the topic in *Zoom*, his online *New York Times* column. But for him, it's also personal. "Plain and simple," Morris explained. "I don't like the fact that these guys took the hit for the war. I think that's wrong."

Standard Operating Procedure recently premiered in competition at the Berlin Film Festival, where it won the second place Silver Bear Grand Jury Prize. Historically, it's the first documentary ever selected to compete with narrative films at the Berlinale.

For Morris, an intellectual, historical, and existential provocateur, the topic of *Standard Operating Procedure* is in many ways a perfect fit. Incorporating themes of his past films, including *The Thin Blue Line* (1988), *Mr. Death* (1999), and *The Fog of War* (2003), it's a murder mystery and a crime story; it's political and personal; it has elements of the outlandish and the absurd. The film also raises philosophical and metaphysical questions, and it examines war—American war.

The fact that *no actionable intelligence* was gained from the Abu Ghraib detainees is one of the film's most shocking revelations. But although illustrative, stylized reenactment footage is used to emphasize the emotional content of the interviews, this key point is simply stated; it is not underlined, bullet-pointed, or even highlighted onscreen. Morris assumes that his audience (much like viewers of contemporary medical television drama) enjoys sophisticated professional jargon and does not need a primer. Viewers are expected to be knowledgeable and to rise to the occasion, gauging the first-hand testimony for themselves.

A passionate historical scholar and meticulous researcher, Morris sometimes takes the unusual depth of his own knowledge for granted. If viewers have not recently read the Geneva Conventions, for example, they may not realize that Javal Davis's account of the daily conditions at Abu Ghraib amounts to, as Morris says, "a concentration camp in Iraq." Nor does the film argue that cover-ups of Abu Ghraib merit a full-scale, front-page investigation, one that he believes should far exceed the current examination of the destruction of the Zubaydah tapes. The treatment of the women soldiers at Abu Ghraib is brought up in the film, though Morris's understanding of the way they were "used" and "degraded" because of their gender as part of regular military interrogation practice is not made explicit.

The balance of how much context and "factual" background information to provide with nuanced interview portraits can be a delicate one. Clear, structured arguments and ample exposition within subjects' interviews was needed in *The Thin Blue Line*, for example, a film which helped exonerate a man on death row for a twelve-year-old Texas murder charge.

Mr. Death, on the other hand, was initially intended to be anchored on a single interview subject: Fred A. Leutcher, self-made "expert" designer of execution equipment. But when Leutcher argued on film that the Holocaust never occurred, he proved so persuasive that after a test screening for a Harvard class, Morris was obliged to include other interviews to counter Leutcher's argument.

In order to fully appreciate *Standard Operating Procedure*, viewers would likewise do well to watch the film in the context of independent historical and political study. But it's a rare privilege to have access to the intimate and powerful first-person documents that Morris has created. The intensity of the interviews is facilitated by the Interrotron, an "interviewing machine" of Morris's own invention. Speaking to his image on a live teleprompter feed rather than to the director himself, interviewees are recorded gazing directly into the camera. (In the past, Morris has compared subjects' experience of being interviewed via Interrotron to "watching a TV set that really cares and wants to know more.")

Thus, instead of a traditional subject/camera/interviewer triangle, the Interrotron captures intimate conversations wherein interviewees make eye contact with their future viewers. *Standard Operating Procedure* contains arguably the most effective, moving interviews that Morris and his Interrotron have ever produced, and even he admits that, "There are a lot of the interviews in this film that I really, really am proud of." More than a movie, the film is an essential American resource, its interviews indispensable primary source material for current and future generations of scholars and citizens.

LB: *Why do you think the soldiers took the photos at Abu Ghraib, and why did they smile?*
EM: Part of the reason for making the film was my interest in that question, "Why would they take these photographs?" One thing that interested me was Sergeant Joseph Darby—who is not in the movie, but whom I did interview. Darby has been profiled again and again and again and again: the hero who turned in the photographs.

The story of Joseph Darby is very complex, and the story that has emerged in the media is not exactly what I would call the "real" story. But it's interesting: Sabrina Harman takes these pictures of the body of murdered Iraqi detainee Manadal Al-Jamadi packed on ice. Under another set of circumstances she could have won a Pulitzer Prize, and it is because of the photograph that we are aware of a murder she has nothing whatsoever to do with. She is in no way culpable for the crime. She simply took a picture of a corpse after the fact.

And because of that fact, because she took the photograph, and because the photograph was disseminated and shown around the world, she became the goat. Darby the hero, and Sabrina Harmon the goat. Darby turns the pictures in and he becomes an American hero. He gets the J.F.K. Profiles in Courage Award. Sabrina *takes* the picture which reveals the murder, and she gets, as Hunter Thompson would describe it, "The 2,000-pound Shit-Hammer."

And the story is filled with strange ironies. The whole story. I find it amazing. In a way it's a very similar irony to listening to [Army Investigator] Brent Pack tell you how the hooded man on the box with wires, nicknamed Gilligan, was standard operating procedure; and the pyramid, or the leash, is a criminal act. Well, the question, again filled with irony: Why is one a criminal act? Why is one standard operating procedure?

There are technical arguments you could make about the nature of the prisoners, but what is clear is that the army, as a matter of policy, was involved in using American females to degrade Iraqi men. They were putting them in stress positions; they were stripping them naked; they were hooding them. The use of women, American female soldiers, to degrade the enemy—there's something incredibly sick about all of it. And the idea that these ideas solely came from the "bad apples"—that it came from Chuck Graner, and Ivan Frederick, and Lynndie England et al.—is just simply wrong. It's just wrong.

One thing that is just so clear is that when these guys arrived at Abu Ghraib, and they started work in what was known as the hard site, Cellblock 1A, this stuff was already in place. They didn't create this world; it existed in advance of them. And part of what the movie is about is how they *reacted* to all of this. It's almost a *Heart of Darkness* story. You find yourself in the middle of this surreal world; nightmare. . . . So I think that's really, really interesting.

But, why would they take the photographs? I don't think there is one reason. There's a theory that when we're dealing with human behavior, there are unitary reasons. There is one "why" that tells you, such and such happened. Why did it happen? You truck out a specific reason that explains everything. I sometimes think of a deck of cards; I think of a whole set of layers. Sabrina writes, very early on, that she's taking the photographs because she wants a record, and she wants to expose what the American military is doing in Iraq—and I think that's correct. Part of it is, "This is unbelievable, I should take a picture of it," and "This is wrong, I should take a picture of it"—because from her letters (and the letters were written from Abu Ghraib) she indicates clearly that she knew this was wrong, and that it was disturbing.

So there are two reasons, and then there are other reasons. Graner, I was told, had—you know, whether it's real or psychosomatic—believed that he had gotten sick from *Gulf War I*, and if he *had* photographs of certain things that happened to him, he would be in a better position to prove his case to the military. I also believe that there was a concern on the part of many of these people, Graner in particular, that these orders should have been given in writing—they were *not* given in writing—and that by taking pictures, they were offering some kind of protection for themselves: yet one more irony.

In terms of why they smiled, there was an evolution—that I think is an important evolution—from photographs that were vérité photographs. From when Sabrina starts taking those vérité photographs of Taxi Driver with panties on his head—those are vérité photographs. She sees this, she takes a picture of it.

The iconic photographs, the photographs that became really, really, really famous, aren't *vérité* photographs. They're posed photographs. They're photographs that were taken *for* the camera, and probably they were posed because a camera was present. They were *created for* the camera—which is *another* interesting phenomenon. Lynndie England with "Gus" on the leash; the pyramid; the picture of Lynndie pointing at the guy's dick with the cigarette dangling out of her mouth; the picture of Sabrina with the thumbs-up, looking into camera, in front of Al-Jamadi's body: All of those are photographs taken very self-consciously. I sometimes think of them as *tableaux vivants*, like Cindy Sherman gone to hell. That they were taken as kind of some crazed art project for the camera.

I think it's complex! The hope is that the movie captures the complexity of the situation and the complexity of the characters. That's the hope: That it makes you think about the question of why these photographs were taken; that it makes you think about who these people are that took the photographs, without really necessarily giving you a clear answer—because I don't think there is a clear answer. I don't think I'm just simply being coy; I just think that the pictures were taken for lots of reasons.

LB: *This is an ambitious subject, especially because of how topical and public the subject of Abu Ghraib has become. Did you feel an added sense of responsibility in tackling this story than you did, for example, with a subject like pet cemeteries in* Gates of Heaven?

EM: Yes; they're stories where people don't really care about whether what they get is true, or false. I mean, *The Thin Blue Line* is a story where the issue of truth and falsehood enter clearly into it. They enter in *Mr. Death* as well. And they certainly enter into this film.

It's different in that these are really current politics. It's not removed. There's nothing removed about this at all. It's ongoing. I wanted to do something about the war; I wanted to do something about photography; the photographs interested me. I also was interested in the fact that I thought that people hadn't really dug in. They hadn't tried to *investigate* Abu Ghraib, as if Abu Ghraib was just revealed entirely in the photographs.

LB: *How did you go about investigating this case? Where did you begin, and how did you organize your search?*

EM: It's kind of the same way I always do anything: I interview people. This started with Janis Karpinski, two years ago, and a very, very long interview. At first I thought, "I'll make a movie out of Janis Karpinski like I had made a movie out of Robert S. MacNamara." From Karpinski, I interviewed one of the "Seven Bad Apples," Javal Davis; I interviewed interrogators; I interviewed the two prison authorities who came to work for the Coalition very, very early on. Amazing stuff. They were in the movie for a long time, but again, just *too much stuff!* And I think it works as a movie around these very specific characters. There's a lot of them to begin with, let alone trying to cram more people into it.

So yes, interviews! As we would talk to people, each person we would talk to we would ask: do you have any records? File transcripts? Photographs? As we went along, we accumulated this amazing archive. Philip Gourevitch [co-author of a book with Morris produced in tandem with the film] says there are a million and a half words of transcript. We assembled un-redacted copies of various reports, and transcripts, affidavits. I probably have over 3,000 photographs from Abu Ghraib. There's just a lot of material, to say the least.

And I could go on with it, I suppose. I mean I . . . I feel a little overwhelmed. I've been thinking of writing about it for the *Times*. . . . You know, it amazes me. I sometimes think, if you don't *really* make people see it clearly, they won't see it. You read articles in the *New York Times* about the destruction of these Abu Zubaydah tapes—whatever it is, two tapes? supposedly of the interrogation of Zubaydah, and "how dare they destroy this material." Part of Abu Ghraib is they destroyed *everything*. There was this amnesty period. Hard drives were erased; material was destroyed. A lot of the records of what happened there are . . . are *gone!* That there was just not a minor cover-up but a *massive* cover-up in connection with this whole story that people are just not aware of.

Again, I'm not making a movie about torture, per se. I think a lot of people have a problem in that they think this has to be a movie about X, because all the other movies have been about X, and that's that people write about X—and so this has to be about that too, or if it isn't, then they . . . I don't know, it's strange . . . but it's different, I think, than what people expect. I made the McNamara movie about a guy at the top. This is about the guys on the bottom.

LB: *Can you talk about the re-creations in this film? I think they're more elaborate than the ones you've done before.*
EM: Are they really that elaborate? In the end, a lot of the more elaborate stuff we didn't use. But . . . maybe they are. They *are* more elaborate than anything. They were certainly more costly than anything I've done before. It's such a huge discussion whenever people ask me about the reenactments. In a way, it's a whole philosophy about film and about the nature of evidence, et cetera.

Part of the idea . . . on some very fundamental level, everything that we know about the world is through the process of reenactment. Consciousness, probably, is a reenactment of the world inside of our skulls. This is, again, a very long-winded discussion, but we don't apprehend reality directly. We frame a picture of reality inside of our heads. The world isn't inside of my head—I'm inside of the world. What I'm trying to do is to break the world down and look at it. To scrutinize it.

I believe the reenactments work really differently in *Standard Operating Procedure*. They were certainly intended to work really differently than in *The Thin Blue Line*, although there are elements in common. *The Thin Blue Line* forces you to think about certain possibilities. The milkshake encourages you to think about the questions, "Was the policewoman outside of the car? At what point was the milkshake thrown? What did the people see who claimed to have seen the crime that night?" It takes you back into what people said, the first-person accounts, and what we know about the story, and whether it makes sense. It forces you to scrutinize the world in a different kind of way than you would ordinarily.

Photographs cause us to scrutinize the world in a different way than we would ordinarily because they decontextualize things; they grip things really squarely out of reality; and they feature them; they frame them; they freeze them; and they decontextualize them. And each of those moments—whether it's Lynndie with Gus on the leash, or the pyramid, or Gilligan on the box—the movie wants to bring us into some kind of reflective mode, where we're thinking about the first-person account.

So here you have Sabrina Harman telling you the story of Gilligan. You see the pictures that were taken of Gilligan; the two pictures that she took of Gilligan, and the one picture taken by Ivan Frederick. And then we're taken *into the moment* in a stylized, aestheticized way, but in a way where my hope is that we are forced to think about the photograph, and the circumstances under which the photograph was taken. That's the hope.

It's a way of slowing down. In the same sense that a photograph freezes reality, I liked all of these quasi-photographic moments. We use this camera, the Phantom V9, which runs at a thousand frames a second, so these images—whether it's the Nerf football, or the water coming out of the showerhead, or the dog—all of these things are forty times slower than sound speed. It's almost like a photographic moment. You're in this strange kind of world. . . . It's an essay on the photographic moment and the nature of evidence, in part.

LB: *Watching the film I could see, even with such a vast amount of information, how frustrating it must have been not to have Graner and Frederick. Did you ever think of holding the film till you could get them? Their absence is such a presence.*

EM: Of course I did! But the film seemed to work without them. Lynndie England was the essential interview. She was the last interview that I did. I interviewed people subsequent to her, but they didn't go into the film. She was the last interview that went into the movie, and it was an essential interview; I can't imagine the movie without her. Yeah, it's a girl's film . . . because it has Sabrina, Lynndie, and Megan Ambuhl. And Janis Karpinski! There were women, of course, in *Thin Blue Line*. I remember when I made *Vernon, Florida*, someone criticized it because there were no women in it. And my answer—which by the way is truthful—is that women were too smart to appear in front of camera!

But women play such an essential role in this whole story. It's not an incidental role. It's impossible to conceive of this whole nightmare without women and some kind of crazy *use* of women that in itself is really, really, really interesting.

LB: *Is what you're saying that you think that they were used—because they were women, because of their sex—by the military?*
EM: I don't think that there's any argument about it. I mean, it's interesting that you can say the army has become emancipated because now women play a more prominent role in war. But think of how the women were used in this instance.

LB: *Fall guys . . .*
EM: They were used by the military explicitly to degrade Arabs, which is (not to sound so obvious) kind of degrading to the women involved. There's something so strange and deeply atavistic; it's not progressive at all. It's like a return to some kind of caveman mentality. The whole way in which sex has played itself out in this war, and in this story in particular, is endlessly interesting to me. I mean, it's part of it. Clearly part of it. You have these weird love triangles, Lynndie-Megan-Graner; you have Ivan Frederick asking these guys to masturbate in front of Lynndie and Sabrina; you have the photography; it's all . . . strange isn't the right word; in a way it's *not* strange, it's just really disturbing and crude.

Yes, it's an interesting story. It still interests me. I always think if I've done my job correctly, I'm still as interested at the end as I was at the beginning—and that's certainly true here. It's interesting how the pictures entered the public world, and how they were interpreted, and how people never wanted to look further, past the pictures, into Abu Ghraib itself. They prevented people from looking further, oddly enough. They provided a cover-up, in the deeply ironic sense.

Are we aware that they were kidnapping people's children and holding them prisoner in order to get confessions? Are we aware that there were problems of actually feeding the prisoners at all? There were all kinds of problems with the food; there were people not getting fed; it was open tent-cities there for many of the prisoners; mortars being lobbed in; prisoners being killed.

I mean, one of the prohibitions of the Geneva Convention is you don't put a prison, prisoners of war, you don't put *anything* in a free-fire zone where the prisoners can easily be killed. That itself is a no-no, you know. . . . And the list just goes on and on and on and on. We had a concentration camp. We had, for all intents and purposes, a concentration camp in Iraq. And it wasn't a concentration camp created by Lynndie England.

I guess one way of thinking about it is: it's not that these guys are *innocent*, but they *exemplify* a problem, rather than they themselves are the cause of the problem. That's probably a good way of putting it.

LB: *Sabrina Harman was married and gay at the time this happened. Was she out to her company?*

EM: Everyone knew she was gay. I think actually, in a certain sense, although nothing saved any of these people, it saved her from having to get involved this kind of heterosexual mess. It saved her from that.

LB: *It's a pretty unusual portrait of being gay in the military.*

EM: Yes, they knew; everyone knew she was gay. I mean by "everyone," many, many, many, many people knew that she was gay. It was no secret. She talks about wanting to be tougher. Wanting to be able to carry the burden of being a soldier. Wanting to inure herself to the pain of others. There's this weird conflict in Sabrina that's really, really, really interesting.

Someone said to me that they found Sabrina "hard to understand." And I think that Sabrina *is* hard to understand. You know, on one occasion, you hear her talking about herself as a muckraker, as a journalist; on another instance, she's taking all of these, these, actually *movies* and still photographs of the people stacking, of the prisoners in the pyramid. Then she says she has to leave, she has to make a phone call to Kelli, blah blah blah. Sabrina is an endlessly interesting character for me. Before joining the military, she wanted to be a forensic photographer.

LB: *She is now, officially, a forensic photographer.*

EM: That's what's so funny: she is now one of the great forensic photographers of our era. I also took a scene out of the movie that was in for a long time—and I took it out for a whole mess of reasons—but Sabrina has all of these tattoos of Abu Ghraib images on her body.

LB: *Based on the photos that she took?*

EM: Yes.

LB: *Where are they?*

EM: Where are they? They're on her arms . . . the ones that I've seen are all on her shoulder and on her arms.

LB: *I can understand, I guess, wanting to make external what you've seen. Maybe it's a similar impulse, you think, to having taken the photos?*

EM: Maybe. I've never understood tattoos. I've never had the urge to have one. In fact, I have the urge *not* to have one. But I am endlessly fascinated by it.

LB: *By just what, exactly?*

EM: Why people get them. . . . I also think that I am so much concerned about covering my body up that the whole idea of someone using their body as a billboard in any way shape or form, it just kind of violates . . . I think it's really deep, too! I think it has a lot to do with body image, and self . . . and it interests me! The whole idea of *marking yourself*—the idea of putting Gilligan, which is this central iconic image of the war, and an image that you participated directly in—on your body. . . . When I was thrown out of graduate school, did I want to have tattooed on my back the scene? Aghhhhh! They also each have a tattooed number. They're the "Seven Bad Apples," so they have an apple with a number in it! Or many of them do . . . maybe it's just the girls . . . ?

LB: *Are you serious?*

EM: Don't I look serious? See look, you look shocked! Wait a second, here's something that would interest you: We went to the MPAA because we were after an R-rating for the film (which we then got). The woman who's Ms. Big, who's the head of the MPAA, tells us that horror movies have changed recently.

LB: *Post–September 11 horror?*

EM: Yes. I kept saying to her that I thought that at the center of this war, this war in particular, was humiliation and sexual humiliation. That was at the core of the whole Iraqi War. Now, I think it may be at the core of Bush's personality . . . but that's another thing.

She then said, "You know, most of the horror movies that now come out are about humiliation." She said all the *Hostel*, the *Saw* stuff, they're all about. . . . It's not just about eviscerating the guy, it's about humiliating him thoroughly, debasing him thoroughly first . . . before you eviscerate him." I thought that was a really, really, really interesting thing. Because if I actually believe—as I do—that humiliation is so much a part of this current war, and maybe so much part of the current zeitgeist in general, it would be odd if horror films *didn't* reflect it. And it's interesting that independently, she's telling me that they do. It's a complete resurgence, the resurgence of the horror movie. Well, there's a resurgence of just plain—I think, in the American world—of just plain meanness. Meanness and aggression.

You know, my argument about Shock and Awe: People ask, "Why were there no plans about what to do *after* you rained a series of bombs on Baghdad?" The answer is: There were no plans because that was not of interest. The interest is in humiliation. The interest is in showing that you're more powerful than the other guy; that you can humiliate the other guy; that you can debase him. The rest of it is not your concern! You're not thinking about it! It's a war of "I'm bigger and tougher," you know, "My dick is bigger than yours." It's a very weird, weird kind of political world that we've entered into. The caveman world.

I watched—you know, because I was trying to do a horror movie for Sony—

LB: *You were?*

EM: Yes; I still am.

LB: *Well,* this *is a horror film.*

EM: That's how I pitched it to Sony! I said, "I want to make a nonfiction horror movie." But I was trying to sell a—who knows what it is, whether it's a "traditional horror movie" or what it is . . .

LB: *What was the idea? What was the title?*

EM: Well, it was *Nub City.* You know, years ago I was going to do this thing; I had gone to Vernon, Florida, which was the town were people . . .

LB: *They cut off their limbs in an insurance scam, in the Nub City idea, right?*

EM: Yes. The script was about an insurance investigator—it was actually a standard, if you like, *Psycho*-type of structure. A young insurance adjuster comes to this weird town in the middle of fucking nowhere, in the swamp, investigating a strange claim. He finds out too much stuff, is horribly murdered, and disappears. Then a crack insurance investigator comes down to find out what happened, and then he become involved in this horrendous nightmare of a town that has gone insane. That's it. Ha!

LB: *What would that look like? Would it look the way the reenactments do, except a whole movie of them? Who would inspired you for a project like that?*

EM: Myself! I don't have to imitate anybody . . .

LB: *Oh, I'm not suggesting that! Tell me, which filmmakers have you been inspired by? I know you're a huge film buff.*

EM: There are so many people who make films; so many whose work I detest, and so many that. . . . I still have this unending love for Bresson. I had never seen *L'Argent* (1983), and I saw it about six months ago. I thought *L'Argent* was just *fantastic*. I gave it to my editor at the time— it really, really annoyed me—he said, "Oh, it's so eighties." And I said, "Yeah, exactly. It's so eighties . . . like Plato is so classical antiquity." It's like, what the fuck kind of remark is that, "It's so eighties?" You know? It's like, fuck you!

LB: *Does that mean he thought it was dated?*

EM: I think it means that he was saying something really, really, really stupid. Yes, I think he was saying that he felt it was dated, among other things. I am always unendingly interested in Bresson's perversity. It is the cinema of perversity. You expect to see something; it's never shown; something else entirely is shown from what you expect. The framing is always different from what you think it should be—and always brilliant. It does, it does so many things so well, and so unexpectedly.

LB: Standard Operating Procedure *could be a double feature with* Joan of Arc *(1962).*

EM: Ha! I think Bresson's *Joan of Arc* is just unbelievably great. That's you know, a kind of movie about sexual perversity. It has that dark. . . . It's deep sexual; deeply screwed up in a way that the Dreyer is more formal. There are so many filmmakers I love, it's not just. . . . But I would like to make a horror film. And I don't think there's anybody that I'd like to emulate. I'd like to do something different and strange.

See No Evil: Errol Morris Interviews Errol Morris on *Standard Operating Procedure*

ERROL MORRIS/2009

Q: *Since you did this last interview, Mr. Morris,* Standard Operating Procedure *was released in theaters and then on DVD. The reception to the movie seems very different than the reception to* Fog of War. *Why do you think that's the case?*

A: It's impossible to predict how people are going to view a movie. With *Fog of War* there was a sense that we were heading down a road very similar to the road to Vietnam. Call it a feeling of *déjà vu*. I never imagined that there would be such a connection between the past and present. But, as I worked on the editing of the film, it became, ironically, a movie about current affairs. I could never have known this in advance. But the success of the movie was because it had a *sufficient* historical distance from the present. It was simultaneously contemporary and removed from the current events by over forty years or more. *Standard Operating Procedure* is not removed at all. We're still mired in that same war that started in 2003, with the hope that a new president will find a way to extricate us from what has become a quagmire. It's very hard for an audience to look at *Standard Operating Procedure* and to see it independent of their political views about the war. It's probably asking far, far, far too much. Still, I like this movie best of all.

Q: *Really?*

A: I wanted to make a movie about photography. I had been thinking about it for many, many years—long before *The Fog of War*. I had gone all the way to the Crimea in 2004 to research a pair of photographs taken in

---

Conducted January 20, 2009. Reprinted with permission by Errol Morris.

1855 by Roger Fenton, and had initially thought it could be the basis for a movie. [Instead, it became a series of essays for the *New York Times* and a book published by Penguin Press.] The Abu Ghraib photographs are among the most seen photographs in history, and yet, we knew so little about them.

Q: *But why photographs?*
A: Because they provide a way into history. We often think of history as a synopsis. You start at the beginning, and you work your way, gradually, through to the end. And, in the process, hopefully you capture the pattern of cause and effect of one event on another on another on another, and so on and so forth. Photography gives us a different window into history. Instead of starting at the beginning, we enter at some arbitrary point. We enter at the moment the photograph was taken.

Q: *So do you like the nonlinear quality of it? Are you fighting against history as a series of cause and effect?*
A: Well, nonlinear has become such a catchword for everything—postmodernism, nonlinear, this, that and the other thing. It's not so much nonlinear, because it's not about taking events out of order. It's about walking into something in the middle and fixating on it. It's also about this belief that you see the whole in an individual part, in an individual detail. That by obsessing over an individual part you capture something of the complexity of the whole. You capture things that you might overlook otherwise, that you might never notice otherwise. It is a different way of doing history. It's a different way of entering the landscape of history. I sometimes think of it as reaching into a photograph. You're looking at a photograph, and you actually pull the emulsion apart and walk into the historical reality that it depicts.

Q: *You get a sense of this in* Standard Operating Procedure *with the metadata. Do you want to talk about the element of chance, that only remnants of history are preserved?*
A: We leave behind us this trail of debris, of detritus, of ephemera, of written material, printed material, drawn images, photographic images, and so on and so forth, the evidence that we were once here, that we thought certain things or believed certain things or went to certain places, or did certain things. I have all kinds of excuses for why I made *Standard Operating Procedure.* Susan Sontag had written this essay that appeared in the *New York Times Magazine*, titled after her book she had written, *On Regarding the Pain of Others.* This essay was entitled "On Re-

garding the Torture of Others." And it was her reaction to the Abu Ghraib photographs. And it was very, very angry, and very well written. But she clearly understood, right from the very beginning, that there was something incredibly important about these images as images. That they were worth studying in their own right. We take images in an unreflective way, for the most part, maybe because vision has always been privileged. We accept what we see. We believe what we see. And these images were a way into the historical reality of Abu Ghraib. Of what happened there in the fall of 2003. I remember my own feelings, seeing these images for the first time, this kind of puzzlement. What am I looking at? It's like suddenly, you've lifted up a rock, and you're seeing this whole world underneath. Good God, what is going on here?

Q: *But don't you think, very quickly, that people were told what to look at? A perceived view was provided?*

A: They didn't even have to be told. People, very quickly, came to their own conclusions about what they were looking at, and what it meant. And I felt, from early on, wouldn't it be interesting to take these photographs and use them as the center of an investigation into what *really* was going on in the fall of 2003 at this American-run prison in the middle of the Sunni Triangle? But I always was starting with the photographs. The intention was to put the photographs at the center of the story.

Q: *What were the most interesting things you found out? Not the smoking gun, necessarily . . .*

A: That the photographs, the picture taking was an act of disobedience. Everybody thought that these soldiers were incredibly stupid. Why would you take these photographs, unless you were incredibly stupid? It has its own kind of syllogistic reasoning.

Q: *Darwin Award winners . . .*

A: Yes, Darwin Award winners. The reasoning is simple, "To take pictures there was incredibly stupid. They took pictures there. Therefore, they were incredibly stupid." Raymond Krol, one of the military intelligence specialists who was interviewed in the movie, says it explicitly. For him, and probably for everyone else, it has a self-evident quality to it. This was stupid. But there is a problem with this assumption. It's wrong.

I may not be able to give you a definitive answer as why these photographs taken. But the soldiers were well aware that they were doing things that were wrong or morally questionable, and they wanted a record of it. Simple as that. They, themselves, were uneasy about their whole position.

Now I'm not saying that this explains everything. But it tells you that the photographs exist for a different reason than we may have thought.

I'll give you just a couple of examples, because there are different people involved, here. And different people usually do things for different reasons. These soldiers were not just a group of automatons, all acting for the same reason, as if they had only one reason for doing what they did. These were people who were quite different. I believe that Sabrina Harman did take the pictures, in part, because she wanted a record of what was going on there. Chuck Graner, by all accounts, felt that he had been badly used by the Army in Gulf War One, had suffered injuries as a result of things that he had been asked to do, had been denied certain medical benefits, and wanted a record of what he was asked to do so that he could prove that he had to do it. Ironically, he may have taken the photographs to protect himself and ended up incriminating himself in the process. This is not to say that nothing excessive was done there, but it is to say that the photographs don't exist as an act of stupidity. It's far, far, far more interesting than that.

Q: *Well, do you think the act of taking photographs influenced or changed the actions in the photographs?*

A: Photographs can change everything. These photographs did. They certainly influenced public opinion. But you are speaking more specifically about the people who took the photographs, and the soldiers that are in them. It's really not so surprising. People who are aware of a camera act differently because they're aware of a camera. It's another set of eyes in the room.

Q: *Yes, you wrote about that in your* New York Times *blog, particularly with the thumbs up and the smile.*

A: I'm endlessly fascinated by how people see themselves and how others see them, and the disparity between the two. And photographs can play a very strong role in that, as well. A friend of mine, Charlie Silver, who I worked with on *The Thin Blue Line*, keeps bringing up my interview with Michael Randell, who was one of the three so-called—quote/unquote—eyewitnesses to the murder of Dallas police officer Robert Wood. I had Randell's statement written at the time of the murder, detailing what he saw. I interviewed him over ten years after the fact. He gave me an account in an interview that appears in *The Thin Blue Line*. And, at the very end of the interview, I asked him to read out loud the statement that he had made over a decade earlier. It was one of the truly surreal experiences to watch him reading this document. Charlie, my friend, keeps going back to how Michael Randell looked, as he read the statement, and realized that the account that he had given was completely different than the account that he had given to the police. Oddly enough, the account that he gave me ten years after the crime was more believable than the account that he gave to the police at the time of the murder. It wasn't as though somehow, in the intervening years, he had forgotten what happened, it was quite the opposite. It's like he had . . .

Q: . . . *polished it?*
A: No. He had forgotten how he had lied about it. . . . So, it's always interesting to sort of compare people's memories, their own first-person accounts with other accounts. . . .

Q: *All that brings up* Fog of War, *then. McNamara was giving his own* . . .
A: Yes, his own recollection.

Q: *And then you showed the memos.*
A: *Standard Operating Procedure* is very much in that mold. I'm very puzzled with all of these reviews that came out, many people wrote that I had failed to address the real issues in the story. That I had failed to follow the story up through the chain of command, to Carbone, Rumsfeld, Yoo, Addington, Cheney, etc. And somehow, as a result, the movie was incomplete. Well, I don't quite see it that way. I was telling a very different kind of story, a story of memory and of photographs. We want, desperately, to simplify why people do what they do. We want some kind of pat explanation. But the attempt to actually uncover who people are and why they act the way they do is endlessly more interesting than simply demonizing them or coming up with a set of simple explanations.

I'll give you one example. People always raise these two very famous experiments in social psychology in connection with Abu Ghraib—the Stanford Prison Experiment (SPE) conducted by Philip Zimbardo and the Milgram experiment conducted by Stanley Milgram. They are both about obedience to authority—obedience to authority in a laboratory setting—where people are asked to administer electric shocks or asked to play the role of prisoners and guards. The end result is that in both experiments abuses occur. But you can't use these experiments to explain Abu Ghraib. You can't explain why people obey authority in a situation where obeying authority is given, where it is absolutely the norm, where it is essential. This is the military. Of course these people obey authority. They are *trained* to obey authority. We're talking about privates and corporals and sergeants. These aren't people who make policy or control policy; these are people who are *required* to follow orders. You don't need a social psychology experiment to tell you why people follow orders in the military. If anything, it would be the opposite. You would need to explain why people don't follow orders. Without a chain of command, without following orders, there would be no military.

Q: *Right. It's not a place for independent thinkers.*

A: But what you have here *is* independent thinkers. That's what's so interesting. You have people who actually are disobeying authority, but we don't recognize it as such. The taking of the photographs was disobeying authority. It was a breach with authority. They provided a window into policies that the military and the government did not want people to know about. They opened a Pandora's box and allowed us to see into the recesses, the dark recesses of administration policy. Ironically, Zimbardo's SPE and Milgram's electric shocks help to explain not the behavior of the soldiers at Abu Ghraib—but why we, the people of America, sat back and allowed these things to happen in our name, in our democracy. Presumably, we, the public, are not (unlike soldiers) trained to follow orders. We could have stood up and protested.

Q: *Do you think the movie will be seen differently after time passes, when it can be viewed as a historical event?*

A: I don't know. And anything I said would be so deeply self-serving, I hesitate to answer the question. I don't know. I know that I make movies because I have questions. And they're not necessarily questions that I can answer easily, and maybe I never can answer, either to my own satisfaction or the satisfaction of others. I often think I've done a good job with a movie if I've been able to capture the underlying complexity of what I am describing. If I've done that, then I feel that it has not been an effort in vain.

Musings on the Universe

ERROL MORRIS

The Grump

No. 1: SANTAYANA

Santayana said, "Those who cannot remember the past are condemned to repeat it."

Really? Human nature being what it is, isn't it hopeless to expect that we can do better regardless of whether we remember anything or not? And what if what we remember leads us to false analogies and misunderstandings?

I prefer: "Those who cannot remember the past are condemned to repeat it without a sense of ironic futility."

Or how about this: "Those who cannot condemn the past repeat it in order to remember it."

No. 2: THE GORILLA-PLOY

You have had some trouble figuring out why people are acting in a confusing or contradictory fashion. You can't provide a plausible explanation of their behavior. Just imagine that they are gorillas. Or, if you prefer, some other kind of monkey. I find this very helpful. Once we have dispossessed ourselves of the notion that we are rational, consistent, or even make sense, then we are in a much better position to analyze our own behavior and the behavior of others.

Big monkeys. That's what we are. And by that I mean no disrespect to monkeys.

No. 3: CURSE THE DARKNESS

A Chinese proverb: "Don't curse the darkness, light a candle." Used by Adlai Stevenson (1900–65), praising Eleanor Roosevelt in an address to

From www.Errolmorris.com. Permission granted by Errol Morris.

the United Nations General Assembly in 1962: "She would rather light candles than curse the darkness, and her glow has warmed the world." While intending no disrespect for either Adlai Stevenson or Eleanor Roosevelt, I disagree.

I can think of several reasons why it makes more sense to curse the darkness. First of all, cursing the darkness is satisfying in its own right. I can't begin to tell you the immense amount of pleasure I get from cursing all sorts of things. Including the darkness. On the other hand, lighting a candle can have a number of deleterious consequences.

1. You could burn yourself.

2. You could cause a fire, e.g., burn down the house.

3. You could drip hot candle wax on good furniture or perhaps a fine tablecloth. We all know how difficult it is to remove.

4. The candle could be one of those ghastly scented candles, patchouli oil or sandalwood. And once one of those things is lighted, it's too damn late. You're stuck with this foul odor that can linger on for days, if not weeks. In short, if you're not completely familiar with the candle why take the chance?

5. The candle provides only minimal illumination. Hardly worth the effort. You can't really read by it without worrisome eyestrain. In short, why bother? Or if you must read by it, consult an ophthalmologist. And that's expensive.

6. It's cheaper to curse the darkness than to light a candle. You don't need matches. You don't need a candle. You don't need anything except a bad disposition. Why not be self-sufficient and do with a little less?

No. 4: OXYMORONS

Oxymorons. What are they? I grabbed a definition from the American Heritage Dictionary.

ox-y-mo-ron

A rhetorical figure in which incongruous or contradictory terms are combined, as in *a deafening silence* and *a mournful optimist*.

Well, I have my own example.
How about . . .
A nice person.

No. 5: MISANTHROPE'S CREED

One's company, two's a crowd.
Or if you hate yourself, along with everybody else, how about:
Zero's company, one's a crowd.

No. 6: THE LAST DINGDONG OF DOOM

I have always been perplexed by Faulkner's Nobel Prize Banquet Speech. Faulkner said: "I decline to accept the end of man. It is easy enough to say that man is immortal simply because he will endure: that when the last dingdong of doom has clanged and faded from the last worthless rock hanging tideless in the last red and dying evening, that even then there will still be one more sound: that of his puny inexhaustible voice, still talking. I refuse to accept this. I believe that man will not merely endure: he will prevail."

Not merely endure? Will prevail? Could an explanation be that it was written in 1949, not long after the end of World War II, and people needed something to hang on to?

But wait a second. Who says that man should even endure, let alone, prevail? (And his statement: I refuse to accept this . . . Could this bold assertion be just one more example of what he, himself, calls: our puny inexhaustible voices, still talking?)

I went back to Faulkner's speech. It is beautifully written, exquisitely written.

The lines preceding the famous quote are strange, moving—lines that speak to a time over fifty years in Faulkner's future—the present.

Allow me to quote what Faulkner said: "Our tragedy today is a general and universal physical fear so long sustained by now that we can even bear it. There are no longer problems of the spirit. There is only the question: When will I be blown up?"

Here. Here.

Although Faulkner left this as a rhetorical question, I would like to provide an answer:

Soon.

Very soon.

No. 7: PANDORA AND THE BOX

The story of Pandora and the box is well known. The story has a simple beginning. Pandora was presented with a box and asked not to open it.

Well, big surprise. She opened it. And out popped every imaginable (and unimaginable) pestilence. A cornucopia of horror for mankind.

But there was something left at the bottom of the box.

Hope.

In her book on mythology, Edith Hamilton writes, "It was the only good the casket held among the many evils. . . ." Hope was supposed to make up for all of the other malefactions.

But wait a second.
Why is hope a good thing?
I have a somewhat different theory.
Hope is the final pestilence.

No. 8: ANTI-HUMANIST

I am a secular anti-humanist.

There is a simple reason. Religion is nasty and so is mankind.

Steven Weinberg has written, "With or without religion, you would have good people doing good things and evil people doing evil things. But for good people to do evil things, that takes religion."

I agree in principle. With one qualification: Religion can certainly help good people to do evil things, but good people do evil things even without religion.

No. 9: UNINTELLIGENT DESIGN

I look at the world of fauna and flora around me, and it becomes completely obvious that it cannot be explained by the processes of natural selection.

Natural selection would have done a better job.

That's why I believe in unintelligent design. The sheer idiocy of it all has to be explained by something, doesn't it?

A mentally-retarded creator? A flawed plan? An idea improperly thought out? Or an idea enacted hastily? (Six days, by the way, has always seemed to me to be rushing things.)

Furthermore, wouldn't natural selection have produced creatures capable of appreciating natural selection?

No. 10: THE NON-EXISTENCE OF GOD

Isn't everybody familiar with Anselm's ontological proof of the existence of God? I've always had a problem with it. Anselm's proof hinges on the belief that that which exists is more perfect than that which exists solely in the mind. I beg to differ. Think of it as Morris v. Anselm.

1. God is perfect.

2. Existence is an imperfection. (This is taken from the obvious principle: Better to not exist than to exist.)

3. Therefore, God does not exist.

No. 11: THE UNIMAGINATIVE CARPENTER

Only the unimaginative carpenter fails to blame his tools.

No. 12: BLAME THE MESSENGER

Am I supposed to object to this? Who are you supposed to blame *other* than the messenger? The messenger may be carrying bad news or criminal orders, but how is one to determine where the message comes from? It involves time, effort, and an attention to detail. You might never be able to determine where the message comes from, and then whom can you blame? Blame yourself? Out of the question. Much better to blame the messenger because the messenger is right there, immediately at hand, available. And because of his "lowly" station as a messenger, no one is likely to object. It is a perfectly acceptable and compelling strategy.

For some reason, messengers don't seem to like this analysis.

Reexaminations

No. 1: Why It Makes Sense to Bite the Hand that Feeds You.

1. Preventive bite. Hand is bound to betray you eventually. Get it before it gets you. Remember, every hand is capable of naked aggression.

2. Preemptive bite. Hand is ready to do something. Just look at it. You've got to protect yourself, don't you?

3. Keeps gums healthy.

4. Hand less likely poisoned than food.

5. Tastes good.

6. Why not?

No. 2: Why It Makes Sense to Beat a Dead Horse.

1. Sets an example for other horses that might be watching.

2. Aerobic workout.

3. Horse might not be really dead. (Isn't it better to be safe than sorry?)

4. Tenderizes the meat.

5. Horse is unable to fight back.

6. Provides a welcome relief for tension or anxiety. (Makes you feel good.)

No. 3: Why It Makes Sense to Dig a Hole for Yourself.

1. Great place to hide. If it isn't deep enough, you can just stick your head in it.

2. Start of a new and possibly lucrative route to China. Unexpected income.

3. Opportunity to gain expertise with earth-moving equipment, e.g., a shovel.

4. Shows initiative. Much better than expecting someone to dig a hole for you.

5. Allows you do something for yourself. Haven't you been spending more than enough time doing things for others. . . ?

6. Practice making decisions. Put it just where you want it without having to consult a committee.

7. Put your dead horse in it. (See previous list.)

No. 4: Why It Makes Sense to Have an Albatross Hanging Around Your Neck.

1. Hides ugly food stains on shirt.

No. 5: Mossiness v. Unmossiness

As a child I was told: A rolling stone gathers no moss. For me, this has been a source of unending confusion.

Is mossiness good or bad? One should strive to be mossy. Or unmossy? Which is better? What is the proverb telling us?

For years, I thought that mossiness was bad. That one should strive to be unmossy, devoid of moss, moss-free. If you keep active—if you enjoy an active lifestyle (as opposed to living like a piece of taxidermy; say, a moosehead)—then you will never be encumbered by moss. Moss in this view is like a fungus, an infestation. Please God, don't allow me to become mossy.

Well, to my surprise, it turns out that that the proverb is supposed to be interpreted the opposite way. Mossiness is supposed to be good. Shouldn't one strive to be covered with a fine patination of moss? More mossy. Most mossy. You should strive to put down roots, to establish yourself in a place and then you, too, can become mossy. Moss is a coveted raiment. Please God, make me as mossy as possible.

Of course, some people learned the proverb and were taught what it is supposed to mean. I don't think I was. Maybe, I wasn't listening. Maybe I read the proverb somewhere but no interpretation was given. But it's not just my problem. Other people suffer from this same confusion. Or have to be dispossessed of this false notion. I know because I've asked a lot of people.

And, anyway, why would you think that mossiness was good without someone telling you that was the case? Maybe if you came from the Moss Planet, where moss is the source of all life, where everyone revered moss . . . I don't know.

And what if all language is like this—all words, phrases, and sentences mean the opposite of what you think they do? Or, the situation is even worse, and all words, phrases, and sentences mean something other than what you think they do.

INDEX